THE DREAM FRONTIER

THE DREAM FRONTIER

MARK J. BLECHNER

THE ANALYTIC PRESS

2001 Hillsdale, NJ London

Published by
The Analytic Press, Inc., Publishers
Editorial Offices:
101 West Street
Hillsdale, New Jersey 07642
www.analyticpress.com

Designed and typeset by Compudesign, Charlottesville, VA

Library of Congress Cataloging-in-Publication Data

Blechner, Mark J.
The dream frontier / Mark J. Blechner
Includes bibliographical references and index

ISBN 0-88163-224-4

Printed in the United States of America
10 9 8 7 6 5 4 3 2 1

Dedicated to Erika Fromm,

for whom education was not the filling of a vessel

but the lighting of a fire,

and to the beloved memory of Stephen Mitchell,

the generous giant of contemporary psychoanalysis,

who encouraged everyone around him to

produce their best and most original work.

CONTENTS

ACKNOWLEDGMENTS

My first thanks go to the late Robert Berman, who taught English at the Horace Mann High School in New York. As part of required summer reading, he assigned Freud's *Introductory Lectures on Psychoanalysis*, which launched my interest in psychoanalysis in general and dreams in particular when I was 15 years old. At the University of Chicago, Erika Fromm allowed me to take her graduate courses on ego psychology and psychoanalytic dream interpretation while I was still an undergraduate and gave me a basic understanding of psychoanalytic thinking that has been my foundation ever since (besides encouraging me to read chapter 7 of *The Interpretation of Dreams* five times by the time I was 21 years old). Others who have been influential teachers about dreams from a clinical standpoint are Montague Ullman, Paul Lippmann, Leopold Caligor, Alberta Szalita, Raul Ludmer, John Schimel, Edgar Levenson, Kenneth Frank, and the late Benjamin Wolstein.

Ruth Day gave me a thorough introduction to cognitive psychology and psycholinguistics, which launched my thinking about linguistic and nonlinguistic mental processes. At the Haskins Laboratories and at Yale University, other professors and colleagues nourished my thinking and research into this area, including James Cutting, Alvin Liberman, Wendell Garner, Robert Crowder, and Michael Studdert-Kennedy. At the Bell Laboratories, where I continued my research, I was greatly supported and inspired by Max Mathews, Mark Liberman, and Vivien Tartter.

William Domhoff, a leading empirical dream researcher, has given me excellent advice during the writing of this book and directed me to the huge data base of dreams that the University of California, Santa Cruz posts on the Internet. Neuropsychologists Robert Bilder and Ashok Jansary were invaluable sources of facts and ideas. William Hirst has graced me with his friendship, challenging skepticism, and rigorous scientific reasoning. The Viceroys, my peer supervision group—including Sandra Buechler, Richard Gartner, John O'Leary, Allison Rosen, and Robert Watson—have been an unparalleled resource of intellectual ferment and clinical wisdom for nearly 20 years. They patiently allowed me to conduct all sorts of clinical experiments with them.

Stephen Mitchell, of blessed memory, loved the spark of innovation and did his best to encourage new ideas. He chaired the landmark 1997 interdisciplinary conference, "Building Bridges: Psychoanalysis and the Sciences of Man," which enabled an exchange of ideas between J. Allan Hobson, George Lakoff, Paul Lippmann, and myself, and where I first presented the ideas in chapter 2. My ideas on dreams and countertransference also benefited from Steve Mitchell's rigorous and benevolent support.

While I was writing this book, the William Alanson White Institute's director, Marylou Lionells, was a facilitator of open and creative thinking. My ideas on dreams have been fostered as well by conversations or correspondence with Martin Bergmann, Jerome Blake, Harry Fiss, Jay Greenberg, Marcia Johnson, Douglas Kargman, Sue Kolod, James Kugel, Carola Mann, Tony Meola, David Olds, Schlomo Riskin, Elizabeth Spelke, Donnel Stern, Ruth Szmarag, Philippe Wahba, Christopher Warnke, and Cléonie White. The students who have taken my courses on dreams have contributed enormously to my thinking. I also owe much thanks to Mark Solms and all those who participate in our study group on Neuro-Psychoanalysis, and the New York Psychoanalytic Institute for creating an invaluable forum on psychoanalysis and neurobiology. Jeffrey Blum, Jane Bressler, Sandra Buechler, Richard Gartner, Daniel Kozloff, Catherine Ng, and Sue Shapiro, precious friends and colleagues, carefully read the entire manuscript, as did my excellent editors at the Analytic Press, Paul Stepansky, John Kerr, and Nancy Liguori. Each of them has given me unique and invaluable feedback on my ideas. John Silberman gave me expert legal advice. My family and friends have put up with years of my immersion in work on this book, and I thank them for their great patience and support. While writing the book, I have also been helped in many ways by Alan and Marcia Baer, Carmen Castaneda, Bernadette Church, Janie Coltrin, Beverly Grimes, Barbara Sloan, and Judith Waldman. Most of all, I thank my patients, though they must remain nameless. In their struggles to explore their psyches, they gave me the honor of examining their dreams in depth. Nearly every idea I have had has stemmed from my clinical collaboration with them.

THE DREAM FRONTIER

PART I

INTRODUCTION AND OVERVIEW

CHAPTER 1

THE DREAM FRONTIER

Ich lebe mein Leben in wachsenden Ringen
die sich über die Dinge ziehn.
Ich werde den letzten vielleicht nicht vollbringen,
aber versuchen will ich ihn.

(I live my life in expanding rings
that spread themselves out over things.
I may not complete the last,
but I want to try.)

Rilke, *Das Stundenbuch*

THE TITLE I have chosen for this book, like a dream itself, condenses several meanings. Where and what is the dream frontier? Dreams are themselves a frontier. They are the frontier of human knowledge, imagination, and creativity. They are the breeding ground of the truly new. In dreams we pull together all that we know and all that we have experienced, and then we create new experiences.

Our daytime thinking is hemmed in by language. We usually do not dare to think the literally unspeakable. We dare to say only what is understandable. We do not generally create new words or utter sentences out loud that are understandable only to ourselves. We do the things that are considered sane. For that we are rewarded by the fruits of communication. If we say things that others understand, then they can share our thoughts and respond to our emotions, which gives us all the benefits of interpersonal relations.

But at night, life is different. We close our eyes, shut off our ears, and descend into a realm of existence where we are alone. For eight or so hours, we are freed from the constraints of functioning in a social world. For those precious hours, our minds are free to think about anything without worrying about being understood or judged. Released from the constraints of understandability and reality, we can think up new words, objects, and people, and we can create new situations. We are at the frontier of human experience. Anything can happen. Anything can be thought. Anything can be felt. Anything can be uttered. We do not have to worry about being thought insane. There is no criterion for sanity, because during those hours we are truly alone with our minds.

Perhaps during that time, our brains actually reorganize. Travel into the dream frontier may require a different setup of our mind/brains. We can dream, "I knew she was my mother, even though it didn't look like her." If we said that about someone while we were awake, we might find ourselves in a psychiatric hospital. But alone at night we can entertain such experiences. Or we can dream of "something between a record player or a balance-scale." We need not worry how something can be between those two different objects. It just is so. During the day, if we think such a thing, we correct it to fit with the world. We change it to either a record player or a balance scale, but not something in-between. At night, however, the familiar categories by which we structure our experience loosen their hold. And maybe the effects of our thinking each night on this new frontier carry over into our daytime thinking.

There is another dream frontier: the frontier of our study of dreams. After 100 years of psychoanalysis and 50 years of modern sleep laboratories, we have learned a great deal. But the more we learn, the more we realize the vast unknown scientific frontier that lies before us. Dreams tell us a great deal about how the brain is organized, how the brain organizes our mind, and how our mind organizes our world. We feel intuitively that this is so, but so far we are standing at the beginning of a great voyage into the unknown. The field of oneirology, the study of dreams, has a long history, but in the twentieth century, more than ever before, we started to try to turn folklore and popular wisdom into science. We have only begun and much remains to be done in the future.

Dreams are also a clinical frontier. In psychiatric and psychoanalytic work, dreams are at the frontier of clinical understanding. A patient's dreams are often ahead of any waking understanding of her or his problems. If the clinician is open to hearing dreams, they provide cutting-edge information about the patient. They chart out where a treatment can go and needs to go, and what personal barriers and defenses stand in the way. Dreams also spell out the problems that the clinician may be having in working with the patient. They provide the key to what is truly going on, for no one lies in his dreams.

Immersion in the study of dreams is a source of endless fascination. Those who work there feel constantly thrilled by the unexpected. But to dwell in dreams is also to subject oneself to ridicule. Too much attention to them is thought to be a flight from the exigencies of life. When we call someone a "dreamer," it can be quite pejorative. We are all curious about dreams, but we are also afraid of them. And it is a short passage from fear to ridicule. So the study of dreams is not well supported in our society. Surely, it is thought, there are more important things to explore. When the scientific study of dreams took off in the 1950s, we were promised solutions to serious problems of the everyday world. The study of dreams would lead us to understand schizophrenia, the mind/body problem, and the unconscious. Those were grand promises. When they did not materialize in a few decades, there was a backlash. Perhaps dream researchers were just dreamers. They had bold ideas, but they didn't come through.

In truth, we do not yet know what the study of dreams will bring. The promises from the early dream researchers may yet come true, but they will certainly require many more years. Part of the problem is that brain scientists have been looking at EEGs and PET scans, and hoping from them to tell us what dreaming is. Clinicians and dream interpreters who do not work in a laboratory, but immerse themselves in the experience of dreaming, have not been in regular communication with laboratory scientists. That mutual isolation worked against everyone. The phenomenology of dreams—how they are structured, how they are experienced, how they are remembered or forgotten or changed—all of these things are vast sources of information. They tell us things in themselves, and they should be informing neurobiological research. The exchange of information between those who study dreams in the consulting room and those who study them in the laboratory has disintegrated, to everyone's peril. I hope this book will revitalize that exchange of information.

With that intention, I integrate four main topics: the theory of dream formation, the meaning of dreams, the clinical use of dreams, and the implications of dream phenomena for our understanding of the brain. I not only study each topic separately, but also try to consider them together. At times, I move back and forth among these main topics, trying to draw together findings from clinical psychology and psychiatry, clinical neurology, cognitive neuroscience, and philosophy. If you are a specialist in only one of these areas, you may use the overview of the book to direct you to the chapters that most interest you. But if you do that, you will defeat my intention of bringing all these areas together, for their mutual benefit.

OVERVIEW

Throughout history, human beings have been fascinated by their dreams. People have interpreted dreams probably since they first had them. One of the earliest known dream interpretations came from 3000 BC, in the Babylonian epic of Gilgamesh (Thompson, 1930). Gilgamesh dreamt that an axe fell from the sky. The people gathered around it in admiration and worship. Gilgamesh threw the axe in front of his mother and then he embraced it like a wife.

Gilgamesh was troubled by his dream. He told it to his mother, Ninsun, and she told him what it meant. She said that someone powerful would soon appear. Gilgamesh would struggle with him and try to overpower him, but he would not succeed. Eventually they would become close friends and accomplish great things. She said (Oppenheim, 1956), "That you embraced him like a wife means: he will never forsake you! Thus your dream is solved!" (p. 247).

The dream interpretation technique of Gilgamesh's mother is characteristic of the pre-Freudian approach to dreams. She adheres to the two principles of antiquity: (1) that dreams predict the future (they are "mantic"), and (2) that dreams are a message from God or some other supernatural force or being.

Most Biblical dream interpretation partakes of one or both of these hypotheses. The dream of Jacob's ladder was a mantic dream. It was a message from God that Jacob would father a great people. Later, Joseph interpreted Pharaoh's dream as a prediction of the future of Egypt, which allowed Pharaoh to prepare his country for the impending famine. In the New Testament, Pilate's wife had a dream that Jesus should be let go; unfortunately, Pilate did not listen to her dream.

Freud argued for a different idea, one that is so common today that we may not realize how radical it once was: that dreams are not messages from an external force or being, but that they are instead reflections of thoughts and feelings in our own minds, thoughts and feelings of which we might be partially or completely unaware. The study of our dreams will lead us to understand these thoughts and feelings better. If we take our dreams seriously, we will know things about ourselves that we might not be able to learn any other way.

Dreams are the most private of thoughts—so private, indeed, that their meaning is often not accessible to the dreamer. Here we have the basic dream paradox—the dream is our most private experience, yet to understand a dream fully, we must share it with other people. As von Franz put it (Boas, 1994), "The trouble with interpreting your own dreams is that you can't see your own back. If you show it to another person, he can see it, but you can't" (p. 16).

Dreams are both intensely personal and yet best understood after being made public. There is an old Talmudic story (Berachoth, 9) that Rabbi Bana'ah told his dream to 24 dream interpreters. Each gave a different interpretation, making a different prediction, and all of them were right. This story has several messages. The obvious one is that dreams condense multiple meanings. But also, there is the message that no one person by himself can know all the rich meanings of his dreams or anyone else's. Groups of people are helpful when interpreting dreams. Each person in the group will project some of his own psychology into the dream. But the individual projections will cancel each other out and what remains is a precipitate of meaning that may be more accurate and balanced than any individual interpretation.

The notion of dream interpretation, which has existed for thousands of years, is due for revision. The usual idea of interpretation is that the dream contains a meaning, and interpretation deciphers that meaning. I propose that the processes of dream formation and dream interpretation are not clearly separate. There are several stages in our experience of a dream: after we actually dream it, we sometimes remember it, convert it into a text, tell it to another person, and hear thoughts about it from that other person. Each of these stages *both decodes and creates* meaning. We are all so accustomed to the dichotomy between dream and interpretation that many people balk at blurring the boundary between them. It is a traditional way of thinking that we may have to unlearn.

The unconscious is distinguished by its lack of concern for understanding by others. Because this is so, meanings in the unconscious are organized in ways that we do not usually notice in waking life. Every element in the unconscious is closely allied with its other forms, including the negative. When we hear any word, our mind attends to all of the word's "relatives"—homonyms, antonyms, words that sound similar, and a whole host of words, concepts, images, and feelings related to that word. When I hear the word "black," my mind probably also thinks of white, of black holes, of Black Sabbath, of Bleck(ner), of the beginning of the universe, of shoeshines (bootblack), of black moods, of financial integrity (being in the black), and so on. All of those meanings of black are activated by my brain; then, the one that is relevant to the situation of the moment is selected.

We could ask, "Why should the brain be involved in so much mental activity of which we are not aware, indeed, of which we cannot be aware?" But we could also ask, "Why should we be aware of most of our brain's activity?" Many people assume that consciousness, that presumed glory of thinking man, is the source of our best thinking. But consciousness, for all its virtues, may be limiting; it is intimately linked to the conventions of reality testing and language. Those are absolute prerequisites for our developing the capacity to have thoughts that can be communicated to other people. But the need for communicability may be at odds with the creative, original capacities of mind. And these capacities may be exercised most efficiently during sleep, when the need for communicability is near zero.

In a very vivid way, I discovered this separation of the mind's activity from the experience of self as I wrote this book. I worked on different sections of the book for two years. There was a period of about a month and a half during which I had to set it aside. Then I went on vacation for two weeks and read all of what I had written up to that point. I had the continual experience of being surprised at my own ideas, liking many of them, rejecting some of them, seeing patterns and connections between them. I felt as if the book I was reading had been written by a person whom I found interesting but surprising. That person was, of course, I, myself, but much of it was the "I" that emerged from middle-of-the-night inspirations that were not integrated with my waking thoughts and experiences, although clearly derived from them. The notion of different "I's" involved in our experience is another theme that I examine in this book. It is a theme that crisscrosses through the latest developments in the fields of psychology, philosophy, and cognitive science. We usually think we know what we mean when we say "I" but that may be another tradition that we have to unlearn.

This book explores several new ideas about the formation of dreams and the best way to understand them. Freud proposed that the mind converts the latent dream thought into the manifest dream by a series of transformations that he called the "dreamwork." The dreamwork is a series of operations—such as condensation, displacement, and pictorialization—which convert our thoughts into the experienced dream. A verbal thought, something like a sentence, is transformed into a vivid experience, with visual imagery, kinesthetic sensations, and intense emotions. In order to analyze the dream, Freud suggested that free associations enable us to trace back the various parts of the dream to their sources in the latent dream thoughts, allowing us to understand the latent dream thought as fitting into our waking thoughts.

The analysis of dreams for Freud was a process of undoing the dreamwork. Freudian dream analysis might be called the "undreamwork." We trace the dream back to verbal thoughts.

I am proposing an alternative model that includes Freud's view but adds to it. In my model, the dream is not exclusively a transformation of verbal thoughts. It is also an alternative to them, a way of thinking that is different from our conscious waking thoughts, a private expression of thinking that shows how the mind works when it is not concerned primarily with communication. Dynamic repression is not the main source of the difficulty we have in understanding dreams; rather, the problem is that *the dream is not concerned with communicability.*

This view of dreams shifts our view of the unconscious; it is not only a place of churning drives that are kept out of awareness by repression. That may be a part of it, but not the main part of it. The bulk of our thinking is unconscious, and part of what keeps it unconscious, besides dynamic repression, is that it has meaning without communicability.

Meaning without communicability—for me, that is the essence of dreams. Freud's model of dreams posits disguise and distortion, but I think that much of what Freud considered disguise is merely a lack of communicability. More often than not, we do not try to hide things in our dreams; we just don't cast them in a language that is meant to be readily understood. The astonishing thing about dreams is how honest they are. "We never lie in our dreams," as I explain in the chapter of the same name. We may try to lie while interpreting our dreams during the waking state, but dreams themselves are perhaps the most honest statements that we humans ever make.

After exploring several new ways of thinking about dreams, I move to more clinical matters. What is the best way to understand dreams? The section on "Clinical Work with Dreams" studies many approaches to working with dreams. Dreams have a tremendous amount of condensed information, and we have a choice about which information we extract from the dream. What we look for will determine what we can find.

Before we can interpret someone else's dreams, we must become adept at understanding our own. All of us are, on some level, afraid of our dreams, a condition I call "oneirophobia." We know, consciously or unconsciously, that our dreams are relentlessly precise about the most intimate issues in our lives. All of us who wish to understand dreams must work to overcome our oneirophobia. I suggest several ways of examining your dreams, by yourself, or with a friend, a psychoanalyst, or a dream interpretation group. The aim is to experience the full richness of your dreams in a safe environment.

Once you are comfortable with your dreams, how do you start to work with someone else's dreams? If our view of dreams is different from Freud's, does that change how we work with them in clinical settings? The answer is yes and no. In the hundred years of psychoanalytic dream interpretation, clinicians have learned a great deal about how best to use dreams in psychotherapy and psychoanalysis. I propose a view of dreams as answers to which we must find the question.

Although my view of dreams may be new, it does not invalidate existing methods of dream interpretation. On the contrary, many different procedures of interpreting dreams can be *reunderstood* within my theory. Our focus becomes less on "dream interpretation" and more on "dream contextualization" and "dream clarification." Interpretation says, "Dream X means Y." Contextualization and clarification say, "Here are the dreamer's main concerns, and this is the question posed by the dream. When you know these things, the dream, in its own words, is often understandable."

Dreams provide tremendous amounts of information about the dreamer. But how best to learn those things, and how best to discover them? There are many techniques of dream interpretation that are valid and useful, but, in my view, what is essential to all work with dreams is the collaboration of the dreamer and the dream interpreter. I outline a process of dream analysis that is collaborative in every sense of the word. It enlists the cooperation of the dreamer and the analyst; it recognizes that the dreamer has barriers to understanding his own dream, but that the analyst may have different barriers. It looks to dream interpretation and dream clarification as processes unfolding between two people, which will explain many things about the dream, the dreamer, the dream interpreter, and their relationship.

The dream interpreter does not have to be a clinician. Friends, spouses, and partners can all help us understand our dreams. Although the clinical chapters look especially at work with dreams by a patient and psychoanalyst, the principles apply to any two people who work together on dreams.

Freud's *Interpretation of Dreams* was not just about dreams; it was an attempt to develop a model of how the mind works. I would like in this book to revive the tradition of studying the implications of dreaming for a model of the mind. I especially address those questions in the final section on "Sleep, Dreams, and the Brain." In doing so, I must acknowledge from the start that I am not a laboratory dream researcher,[1] although I am familiar with many of the findings of laboratory science. My firsthand study of other people's dreams, while intensive, is done primarily

---

1. In 1972, at the University of Chicago, I spent a few days at Allan Rechtschaffen's laboratory. But dream research requires nights, not just days. I spent one entire night awake, watching an experimental subject sleeping and dreaming. It was fascinating, but the next few days were hell for me. I was

in the clinical consulting room. Therefore, my suggestions about the implications of clinical data for the neurobiological study of the mind are just that—suggestions.

Nevertheless, I hope my hypotheses and observations will stimulate researchers in cognitive neuroscience to test them in the laboratory. There is a tendency among cognitive neuroscientists to dismiss psychoanalysis as nonscientific and to argue that their hypotheses and data have bearing on psychoanalytic thinking, but not the reverse. In this respect, the approach of the neurobiologist Semir Zeki is refreshing. In his authoritative book *A Vision of the Brain* (1993), Zeki writes the following: "The study of the brain is still in its infancy and many exciting ideas about it remain to be generated and to be tested. I hope that no one will be deterred from asking new questions and suggesting new experiments simply because they are not specialists in brain studies. Leaving it to the specialist is about the greatest disservice that one can render to brain science in its present state" (p. ix).

I accept Zeki's invitation and hope to inspire my fellow clinicians to do the same. This book is an offering to him, and all cognitive neuroscientists, of some observations culled from a long-term immersion in the psychic life of individuals and their dreams.

Most of the current neurophysiological research has provided data about brain function that can be incorporated by clinicians into their theory of dreams. I propose that we also think in the opposite direction: by studying the kinds of "disordered" thinking that can occur in dreams, and considering them in connection with neurological studies of brain damage and experimental research on the brain, we will learn the principles of brain organization. I will suggest routes from phenomenology to biology, instead of just the other way around.

By carefully studying dreams from these perspectives, clinicians who do psychological work with dreams may be able to formulate hypotheses about the kinds of processing of information and emotion that differentiate dreams from waking mental life. These hypotheses may then help guide the research of cognitive scientists about which mental processes are functionally and neurologically separable from one another, and how these processes are reorganized during sleep. Laboratory scientists may then produce data that either confirm or disprove the hypotheses and further our understanding both of psychodynamics and brain function. In this way, we may lessen the gap between psychoanalysis and neuroscience, to everyone's benefit.

---

exhausted and felt jet-lagged. I discovered that my biological clock lacked the resilience necessary for laboratory dream research.

PART II

NEW WAYS OF THINKING ABOUT DREAMS

CHAPTER 2

THE ANALYSIS AND CREATION OF DREAM MEANING

The name generally given to widely accepted error is *tradition*.

Charles Rosen

THE CURRENT GAP between psychoanalysis and neurobiology did not exist when psychoanalysis was founded. Freud's first scientific research (1877) was on animal neurology, the development of the nervous system of the eel. Later, one of Freud's major works was the *Project for a Scientific Psychology* (1895), which attempted to create a model of human mental functioning based on the neurological knowledge of his time. This work is still appreciated and admired by leading cognitive neuroscientists today (Bilder and LeFever, 1998). Pribram (1998) says that "we find that Freud, 100 years ago, was in fact a good scientist and what his science had to offer—even in considerable detail—is not so different from what we today can offer" (pp. 18–19). But over the years, psychoanalysis, cognitive science, and neurobiology have become relatively isolated from one another, although some communication among the fields has continued, especially in the area of dreams.

The psychoanalytic view of dreams has changed dramatically in the hundred years since Freud published *The Interpretation of Dreams*. Many psychoanalysts, from Jung to the present, have questioned Freud's conclusion that all dreams are the fulfillment of wishes. In 1944, the Scottish psychoanalyst Ronald Fairbairn argued that "dreams are essentially, not wish-fulfillments, but dramatizations or 'shorts' (in the cinematographic sense) of situations existing in inner reality." In 1950, Frieda Fromm-Reichmann, transplanted to the United States from

Germany, argued that there were many dreams that do not deal with wish fulfillment (see also Stolorow and Atwood, 1982; Fosshage, 1983). Fisher and Greenberg (1996) surveyed dozens of dream studies, and concluded that while there is good evidence that dream content has psychological meaning, there is none that supports Freud's wish-fulfillment theory.

Even Freud questioned whether all dreams are the product of wish fulfillment. Already in the Dora case (1905), he wrote that the meaning of a dream could be "of as many different sorts as the process of waking thought. . . . In one case it would be a fulfilled wish; in another a realized fear; or again a reflection persisting into sleep; or an intention; or a piece of creative thought" (p. 68). Then, in 1933, he considered whether dreams should be seen, not always as wish fulfillments, but rather as *attempted* wish fulfillments. Finally, in the *Outline of Psychoanalysis*, written near the end of his life (Freud, 1940), Freud proposed two kinds of dreams:

> With the help of the unconscious, every dream that is in process of formation makes a demand upon the ego—for the satisfaction of an instinct, if the dream originates from the id; *for the solution of a conflict, the removal of a doubt or the forming of an intention, if the dream originates from a residue of preconscious activity in waking life* [p. 169; italics added].

Here Freud is suggesting that only *some* dreams aim for the satisfaction of an instinct. Other dreams may try to solve a conflict, remove a doubt, or form an intention.

In his 1988 and 1993 books, neurobiologist Allan Hobson continues to wrestle with Freud's earliest idea that unconscious wishes instigate the dreaming process. He writes (1988): "Once REM sleep and dreaming have been cholinergically triggered, wishes may be expressed and may even shape dream plots, but they are in no sense causative of the dream process" (p. 202). Many contemporary psychoanalysts would agree with this formulation. From a clinical standpoint, the motives behind the formation of a particular dream are much more important than the instigators of dreaming itself. But that much could already be surmised from the first studies that found dreaming to be a regularly occurring experience during the night.

Contemporary psychoanalysts have suggested many motivators for dream formation. Erich Fromm (1951) saw in the dream an attempt to express psychological insights in symbolic language, without the "noise" of cultural convention. Paul Lippmann (1998) sees dreams as responding to both private concerns and social factors. Edgar Levenson (1983, 1991) has shown how dreams often portray the most simple truths about the dreamer's experience, truths so blunt that, in the clinical setting, neither patient nor analyst may fully understand them without first reenacting them during the process of dream interpretation. I have argued (Blechner, 1983) that dreams may express things that are not expressible by any other means, and I will expand that viewpoint in this book.

All of these revisions have one thing in common: they change our theory of how dreams carry meaning and how best to understand that meaning. In this chapter, we will therefore address three main questions: (1) Where is the meaning of the dream? (2) How do we arrive at that meaning when we do clinical dream analysis, and to what degree is that meaning discovered or created? and (3) What is the significance of bizarreness in dreams?

Freud's view was that the mind starts with the latent dream thought, which is represented something like a grammatical, understandable sentence. Because the latent dream thought is threatening and unacceptable, the dreamwork disguises it through various mechanisms, such as symbolization, condensation, and displacement. The result is the manifest dream, which contains the latent dream thought in a disguise that makes it seem less sensible and understandable. This disguise allows the unacceptable latent dream thought, and its source in unacceptable infantile impulses, to be discharged without disturbing the dreamer's sleep.

To the question "Where is the meaning of the dream?" Freud would answer that it starts in the unconscious, as a thought that is logical and grammatical but unacceptable, and it is then disguised by the dreamwork into the manifest dream. To the question "How do we arrive at that meaning when we do clinical dream analysis?" Freud's answer would be that by using the dreamer's free associations, in combination with symbol translation, we can undo the disguise of the dreamwork and *reconstitute* the original latent dream thought. To the question, "What is the significance of bizarreness in dreams?" Freud would answer that it is a byproduct of the dreamwork's transformation and disguise of the latent dream thought.

This basic Freudian theory of the formation of dreams, which dominated psychoanalysis during its first half century, has been seriously questioned during the last half century, not only by clinical psychoanalysts, but also by laboratory dream researchers. Freud thought of dreams as mini-pathological events, but this viewpoint had to be revised when Aserinsky, Dement, and Kleitman discovered that we dream regularly throughout the night, and much more often than we consciously realize (Aserinsky and Kleitman, 1953; Dement and Kleitman, 1957a, b). Usually we are dreaming during periods of "Rapid Eye Movement" (REM) sleep, which occur throughout the night, about every 90 minutes. We also can be dreaming during nonREM periods of sleep, although less frequently and often less vividly.

The fact that dreams occur so regularly, along with other new findings, has led some dream researchers to postulate that dreams do not start with a fully formed verbal thought. One of the best known of these theories is that of Hobson and McCarley (1977), who call it the "activation-synthesis hypothesis." They propose that the basic stimulus of the dream is an image produced during REM sleep by periodic firing of the pons, a structure in the brain stem. Such images, which Hobson and McCarley believe to be random, are then synthesized by the higher levels of the brain into an ongoing narrative. The process is very much like the brain administering to itself a TAT (Thematic Apperception Test), showing itself an image and then elaborating a story based on that image. Antrobus (1991) suggests that the primary input may be even more obscure, for example, just a visual feature, which the conceptual or higher perceptual modules transform into a recognizable object or person.

There are many objections that can be raised about Hobson and McCarley's original theory. It is known that 10% to 15% of dream reports from nonREM sleep are indistinguishable from REM dreams (Foulkes, 1962). Solms (1997), studying patients with brain injuries, found that patients with damage to the pons still dream, whereas patients with lesions to the ventromedial quadrant of the frontal lobes in the white matter permanently stop dreaming.[1] These data suggest that the activation-synthesis hypothesis may have to be revised. Indeed, McCarley (1992) has acknowledged that the activation-synthesis hypothesis does not pose a threat to the psychological interpretation of dreams. It is primarily a theory of the *instigation* of dreams, and he argues that the final dream integrates "the brain stem-induced motor and sensory activation with the particular memories and personality characteristics of the dreamer" (p. 52). This is more in line with Solms's (1999) proposal that REM is an instigator of dreams, although not the only one. Hobson

---

1. This is the same part of the brain in which prefrontal lobotomy is performed, and a regular side effect of that procedure is that dreaming stops (Jus et al., 1973). The unfortunate widespread use of prefrontal lobotomy, once thought to be the treatment of choice for schizophrenia, intractable pain, and other pathologies but now discredited, turned out to be an inadvertent study of dreaming.

(1999) has also proposed a revision of activation-synthesis that gives a greater role to forebrain mechanisms and allows for increased possibility that dreams are meaningful.

But let us consider what Hobson and McCarley's original theory implies about our first two questions: To the first, "where is the meaning of the dream?" the activation-synthesis hypothesis says that we do not start with meaning. We start with a relatively meaningless image that has been generated by neural firing. Then, in the synthesis stage, the higher levels of the mind construct a more coherent narrative out of such internally generated stimuli. So the dream starts as meaningless, and then becomes more meaningful.

What does this theory say about our second question, namely, "how do we arrive at that meaning when we do clinical dream analysis?" In my view, it suggests that when we interpret a dream, we may be continuing the brain's process of creating meaning. In other words, dream interpretation is not taking the dream back to its original sources in the latent dream thought. According to activation-synthesis, there is no latent dream thought at the start of the dreaming process. Instead, if the dream interpretation does decode meaning, the meaning comes only from the synthesis stage of dream formation.

Another theory of dreaming is that of Francis Crick, the Nobel Prize winner for DNA research, and Graeme Mitchison (1983, 1986). They have proposed the theory that dreams are not meaningful; instead, they are waste products. They draw the analogy with large computer systems, which at night perform certain operations to clear out spurious material. In particular, they eliminate "parasitic oscillations" in the cortex, which are a kind of neural analogue to obsessional thoughts.[2] Crick and Mitchison see this sort of housecleaning as the function of dreaming—the brain expelling useless material; and the conclusion they draw is that the analysis of dreams, or any focused attention on dreams, may be harmful.

This thesis was advanced in the journal *Nature*, and was seen as a major challenge to Freud.[3] But the fact is that Freud has already considered it, in one of its earlier incarnations—the theory of Robert. According to Freud (1900),

---

2. This theory raises the question whether those suffering from obsessive thoughts during waking have defective or insufficient dreaming, and hence are less able to eliminate parasitic nodes.

3. As Panksepp (1998) notes, however, this is an interesting theory for which there are absolutely no data.

> Robert describes dreams as "a somatic process of excretion of which we become aware in our mental reaction to it." Dreams are excretions of thought that have been stifled at birth. "A man deprived of the capacity for dreaming would in course of time become mentally deranged, because a great mass of incomplete, unworked-out thoughts and superficial impressions would accumulate in his brain and would be bound by their bulk to smother the thoughts which should be assimilated into his memory as completed wholes." . . . What Robert is clearly doing is to infer from these two features of the material of dreams that by some means or other an expulsion of worthless impressions is accomplished during sleep as a *somatic* process, and that dreaming is not a special sort of psychical process but merely the information we receive of that expulsion. Moreover, excretion is not the only event which occurs in the mind at night. Robert himself adds that, besides this, the suggestions arising during the previous day are worked out and that whatever parts of the undigested thoughts are not excreted are bound together into a rounded whole by threads of thought borrowed from the imagination and thus inserted in the memory as a harmless imaginative picture [p. 79].

Note how similar this is to Crick and Mitchison's hypothesis, except that the computer analogy is not invoked. Actually, this theory has gone through several other iterations. In 1964, Evans and Newman (1964; Newman and Evans, 1965) proposed a similar "brain housecleaning" operation for dreams.

The question of whether dream meaning is decoded or created is not just a theoretical controversy. It has implications for the question of how best to analyze dreams in the clinical setting. It harks back to the old debate between Jung and Freud about using free associations to interpret dreams. Free associations, Jung believed (Jacobi, 1973), "always lead to a complex, but we can never be certain whether it is precisely this one that constitutes the meaning of the dream. . . . We can, of course, always get to our complexes somehow, for they are the attraction that draws everything to itself" (p. 84). Jung felt that Freud's stated procedure of relying primarily on the patient's associations led to a *reduction* of the dream. We will get to a reflection of the patient's complexes, but that is not the true meaning of the dream.

In a way, Jung's view was prophetic for psychoanalysis. In 1967, the members of the Kris Study Group on dreams at the New York

Psychoanalytic Institute came to the conclusion that dreams have no special significance in clinical psychoanalysis (Waldhorn, 1967). They felt that all of the psychodynamics that are derived from dream analysis can also be derived from analysis of a patient's free associations. When Freud wrote *The Interpretation of Dreams*, he had not yet discovered the basic techniques of psychoanalysis, and much of his self-analysis was devoted to the analysis of his own dreams. But, they argued, today's analysts have no special need of dream analysis. Had Jung been alive when this report came out, I presume he would have laughed. He would have said that this so called "finding" was the logical outgrowth of the Freudian process of dream analysis. Free association to the dream takes you back to the patient's complexes, and if that is all that you do in your dream analysis, then of course dreams will yield nothing special to you.

The question of whether dream analysis is useful, harmful, or something else seems especially significant when we study bizarreness in dreams. Is the bizarre material in dreams critical to dream analysis, as Freud thought, because of the intensity of the operation of the dream-work on that material? Or is bizarre material mainly to be dismissed as meaningless, as Hobson has argued, the result of the cortex "making the best of a bad job" in having to integrate imagery and eye movements that are not under its control? Or is there some other, special significance to bizarre material in dreams?

To discuss these questions, I would like to turn to one of Hobson's own dreams, which he recounts in his book *The Dreaming Brain* (1988). It is of special interest to me for three reasons. First, the manifest dream deals with the relationship of Hobson, a neurobiologist, and his colleague Van, a psychoanalyst. It is a good example of what Lippmann (1998) means by a dream that has both private and social ramifications. Second, Hobson uses his dream to consider whether bizarre aspects of the dream have any meaning, let alone whether they have special importance. And third, the dream shows some of the basic metaphors that Lakoff and Johnson (1980) have identified in their book *Metaphors We Live By*, but elaborates and recombines them in unusual ways. Here is Hobson's dream, along with his commentary on it:

> I am in Williamstown, Massachusetts, talking to a colleague, Van, who is wearing a white shirt (he usually wears blue) open at the neck (he is normally neck-tied, and even collar-clipped) and khakis (he usually sports flannels). Casual. Van says, as if by the way, that he attended the committee meeting that had

yesterday considered my candidacy for an invited lecture series. (I know from his tone that he is going to deliver bad news.) The committee has decided against it because "They don't feel that psychoanalysis should be confronted with laboratory data."

I allowed as to how bad an idea that was. "It's the wrong reason," I said. "And their timing is off, because Adolf Grünbaum is just about to publish his important new book in which he insists that this is precisely what psychoanalysis must do." Van ignores this statement, appearing never to have heard of A. G.

Van then begins a gentle pirouette and tosses me a piece of hardware, something like the lock of a door or perhaps a pair of paint-frozen hinges. It is as if to say, "Here, take this as recompense." Despite my scavenger nature, I think I should refuse this "gift," and so I toss it back to Van on his next choreographic spin. He insists that it is meant for me, and the scene changes without clear resolution of whether or not I will keep it.

We go out a door (which is on the corner of the building) to behold the beautiful Williams campus. A red-brick walk extends down a green lawn to the classic white Puritan buildings.

Van says, "They chose Mary" (or seems to say that), "reflecting their priorities, to attract a speaker who might help them with their fundraising efforts."

"That is why you have such beautiful buildings," I note, "and why there is nothing in them" [pp. 232–233].

Hobson then tells us:

The narrative significance of my dream should be transparent. My task is to change the psychoanalytic mind: not only mine, but my colleague's (and, indeed, in this book, my readers' as well). The psychoanalyst, always on the lookout for latent meaning, might be interested in the fact that my father also lives in Williamstown, and wish to see my motives as quixotically oedipal! Also a resident is a mutual friend, Bart, whose first wife was named Mary. Perhaps these are clues to a deeper, formative motive of my dream which is cloaked by the dance with Van (itself a thinly veiled homosexual desire?).

But I think my dream has more clearly and openly to do with my annoyance at my old friend Van, who left me in the lurch at Harvard and went to Williams to take an endowed chair

> in psychoanalytic psychology. I obviously wonder whether he is friend or foe. Is he a faithful ally or a self-serving turncoat? In view of the latter possibility, I get my revenge by accusing him (via displacement to Williams) of mercenary motives that lead to graceful forms devoid of substance. This all seems very transparent to me. Almost naked. Perhaps I also wonder if my theory of dream form will be architecturally appealing but uninhabitable.
>
> So why is Van dressed incongruously? Why does he pirouette? Why does he suddenly toss me a piece of hardware? Why is the hardware "something like" the lock of a door? Why is it "perhaps" a pair of paint-frozen hinges? Why does the scene change? Why does Van "seem to say" that the committee chose Mary? Answers to these questions, which relate to the only features of the report that make it distinctively dreamlike, are all too easily ascribed to defenses whose meaning is to be sought in my mental associations. But viewed as disguises they are inadequate. And viewed as symbols they are unnecessary [p. 233].

I would like to address some of the questions Hobson raises about his dream. My intent here is not to attempt an exhaustive analysis of the dream. Rather, I will focus on those aspects of the dream that are relevant to the theory of dreaming.

Hobson asks us: "Why is the hardware 'something like' the lock of a door? Why is it 'perhaps a pair of paint-frozen hinges?'" We can answer that both of them are means of blockading. They describe different kinds of defensiveness. A lock is an absolute defense. It allows one to choose whether to let others in through the door or not; hinges allow a door to open, but if they are paint-frozen, they work something like a lock, although they are less impenetrable and they do not give one the choice of locking someone else out or not. The paint-frozen hinge is frozen, but this is considered a dysfunction. This part of the dream is a typical dream formation. The lock/frozen-hinge is a composite creation that may represent various gradations and kinds of defensiveness. This defensiveness blocks the passage of information about brain hardware and mental software between psychoanalysis and cognitive neuroscience.

Hobson says that he usually would take the lock/hinge due to his "scavenger nature," but he thinks he should refuse it. He sends it back, but Van insists that it is meant for him, and the scene changes without clear resolution of whether or not Hobson will keep it. The dream may represent the relationship between Hobson and Van, between neurobiology and psychoanalysis. Each of them is defensive, and they are playing a game of "hot potato" with the lock/hinge, that is, with their charges of defensiveness. It is as if Van is saying, "You are blocked, and this lock/hinge symbolizes the way you are blocked," and Hobson sends it back, as if to say, "No, the blockedness is yours, Van."

What is the nature of the barrier between Hobson and Van? Is it something like a lock that a person can choose to open at will, if he is willing to open the latch or if he has the key? Or is it perhaps like paint-frozen hinges, which do not budge even if you want them to? To get frozen hinges to move is a tougher task; you have to soak them in solvent for a long time, which is messy and time consuming. And maybe Hobson and Van, neurobiologist and psychoanalyst, are not sure if they want to engage in that slow, messy process to free up the hinge in their relationship.

Of course, in interpreting the dream in this way, we could also be enacting the dream. As Schimel (1969), Levenson (1983, 1991), Joseph (1985) and I (Blechner, 1995a) have pointed out, that is often the case in dream interpretation. The content of the dream is enacted between the dreamer and the interpreter during the process of dream interpretation. In his commentary on the dream, Hobson doesn't fully engage the possibility of psychoanalytic interpretation. He dares analysts to find formulaic oedipal and homosexual themes in his dream. He seems to have a misconception about psychoanalytic dream interpretation, which is not limited to a few sexualized clichés. My initial reaction to the dream and Hobson's commentary was that it was about Hobson's defensiveness, which he will not acknowledge. But in making that interpretation, I would be, in effect, doing what Van does in the dream, trying to give the frozen hinge back to Hobson, and he could then try to give it back to psychoanalysis. We could easily get into a deadlock (pun intended). So, I think, instead, that interpreting the dream as representing the dialectic between easygoing playfulness and rigid defensiveness, between neurobiology and psychoanalysis, may be more to the point of the dream, and it may get our hinges unstuck.

Hobson also asks us: "Why is Van dressed incongruously?" In the dream Van is dressed more casually than usual. Perhaps Hobson wants Van, that is, psychoanalysis, to be more casual than usual. And, I would like to say, the dream sees the truth—modern psychoanalysis *is* more casual than it used to be. Perhaps Hobson is used to the formality and rigidity of certain psychoanalytic institutions. Perhaps, too, instead of the rigidity and adversarial nature of some scientific disputes, Van's dance signifies a kind of gentility, grace, and openness to mutuality.

Hobson also asks, "Why does the scene change?" Within the interpretation of the dream that we have pursued so far, we can answer because Hobson does not want to deal further with the issue of his, or Van's, defensiveness. But let's look more closely at the scene change. The characters of the dream go from indoors to outdoors.

Here, Lakoff (1993) can be especially helpful to us. If we apply his notion of the unconscious metaphoric underpinning of the dream, we can see the scene change as going out for a "breath of fresh air." This is another attempt to defuse a confrontation. *The shift captures the affective essence of the dream, which may be the dialectic between easygoing playfulness and aggressive confrontation.*

Thus, in my view, the central image of the lock/hinge, with all of the words modifying it, is not a random bizarre creation. Instead, it forms the nexus of meaning in the dream. This question, of whether bizarre dream formations have special meaning, is crucial in my opinion. It touches on the fundamental question of why we need to dream, and of whether dreams have a special place in our thought processes. I would now like to suggest an alternative to both Freud's view of wish fulfillment and Hobson's view of periodic biological causation.

In my view, what is extraordinary about dreaming is that it allows us to have thoughts that cannot be put into words. Dreaming allows extralinguistic thinking, thinking that extends beyond the bounds of language, with much fewer constraints than most waking thought. Psychoanalysis has focused in recent years on what Bollas (1987) calls "the unthought known" and Stern (1997) calls "unformulated experience." Both of these concepts imply that the thoughts could be expressed with words, but are not. In my view, dreams allow us to express literally unspeakable thoughts, thoughts that cannot be expressed in words because we do not have the words to say them. And that is why dreams can tell us things that free association cannot.

Thus, the dream allows the mind to think without the constraints of language. Language is certainly crucial to formulating thoughts in ways that can be communicated easily and efficiently from one person to another, what Sullivan (1953) called the syntaxic mode of thought. But language is also very constraining of thought. Dreams allow us to supersede the constraints of language; dreams allow us to think the unspeakable. (I mean unspeakable, here, not only with its connotation of something taboo, but more literally, as something that cannot be spoken because it is not expressible with words.)[4]

Psychoanalysis was founded on the idea that translating the neurotic symptom into something spoken in words would lead to cure. This was the principle behind the treatment of hysteria. The bodily symptom was expressing something that could not be spoken. But the source of this "unspeakability" was usually dynamic repression; in other words, it could not be spoken because certain emotions, like guilt, or cultural taboos, militated against its being spoken. For instance, women who had been sexually abused were under strong cultural pressure not to speak about it. But the unspeakable thoughts that are reflected in dreams may not all be subject to repression or dissociation because they are unacceptable; it may be, rather, that they cannot be spoken because they employ concepts for which we do not have words in our language.

According to the Whorf-Sapir hypothesis (Whorf, 1956), language shapes and limits the kinds of thoughts we can have. In waking life, it is very hard for us to think of things for which we have no words. The Whorf-Sapir hypothesis holds that speakers of different languages may have different thoughts because they have different vocabularies that allow those thoughts.[5]

A good example of the way language limits thought is very salient in today's cognitive neuroscience. In our language, we have the words "mind" and "brain." These two words enforce the Cartesian viewpoint that the mind and brain are separate. When we say "brain," we mean the bodily organ. When we say "mind," we mean the collection of mental processes and faculties. But many of us are becoming more and more uncomfortable with this division. The aim of modern neuroscience, as well as Freud's aim in his *Project for a Scientific Psychology*, is to be able to account for mental events in terms of neurobiological processes and vice versa, so that ultimately we will understand them as unitary phenomena. And so, many of us have come to talk about the "mind/brain." This compound term is the closest we can get in English these days to bypass Cartesian dualism. Maybe someday we will have a single word for the mind/brain. Perhaps we will say "mind/brain" often enough, and it will be slurred into a new word like "mibron." Or maybe a com-

---

4. Since I am also a musician, I have always had good reason to believe this. Music allows mentation that is both highly structured and significant, but still nonlinguistic (Blechner, Day, and Cutting, 1976; Blechner, 1977; Jackendoff, 1987).

5. The factual accuracy of Whorf's examples concerning the number of Eskimo words for snow has been seriously questioned (Martin, 1986; Pullum, 1991).

pletely new word will be coined. Maybe someone will create such a new word in a dream.

In my view, dreams allow us much more flexibility in our thinking because we are free in our dreams to think thoughts that extend beyond the bounds of language. When we try to report such dreams, we inevitably have to resort to language, but the vagueness or complexity of these descriptions shows how far the dream has ranged from the constraints of language—as when Hobson says "something like" a lock or "perhaps" a hinge. We then often characterize these parts of the dream as bizarre. But they are the truly creative and informative aspects of the dream. Ideally, in interpreting them, they should not be reduced to phrases that sound more linguistically coherent but are further from the original dream percept. Perhaps they should not be interpreted at all.

Not interpreted at all! This does not sound like proper psychoanalysis. But I mean that some percepts, especially the more bizarre ones, should be left intact, in their original wording. Instead of translating them, we can make their meaning clearer by describing the overall context of the dream, perhaps as a question.

In this way, dream analysis may be like the game *Jeopardy!* in which you are provided with the answer and you have to come up with the right question. In dream interpretation, if you provide the right question, the dream image will function as the answer. If you set up the right context, then the seeming nonsense will make sense.[6]

Lakoff and Johnson (1980) provide an excellent example of this from waking life. They propose the sentence: "Please sit in the apple-juice seat." While in isolation this sentence has no meaning, it did in the context of its creation: "An overnight guest came down to breakfast. There were four place settings, three with orange juice and one with apple juice. It was clear what the apple-juice seat was."

One of the questions addressed by Hobson's dream is: "What is the relationship between Hobson and psychoanalysis like?" The answer it provides is, "It is something like a cross between a paint-frozen hinge and a lock, with neither party wishing to hold onto it, work it, or fix it." Actually, when we translate a dream into secondary process language, as I have just done, we make the dream more communicable, but we probably lose something of the original, precise significance of the dream. In this, I agree with the composer, Ned Rorem (1994), who wrote:

---

6. The theoretical basis for this approach to dreams is developed further in chapter 8.

> Dreams are dreams, with their own integrity, not symbols designed to keep us asleep. Like music, whose sense and strength and very reason-for-being can never be explained by mere intelligence, the meaning of dreams forever evades us, not because that meaning is too vague for words but because it is too precise for words [p. 517].[7]

James Hillman (1979) has expressed a similar view:

> For us the golden rule in touching any dream is keeping it alive. Dreamwork is conservation. We have to set aside what we naturally and usually do: projecting the dream into the future, reducing the dream to the past, extracting from the dream a message. These moves lose the dream in exchange for what we get from it. Conservation implies holding on to what is and even assuming that what is is right [p. 116].

---

7. In my private experience, I find this to be true. At different points in my life, I have "mapped" my experience onto music, thus devising "metaphors" that nonmusicians would find unconventional. This started when a close friend asked me, "Which piece of music is you?" and I discovered that I had an immediate answer: I "was" Brahms' Second String Sextet, op. 36. It took time for me to think through how that piece "felt like me" at the time, and I realized that whatever linguistic adjectives I came up with (optimism, tenderness, gentleness) were not as precise as the music itself. The mapping of my emotional experience onto music bypassed language, but felt metaphoric nevertheless. Similarly, one of my patients was told by her husband that their relationship reminded him of the last movement of Mozart's Piano Concerto no. 23. She felt she knew what he meant and was very flattered.

There is much to be studied concerning nonlinguistic metaphors—the mapping of one nonlinguistic experience onto another. In such instances, verbal consciousness, the description of the experience in words, is truly an epiphenomenon. Musicians don't need words to work out such mappings. Musicologists, academicians who write about music, take on the task of describing musical experience in words. Some do it better than others, but most musicians agree that words merely approximate something that musicians can communicate with one another through nonverbal, musical means.

Leonard Meyer (1956) was one of the most successful musicologists to describe the processes of music in terms of Gestalt psychology. But his work, although it is written in words, owes its success to its description of musical perception in terms of nonlinguistic functions of perception—the good continuation, Prägnanz, closure, and so on. Such concepts have also been applied to visual form. I expect that people who are more sensitive to the visual arts might be able to map their experience similarly onto individual paintings.

Probably, in Hobson's dream, the object that Van tossed to Hobson was something never before seen and something for which we have no precise word. Hobson relates this in-between quality well. If he had not written it down, over time he would probably have changed this object to fit more neatly into our world of objects, as classified by familiar language. And we would lose something of the dream's essential meaning.

My conception of the extralinguistic capacity of dream thought has been paraphrased incorrectly by colleagues, a number of times, as prelinguistic. I would like therefore to stress that prelinguistic and extralinguistic are not the same. I think dreams are reflective not just of early modes of thought (prelinguistic), but of fully developed, perhaps even advanced kinds of thinking that are not constrained by language (extralinguistic).

Dreams are extralinguistic in several ways. As I have already noted, they can create objects for which we have no name. But they are also extralinguistic in that they step beyond the bounds of conventional metaphor. They create entirely new metaphors, and they also extend and combine commonly used metaphors in brand new ways.

Let me explain what I mean. Lakoff and Johnson, in their book *Metaphors We Live By*, have shown us how our everyday speech is filled with common metaphor. We are usually unaware of most of these metaphors as we use them, although it is easy to bring them to our attention. For instance, they point out that a commonly used metaphor is *ideas are food*. We often say, "We have the *raw* facts" or "His ideas are *half-baked*." But there are limits, at least in waking thought. As Lakoff and Johnson say, there are *half-baked ideas*, but there are no *sautéed*, *broiled*, or *poached ideas*" (p. 109). A sautéed idea feels ungrammatical when used in everyday speech. But not in dreams. In dreams there *can* be sautéed ideas. The understanding of dreams requires us to open our minds to unconventional metaphors, or metaphors expanded into new ranges of detail.

Another common metaphor pointed out by Lakoff and Johnson is *an intellectual discussion is a sport*. We say, "Let's toss around some ideas." With baseball in mind, we may say, "My opponent in the debate threw me a curve ball" or "You hit a home run with that idea." Golf devotees may say, "That point was a real hole-in-one." Tennis players may say, "He's not good on the return." Boxing devotees may say, "Now he's really taking off his gloves." All of these metaphors are easily understandable as idiomatic English.

Hobson's dream takes the metaphor *an intellectual discussion is a sport* and expands it. Hobson and Van play catch, but in a very special way.

While most of us would understand, "In the debate, he threw me a curve ball," we would be startled if, in waking speech, we heard someone say, "In the debate, he threw me a paint-frozen hinge," or "He threw me a lock." But these sentences create a new metaphor: *An intellectual discussion is collaborative construction*. Thus, Hobson's dream joins together two metaphors, *intellectual discussion is sport* and *intellectual discussion is collaborative construction*. The crossover, a conjoint metaphor, produces a game of catch with a piece of hardware, and this hardware is itself a condensation of multiple ideas. Such conjoint metaphor, which may be a special feature of dreaming, is worthy of further study.

CHAPTER 3

SECONDARY REVISION, TERTIARY REVISION, AND BEYOND

Ich glaube an alles noch nie Gesagte.
(I have faith in all that is not yet said.)

Rainer Maria Rilke, *Das Stundenbuch*

IN THE LAST CHAPTER we asked: How, when, and to what degree is dream meaning created? Part of our answer at this point is that whenever we remember a dream and tell it, we are transforming it and creating some of its meaning. And this is something that we do with every dream that reaches consciousness. It is notable that our only waking conscious access to dreams is to *memories* of dreams. So far, a dream of one person has never been observed by another person, although this has occurred in the science fiction movie *Brainstorm*. In that film, a machine was devised that could transmit the experience of one person to another person, either simultaneously as it happened or recorded on tape for future playback.

But so far, real science has not managed to observe dreams in real time. We observe the corollaries of brain function—electroencephalograms, EMGs, patterns of eye movements and muscle movements—but not the dream itself. As Wittgenstein (Kenny, 1994) asked: "Has the verb 'to dream' a present tense? How does a person learn to use this?" (p. 223).

We never *say*, "I am dreaming that so and so . . ." Nor do we say, "She is dreaming that so and so . . ." Present-tense dreaming, in most usage, is ineffably singular and solitary—unless we are speaking of dreaming in the sense of a daydream or a fantasy, such as Martin Luther King's "I have a dream" (which has a different meaning from "I am having a dream").

There has been an experiment that brought us closer to eavesdropping on someone else's dream while it happens. Arkin, Hastey, and Reiser (1966) gave a posthypnotic suggestion for the dreamer to talk in his sleep about the dream while it is happening. In most of the awakenings after such sleep-speeches, the remembered dream was very close to the dream described during sleep. This is probably the closest anyone has come to taking part in someone else's dream while it occurs.

But even in this case, the dreamer *spoke* about his dream as it happened. That is different from the dream experience itself. When we recall a dream or speak about it, we can already see the process of transformation occurring—the transformation from something sensory and experiential and relatively nonlinguistic to something that is primarily linguistic, with the sensory and experiential elements translated into a linguistic text (more or less). We often work in psychotherapy with the "dreamtext." But no one dreams the dreamtext—that text is already a transformation of the dream experience. *If interpretation is the transformation from one system of meanings into another, then the translation of experience into text, which we all do when we recall and when we tell a dream, is already part of the process of dream interpretation.*

Freud introduced the concept of secondary revision to address the process by which we fill in gaps in the dream narrative to have it be more coherent and make more sense. Secondary revision is like waking confabulation in psychotic and neurologically damaged patients (Blechner, 2000b). The patient makes up material to fill in the gaps.

Freud (1900, p. 489) argued that we can identify the work of secondary revision by several signs. The interpolated parts of the dream can be identified by:

- The ease with which they are told,
- Introduction by an "as though,"
- A lack of vividness,
- Placement at points of juncture between two dream parts, and
- Less easy retention in memory than genuine derivatives of dream thoughts.

Secondary revision is one of the thornier aspects of Freud's dream theory, yet it is also one of the most important. Freud changed his mind about secondary revision several times in his career. He claimed at first that it was part of the dreamwork, and, in *The Interpretation of Dreams*, devoted an entire section of his chapter on the dreamwork to it. Even in that chapter, however, he started to have doubts and identified secondary revision with the processes of waking thought:

> The following consideration makes it highly probable that the psychical function which carries out what we have described as the secondary revision of the content of dreams is to be identified with the activity of our waking thought. Our waking (preconscious) thinking behaves towards any perceptual material with which it meets in just the same way in which the function we are considering behaves towards the contents of the dreams. It is the nature of our waking thought to establish order in material of that kind, to set up relations in it and to make it conform to our expectations of an intelligible whole. In fact, we go too far in that direction. An adept in sleight of hand can trick us by relying upon this intelligible pattern of the sense-impression that are offered to us. We often fall into the strangest errors or even falsify the truths about the material before us [Freud, 1900, p. 499].

Later in his career, Freud (1913, 1923c) moved toward a conviction that secondary revision was definitely *not* part of the dreamwork proper:

> Before the manifest dream is arrived at, they are submitted to a process of secondary revision which seeks to give the new product something in the nature of sense and coherence. Strictly speaking, this last process does not form a part of the dreamwork [1923c, p. 241].

Sometimes Freud thought that secondary revision is only a kind of patchwork; it fills in the holes in the narrative structure, cleaning it up and making it more coherent. At other times he thought that *most* of the narrative structure of the dream came from secondary revision.

The rejection of secondary revision as part of the dreamwork became integral to Freud's theory of dreams. It fit his claim that the overall narrative structure of the dream, being something patched on afterward, is not central to the meaning of the dream. He called the narrative structure of the manifest dream "an unessential illusion." This viewpoint supported his rebus-like approach to interpreting dream elements, in which the dream interpreter ignores the narrative structure of the dream and decodes each element of the manifest content via the dreamer's associations to uncover the latent dream thoughts.

If we see dream meaning as something that is constantly evolving, we can combine both of Freud's views about secondary revision. Secondary revision may go on as a subprocess of dream formation, and it can continue after the dream experience. Part of the complexity of secondary revision is that it is not a one-time process. Each time we recollect or tell a dream, there is more secondary revision. The process of smoothing out or altering the dreamtext is inevitable. It goes on with all dreams, even in the Bible.

Consider, for example, Pharaoh's dream in Genesis. The Bible tells the dream twice, first when Pharaoh dreams it, then when he tells it to Joseph to have it interpreted. If you look at the two tellings of the dream, you will see that they have small but significant differences. In order to make this clear, I have juxtaposed the two versions of the dreams side by side and underlined the parts of the second recounting that are significantly changed (see facing page).

The second telling is longer; the two dreams are now joined into one, and some of the wording is more extreme. The second version also adds that after the lean kine eat the fat kine, they are no fatter than before.

Freud was aware of this tendency to alter dreams with each telling and argued that when a dream is told twice, the altered sections are especially important areas of repression and may be key to the interpretation. This was something that Joseph knew. He interprets the dream thus [my commentary is in brackets and italics]:

> The dream of Pharaoh is one [*which Pharaoh's retelling of the dream had made clear*]: God hath shewed Pharaoh what he is about to do. The seven good kine are seven years; and the seven good ears are seven years: the dream is one. And the seven thin and ill favoured kine that came up after them are seven years: and the seven empty ears blasted with the east wind shall be seven years of famine. [*The fact that the lean kine do not fatten by eating the previous kine reinforces this interpretation that they succeed them in time, but do not profit from them.*]

This then becomes the essence of Joseph's advice to Pharaoh:

> This is the thing which I have spoken unto Pharaoh: What God is about to do he sheweth unto Pharaoh. Behold, there come

THE TWO VERSIONS OF PHARAOH'S DREAMS

FIRST RECOUNTING OF PHARAOH'S DREAMS (when he has them) [Genesis 41:1–7]	SECOND RECOUNTING OF PHARAOH'S DREAMS (when he tells them to Joseph) [Genesis 41:17–24]
And it came to pass at the end of two full years, that Pharaoh dreamed;	And Pharaoh said unto Joseph, In my dream, behold, I stood upon the bank of the river:
and, behold, he stood by the river.	
And, behold there came up out of the river seven well favoured kine and fatfleshed; and they fed in a meadow. And, behold, seven other kine came up after them out of the river, ill favored and lean-fleshed; and stood by the other kine upon the brink of the river. And the ill favoured and lean-fleshed kine did eat up the seven well favoured and fat kine.	And, behold, there came up out of the river seven kine, fatfleshed and well favoured; and they fed in a meadow: And behold, seven other kine came up after them, poor and very ill favoured and leanfleshed, such as I never saw in all the land of Egypt for badness. And the lean and the ill favoured kine did eat up the first seven fat kine: And when they had eaten them up, it could not be known that they had eaten them; but they were still ill favoured, as at the beginning.
So Pharaoh awoke.	So I awoke.
And he slept and dreamed the second time:	And I saw in my dream [NB. he now describes it as one dream],
and, behold, seven ears of corn came up upon one stalk, rank and good.	and behold, seven ears came up in one stalk, full[1] and good:
And, behold, seven thin ears and blasted with the east wind sprung up after them.	And, behold, seven ears, withered, thin, and blasted with the east wind, sprung up after them:
And the seven thin ears devoured the seven rank and full ears. And Pharaoh awoke, and, behold, it was a dream.	And the thin ears devoured the seven good ears: and I told this unto the magicians; but there was none that could declare it to me.

1. This difference is not due to the translator; it exists in the Hebrew text: "Briot" in the earlier telling vs. "Melayot" in the later telling.

> seven years of great plenty throughout all the land of Egypt; and the famine shall consume the land; And the plenty shall not be known in the land by reason of that famine following; for it shall be very grievous. And for that the dream was doubled unto Pharaoh twice; it is because the thing is established by God, and God will shortly bring it to pass [Genesis 41:25–32].

And so, Joseph's advice is to store up supplies during the seven fat years, so that there will indeed be food during the seven lean years.

TERTIARY REVISION

The process of dream revision does not stop with the dreamer. When we tell our dream to a psychoanalyst or any other person,[2] that person also will revise the dream as he or she recalls it or tells it. When such revision is done by someone other than the dreamer, I call it "tertiary revision."

If you want to observe tertiary revision, try this test on yourself. Have someone else tell you a dream. Write it down as you hear it and then put it away where you won't see it. Two weeks later, write the dream down again, and then compare your two versions. I think you will find the alterations very revealing. They will bear the stamp of your own psychology; they also will tend to smooth out the unusual aspects of the dream.

There is a fascinating example of this in the psychoanalytic literature. Sullivan twice reported a dream told to him by one of his assistants, once in his book *Personal Psychopathology* and again in *The Interpersonal Theory of Psychiatry*.[3] As with the example of Pharaoh's dream, I have laid out the two versions side by side to make the comparison easier:

---

2. When I first wrote this sentence, the wording that came out of me was "When we tell our dream to a psychoanalyst or any other *third party*. . . ." I realized that the person to whom we tell our dream is a second party not a third party; but I realized my error reflects our experience of dreams as privately interpersonal. They are like stories told to us by someone else (although we know that the author of those stories is ourselves).

3. I am indebted to Mark Siegert for making me aware of these two versions of the dream.

SULLIVAN'S TWO VERSIONS OF HIS ASSISTANT'S DREAM

Personal Psychopathology	*Interpersonal Theory of Psychiatry*
"I can perhaps best illustrate both the fugue and the diminution of self-consciousness by reference to a not too uncommon sort of dream. One of my colleagues in the course of coming to understand himself underwent a nightmare perhaps the most typical of this sort of experience of any that I know. This young man, one of the most talented in dealing with disturbed patients, and one who had come to a belated realization of the homoerotic tendencies in his personality, was at that time engaged to a woman whom later he married. He had come, however, in dealing with his mental content, to look temporarily upon a homosexual *modus vivendi* as a possible, perhaps to be desired, consummation of some of his tendencies.	"To go on to another dream: At one time I had a really marvelous assistant—one of those people without any particular formal education whose gifts and life experience had produced the sort of person who automatically reassured terrified people. He possessed no suitable hooks that panicky young schizophrenics could use to hang their terror on, and he reflected in many other ways the naturally estimable personality structure that would be required for dealing with schizophrenics. In those days there was a great deal I didn't know about the risks attendant upon dealing with human personality, and this young man rapidly became not only my left hand, but, I suppose, most of my left upper extremity. After the pattern of the good-if-they-do not-die-young, he became of great interest to a bitterly paranoid woman. Thanks to the eternal vigilance which we do preserve, however blindly, he was worried about this relationship, and talked to me about it. And I talked to him and talked to her, and counseled delay, because she seemed to be suffering frightfully from his very casual heterosexual life away from her, and I thought that such worries would grow if they were legitimized, and so on. And also I didn't want him upset —he was too valuable.
He dreamed one night somewhat as follows: He stood on a plot of lush green grassland. It was most beautiful and agreeable. He had observed incidentally that it was at the lower level before a huge concrete dam that towered far above toward the zenith.	Whereupon he dreamed a dream. Some of you may have been in the environment of Baltimore and have seen Loch Raven. Loch Raven is one of those monolithic concrete dams which produce very beautiful artificial lakes behind them. And this monolithic dam is quite

As he was enjoying himself, to his astonishment, a band of water appeared between his plot of land and the foot of the dam. As he watched this, it widened. At the same time, astonishment gave way to fear increasing toward terror. Synchronously, someone far above on the top of the dam called to him. [His associations place the person as his fiancée.] He struggled with himself; he was in panic; he wished to go to her—to be on the solid concrete monolith. He leaped over the widening band of water—he found himself, even as he was making the wild effort to jump the broad band of water, leaping from the edge of his bed into a pool of moonlight on his bedroom floor. The crash did him some injury, but it was some time before he could rid himself sufficiently of fear, and 'recover sufficient touch with reality' to discover the hurts, calm himself, and return to sleep. The self is abundantly evident in this dream. The self-consciousness, as an approving reference system concerned in our appraisals of personal reality, however, was slow in full recovery from the dream-situation. In the schizophrenic fugue, the state of awareness throughout is very like that of the moments following the 'awakening' of the dreamer, varying only in the sense of greater reduction at such time as the patient is 'wholly out of touch with reality' (generally in panic) or engaged in very troubled 'sleep'" [Sullivan, 1972, pp. 288–289].

impressive—very high, with a wide sluiceway. The dream is set at the foot of the Loch Raven dam. There is an island, very small, very green —a lovely island—not far from the shore, on which this assistant of mine and I are walking, engaged in conversation. He gazes up at the dam and sees his fiancée at the top of it, and is not particularly distracted in his conversation with me.

Then he observes that the area of water between the island and the shore, over which we had stepped, is rapidly widening.

He awakens in terror, finding himself leaping out of bed into a pool of moonlight in the bedroom [Sullivan, 1953, pp. 336–337].

You can see some of the dramatic changes: in the information preceding the dream, Sullivan stresses the homosexual conflict in the first telling, but completely omits it in the second telling, in which the woman is distressed by the dreamer's "very casual heterosexual life away from her." Then in the dreamtext itself there are changes, most notably in the degree of conflict the dreamer is feeling, especially about his choice between Sullivan and the woman. In the first telling, Sullivan is not mentioned as being part of the dream, and the dreamer is in panic; in the second telling, he is not particularly distracted in his conversation with Sullivan, who is present in the dream.

Ferenczi (1913) told us that "one feels impelled to relate one's dreams to the very person to whom the content relates." It may be that the dreamer told Sullivan the dream because of the conflict he was feeling, and Sullivan's own conflict led to the tertiary revision.

Secondary and tertiary revision are not fundamentally different processes, but whereas secondary revision involves an intrapsychic elaboration of the dream, tertiary revision is to some degree interpersonal. The process of dream revision does not stop even with tertiary revision.[4] Dreams can continually be told and retold to as many people as will listen. In fact, one theory of myth formation is that myths start with one person's dream. As the dream is retold by one person to the next, it changes, as in the child's game of "telephone." With each successive telling, a few idiosyncratic and personal details are stripped away, and the core elements that are relevant to the larger group are retained or amplified. In the end, we have a revised dream story that functions as a parable for all the members of a society.[5]

---

4. There are many examples of secondary and tertiary revision in literature. Interested readers may wish to analyze the secondary revision in Oblonski's dream in Tolstoy's *Anna Karenina*, and the tertiary revision about the same dream in Vladimir Nabokov's essay about Oblonski (Nabokov, 1981).

5. The Jungian technique of relating a dream to a myth achieves a reverse version of this process. The myth, which may once have started as the dream of an individual, is now used to reflect back on an individual's dream and to highlight and amplify its universal themes.

CHAPTER 4

WHO CREATES, HAS, REMEMBERS, TELLS, AND INTERPRETS THE DREAM?

Will you know how to dream of what you do not see?

Olivier Messiaen

MANY OF THE new developments in cognitive neuroscience are teaching us that our language for speaking about human experience is inadequate and imprecise. We are discovering that our way of speaking about ourselves is based on the illusions of our conscious experience. As we come to unravel the workings of the mind/brain as measured extramentally (i.e., by methods of measuring brain activity from the outside, such as EEG, PET scans, etc.), we discover that actions of the mind/brain often do not coincide with conscious awareness of those actions.

These findings have led us to reconsider what it means to act, to have a will to act, and to be conscious; in the process of this reconsideration, the word "I" has come to be extremely suspect. When we say "I," we think we know what we are talking about. But the more we know about the mind/brain, the more we learn that the word "I" is very inadequate in formulating sentences that are true.

For example, there are studies that show that the brain initiates action *before* we are aware that we want to do it. Thus, the will of the brain *precedes* the conscious will. Consider the experiments of Libet and his colleagues (1983), in which brain activity is monitored electrically. The subjects are asked to flex a forefinger vigorously any time they choose. The subjects consciously make up their minds to move their fingers about 200 milliseconds (msec) before the actual movement. But the electrodes in their scalp detect a spate of mental activity *350 msec before* the person makes the conscious choice to move his finger. Thus, the brain makes the decision to move the finger before the person is aware of having made such a decision. The brain first makes the decision, and our consciousness of the decision follows shortly thereafter.[1]

Consciousness thus may be, in some instances, a process of *monitoring* brain activity, rather than *directing* of brain activity. Even when we think we are consciously making a decision to act, the decision may already have been made in our brains. Does that mean that "I" did not make that decision? Only if "I" does not include my brain. But in the kind of speaking that we are used to, when we use the word "I" as the subject of a sentence, we are accustomed to thinking of a consciously-directed activity, such as when we say, "I wrote, I said, I walked." We don't usually say, "My brain decided I would walk, and then I became aware of my brain's decision, and, not having vetoed it, my legs began to move."

It may be necessary for us to change how we think of "I." Instead of a unitary self, there may be many aspects of "I," including various sections of "my brain." If, following some stressful news, we have stomach cramps, how shall we most accurately describe the experience? We would find it awkward to say, "My brain decided to cause me to have stomach cramps," but that sentence may be close to the truth. If the brain is part of "I," then a paraphrase of that sentence is "I caused me to have stomach cramps," which sounds strange and awkward. The "I" refers to my brain, and the "me" refers to my total organism, including my stomach and my awareness through my brain of my stomach. We are accustomed to saying "I had stomach cramps," but the causation, if it is unconscious, is usually not linked with "I." It would perhaps be more precise to say, "Part of my brain caused my stomach to cramp, and part of my brain perceived those cramps."

---

1. Freud (1923b) anticipated this question when he wrote: "But what about those internal processes which we may—roughly and inexactly—sum up under the name of thought processes? They represent displacements of mental energy which are effected somewhere in the interior of the apparatus as this energy proceeds on its way towards action. Do they advance to the surface, which causes consciousness to be generated? Or does consciousness make its way to them?" (p. 19).

DREAMS AS STORIES THAT WE TELL OURSELVES

The questions of agency and experience are even more complicated when it comes to our dreams.

We experience dreams as if they are a story that is authored by someone else. By whom? The ancients thought that they were messages from the Gods. Freud told us that they were messages from our unconscious. If Freud is right, it leaves us with an astonishing experience. The dream is told to us by our own mind, and yet it feels interpersonal. It feels as if we are experiencing the dream without awareness of its source and, usually, without any control about how the dream goes. It feels as if it comes from someone or somewhere else, but it is ours. So the dream becomes a prime example of an experience in which our own mind is experienced as if it is another person.[2]

Dreaming is an involuntary creative activity. In our dreams, all of us are bards, storytellers, weavers of new experience. We know that "we" do it, but we feel that the I that we experience, as our intentional conscious willful self, is usually not involved in the dream's creation. Instead, some other I, our night-I, or our unconscious-I, with an intelligence and inspiration at least as good as our waking life and maybe better, takes over. This aspect of experience is made explicit in certain languages like Greek, in which one says, literally, "I saw a dream."

The neurologist V. S. Ramachandran, who directs the Center for Brain and Cognition in San Diego, reports having a dream in which someone was telling him a very funny joke that made him laugh heartily in the dream. This dream suggested to Ramachandran (Ramachandran et al., 1996) that "there must have been at least two mutually amnesic personalities inside me during the dream" (p. 44). The experience of laughing heartily at a joke requires an element of surprise. Who told the joke in the dream and who laughed at it?

Ramachandran asserts that his dream proves the plausibility of multiple personalities. But in another way, *most* dreams suggest the experience of multiple personalities, since the personality that creates the dream scenario and the personality that experiences it seem separate to us, and our dreams can surprise us in many ways, besides jokes. It is very common, in dream reports, to find the word "suddenly." We often experience sudden surprising shifts in dreams that may frighten us, delight us, or intrigue us. But the experience of something happening

2. An exception to this is the "lucid dream," in which the dreamer can feel a certain level of awareness that he is dreaming and sometimes an ability to control the progress of events in the dream (van Eeden, 1913; LaBerge, 1985).

in a dream that seems "out of the blue" increases our sense of some strong independent force directing the dream narrative. If we were conscious of concocting the dream ourselves, those sudden shifts would not feel so surprising.

We need new ways of speaking about dreams, but they have not yet evolved or been invented. I say, "I dreamt." If I say, "I had a dream but I don't remember it," the implication is that at one point I was conscious of the dream, but now I have forgotten it. We don't usually say, referring to a dream that was *never* conscious, "I had a dream but I don't remember it. I never remembered it, or at least I don't remember ever remembering it." This statement, however, is often the true state of our dream life. In 1953, Aserinsky and Kleitman discovered that we dream regularly throughout the night, although we do not remember having had most of those dreams. Since the discovery of Aserinsky and Kleitman, it would also be correct to say, "I had more than five dreams last night, and I don't remember any of them." In this case, the conviction of having had dreams is based on the knowledge of the regularity of dreaming, rather than on the firsthand conscious experience of dreaming.

Someone who knows the experiments of Libet et al. (1983) might say, "I decided to do it before I realized that I decided to do it," but in our world, so far, such a sentence would sound strange. The different "I's" in the sentence have different referents. We do not yet have different words in our language to refer to those different I's; we do not have nouns to discriminate the "I-ness" of our unconscious brain activity that precedes the more familiar "I-ness" of the conscious sense of willing.[3]

In this respect, philosophy helps us analyze the inadequacy of language to describe the phenomena that we know in the world. There may have to be a branch of philosophy that is involved with expanding language, creating language that will cover the full extent of what we can know.

The histories of philosophy and psychiatry have often conflated the notion of the self with the notion of the *conscious* self, but not always. Even Socrates, in the *Meno*, attempted to show us that learning may not be a process of willful accumulation and sorting through of knowledge, but might be a conscious discovery of what the mind/brain already knows unconsciously.

---

3. Richard Restak (1991) brought this problem to our attention with his clever book title: *The Brain Has a Mind of Its Own*. In 1911, the Frenchman Claparède invented the term "moïté" which David Rapaport (1951) translated as "me-ness," but this word has not entered common usage.

In the nineteenth century, there was an attempt to solve this problem of terminology by calling the conscious self the "I" and the part of the organism that is not under conscious control, the "it." In *Beyond Good and Evil*, Nietzsche (1886) wrote: "A thought comes when 'it' wishes, and not when 'I' wish, so that it is a falsification of the facts of the case to say that the subject 'I' is the condition of the predicate 'think.' *It* thinks" (p. 24).

George Groddeck (1923) expanded this notion in *The Book of the It*, arguing that most physical illness is the expression of mental conflict that is largely dissociated. One of Groddeck's examples is that of morning sickness. According to Groddeck, no matter how much the pregnant woman consciously looks forward to the birth of the child, she also fears the birth and may, in varying degrees, wish to be rid of the fetus. This is expressed in the nausea and vomiting of morning sickness. The mother has these feelings, but they feel alien and unacceptable, and are therefore attributed to the "It" rather than the "I."

Freud (1923b) took this argument further in designating three "regions" or agencies of the mind—the "I," the "It," and the "Super-I." These were translated by James Strachey as the ego, the id, and the superego, which gave them a pseudoscientific sound. But in German, the word for the id was the same as those used by Nietzsche and Groddeck, das "Es" (the "It"), and Freud's German readers readily see the link from philosophy to psychoanalysis, which readers of the English translation may miss.

Freud, and most of us who have followed him, referred to "*the* unconscious" but rarely, if ever, "*the* conscious." This distinction has become entrenched in our language; psychoanalysts speak about "the contents of the unconscious," which sounds perfectly grammatical. To speak about "the contents of the conscious" does not sound grammatical to most people. Why did "the unconscious" become reified with the definite article? It may be that the unconscious, feeling foreign, was conceived of as a thing. "The conscious," much more familiar to us, already had a very personal name: "I." Still, the various forms of unconscious mentation do not have names, especially when one speaks in the first person. We resort to adverbs. We can say, "I wanted to do it unconsciously." We do not, in ordinary English, say "It did it," referring to our unconsciously determined actions (although Nietzsche and Groddeck did write such sentences).

The "I" in Freud's schema, and in popular thinking, at first was identified with the conscious ego. Freud later recognized the need to divide the I, the ego, into conscious and unconscious portions. In *The Ego and the Id* (1923b), which should be titled in English, *The I and the It*,[4] Freud separates three kinds of unconscious processes: (1) the preconscious, which is capable of becoming conscious; (2) the repressed, which is actively kept out of consciousness, by forces which can be undone by psychoanalysis; and (3) a third unconscious, which is not repressed, but which involves functions that are nevertheless out of awareness, and not accessible to consciousness. This latter part of unconscious ego functions, about which Freud commented "and Heaven knows how important a part," has become the increasing focus of attention in recent years by cognitive neuroscientists (Kihlstrom, 1986; Libet, 1993).[5]

There are various kinds of unconscious mental experiences, which can and cannot become conscious, for various reasons. We have:

1. dynamically repressed thoughts, by reason of being *inadmissible* to consciousness;
2. dissociated thoughts or emotions, admissible in certain states of consciousness, but in which the connection with other thoughts (or emotions) is not conscious;
3. thoughts that are unthinkable in linguistic consciousness, but may be experienced nonlinguistically, either emotionally, musically, or in some other format;
4. "unformulated experience" which are thoughts that *could* be described by linguistic consciousness, but are not;
5. thoughts that are completely incapable of being conscious in any format, whose nature we cannot describe, and whose existence we can never prove, although we can surmise them to go on in various realms of mental activity, such as some forms of waking unconscious processing of which we are never aware.[6]

---

4. It is a valuable exercise for English readers to recast some sentences from *The Ego and the Id*, with "Ich" translated as "I," and "Es" translated as "It." If the whole paper were thus retranslated, I think it would be understood quite differently by contemporary readers.

5. Many of the basic concepts of psychoanalysis are being rediscovered and renamed by cognitive scientists, often without acknowledgment of their psychoanalytic predecessors. The "observing ego" reappears in Mesulam's (1998) "commenting self," and the structure of adult thinking on a fundament of bodily experience is rediscovered by Lakoff and Johnson (1999).

6. This last category would not include "nonmental" cerebral processes of which we *never* could become aware. Libet writes about this (1992): "The broad view of unconscious mental functions extends far beyond a more limited one of Freudian 'repression' of emotionally difficult thoughts. However, it would not include those cerebral operations which are 'nonmental,' in the sense that they

Which aspects of dream formation and dream experience correspond to these varying levels of consciousness? You realize the difficulty of this question if you try to speak of the dream experience in the first person. For example, if you accept Freud's model of dreaming, you might say: "Part of my brain has a thought (the latent dream thought) which another part of my brain knows will be disturbing, and so it censors the original thought and transforms it into a format that is largely unrecognizable (the manifest dream) through a process known as 'the dreamwork.' The manifest dream does not disturb me, and so I can continue sleeping." All of these are different parts of "I": the thinker of the latent dream thought, the perceiver of its troubling content, the censor which transforms it through the dreamwork, and the "I" that finally experiences the censored and transformed product, the manifest dream. Then there is the "I" that remembers the manifest dream in waking life and mulls it over to extract the latent dream thought.

If you accept the activation-synthesis model of dreaming, you might say: "My brain goes into a different state, during which a part of my brain starts firing out a random image, and another part of my brain works with that image and tries to weave a story around it. I (or still another part of my brain) see and feel that story as a kind of visual-kinesthetic experience."

The question of agency in dream formation, of "who does what" in the dream, has troubled many psychoanalysts. And among those who adhere to Freud's theory of dream formation, none has come up with a satisfactory answer. Roy Schafer (1983) asks:

> Who does the dream work? The dream work doesn't just happen. It makes little sense to state or imply, as Freud did, that it just does itself. Saying that the primary process does the dream work is unacceptable. This is so not only because one would thereby remain in the realm of mechanistic discourse, but also because saying so would be inconsistent with one's being as impressed with dreams as one often is, in that the prevailing conceptualization of primary process emphasizes energic mobility and not creative synthesis. And in modern psychoanalytic

---

do not ever achieve a potentiality to rise into awareness; these would include control processes for blood pressure, heart rate, automatic postural adjustments, etc." (p. 264). This is a fascinating definition of mental, that is, cerebral operations which at least have a *potentiality* of rising into awareness. If an advanced practitioner of yoga learns to control his heart rate, does that mean that he has made his heart rate a "mental" function?

> theory there is, following Freud, no longer a hypothetical system *Ucs.* to do this work; metapsychologically, the matter must now be conceptualized structurally.
>
> From the structural standpoint, then, one would have to invoke the principle of multiple function. One would say that all the constituent structures of the mind participate in the amazing end result that one appreciates as a dream . . .
>
> In his discussion of responsibility for dreams, Freud (1925a) had to say that the dreamer was responsible for the dream. Who else, he asked, dreamed the dream? Just as soon as notions of responsibility enter the discussion, one must depart from metapsychological impersonality and begin to speak of persons [p. 61].

Donald Spence (1982) founders on the same question, and comes to the conclusion that free association *changes* the remembered dream, which is close to my belief that the process of dream interpretation actually continues the process of dream formation and can create, rather than just discover, meaning. James Grotstein (1979) sums up the question wittily with his paper title, "Who is the dreamer who dreams the dream and who is the dreamer who understands it?"

The experience of multiple states of consciousness and agency applies not only to dreams, but also to creative work. Several great creative thinkers have acknowledged that, in moments of inspiration, they feel like the passive vessel of their brain's activity. The composer Igor Stravinsky said something like, "I am the vessel through which *The Rite of Spring* was passed." And Albert Einstein, in a 1932 letter to Erika Fromm (Fromm, 1998), described his experience of developing the theory of relativity as looking for a solution that he felt his mind had already worked out: "the creator of the problem possesses the solution."

When we say, "The thought occurs to me" rather than "I think," we are acknowledging the same subjective sense of passivity with respect to our own brain activity. This grammatical construction, more acceptable in English than the German equivalent ("It thought to me"), expresses our sense of not consciously experiencing the process by which our thoughts are formed.

One of the growing developments in cognitive neuroscience is the recognition that the brain is extremely multi-faceted, with different kinds of processing going on simultaneously. This model is currently known as parallel distributed processing (PDP) (McClelland and Rumelhart,

1986). One of its important features is "multiple re-entrant signaling."[7] This means that the brain's output becomes part of its input—the brain reprocesses its own processes.

David Olds (1994) helped move psychoanalytic theory toward integrating these newest findings of cognitive neuroscience, by highlighting these re-entrant properties of consciousness. He emphasized that "consciousness is one of the brain's *output* vectors. That which is flashed in consciousness then becomes one of the many *inputs* the brain has to deal with, along with sensory input and input from memory and the visceral system" (p. 597). Where we would locate "I" in such a system is extremely complex; perhaps it is impossible.

Consciousness is not just an experience for its own sake. It becomes a way to monitor the brain's activity, and to modify the effects of the brain's output through what is called "re-entrant signaling." Weiskrantz (1986, p. 170) refers to consciousness as a "commentary system." Consciousness does not totally direct our brain's activity. At best, it allows us to modify our brain's activity somewhat, but probably much less than common sense would suggest.

One of the abilities of conscious thinking is the ability to lie. When we intend to lie and a slip accidentally reveals the truth, psychoanalysis has usually thought of that phenomenon as an intrusion of the unconscious into conscious intention. In the next chapter, we will consider how this ability fares in dreaming and what that suggests about "who" dreams the dream.

---

7. Freud wrote (1923b), "All perceptions which are received from without (sense-perceptions) and from within—what we call sensations and feelings—are *Cs.* from the start" (p. 19). We know today that the process of a sensory stimulus becoming conscious is quite a bit more complicated at the start. For example, when we see a house, it is not just that the light waves enter our eye, are transformed into a signal carried by the optical nerve, and then that signal is decoded into a neural representation of house. The information does not flow through our mental apparatus in one direction only. Instead, the flow of information can be multi-directional and re-entrant. Light may start by entering the eye and stimulating the retina. The information may then move to the lateral geniculate nucleus, and then on to the visual cortex. But there are many recurrent feedback loops along the way that feed the partially processed information back into the system. Similarly, the connections with memory can involve many kinds of feed-forward and feed-back mechanisms. We may revive memories of many kinds of houses that we have seen, or even of white boxy objects that we have seen, and these revived memories may actually influence the way we see the house. Also, our cortical processing of the house can influence eye movements to scan the image differently (Keating and Gooley, 1988; Kosslyn, 1994).

CHAPTER 5

WE NEVER LIE IN OUR DREAMS

THE TRUTH OF MANIFEST CONTENT

> If it were given to our bodily eyes to see into the mind of another, we would judge a man far more often by what he dreams than by what he thinks. . . . The dream, which is all spontaneity, takes and keeps the impress of our mind. Nothing emerges more directly and with more sincerity from the very depths of our soul than our unreflective and unconfined aspirations. . . . Our chimeras are what resemble us most.
>
> Victor Hugo, *Les Misérables*

FREUD SAW THE main motivation in the construction of the dream to be the disguise of unacceptable wishes. For him, the dream censor is always disguising and transforming unacceptable thoughts into manifest dream thoughts, which keep the latent dream thoughts hidden.

At one point in *The Interpretation of Dreams*, Freud (1900) went quite far with this thesis:

> The resolution of what are ostensibly acts of judgement in dreams may serve to remind us of the rules laid down at the beginning of this book for carrying out the work of interpretation: namely, that we should disregard the apparent coherence between a dream's constituents as an unessential illusion, and that we should trace back the origin of each of its elements on its own account [p. 449].

I propose something quite different: Our dreams are not concerned mainly with disguise and censorship. They are, in fact, our most honest communications, perhaps the only human communication in which we cannot lie. We can lie *about* our dreams, but not *in* our dreams. In light of Freud's theory that dreams disguise the underlying latent dream thought, it may seem a bit ironic for me to claim that we cannot lie in our dreams.[1] But I believe it to be so. We always tell the truth in our dreams, although their message may not be accessible to all. Because dreams represent the truth through means that differ from our waking thoughts, their meaning may be unclear to the dreamer. And since the message may be something that is dissociated for the dreamer, she may not see the meaning that may be obvious to another person who does not have the need to dissociate the same content. This is what the Jungian analyst Marie-Louise von Franz meant when she said, "No one can see his own back."

Dreams are not crafted to disguise, nor are they crafted to be readily understood. They merely speak in their own language, which is designed to be meaningful without necessarily being communicative. Some effort and interest is required for the waking mind to understand them. But our dreams tell many truths about us that we might not reveal in waking speech. Since many people do not realize what is in their dreams, they may reveal things about themselves by telling a dream that they would otherwise prefer to keep secret.

Very often, patients who cannot or will not share critical information with their psychoanalyst may reveal such information in their dreams. In some cases, the dreams are a few months or even a few years ahead of the material that is discussed openly in the treatment. The analyst may hear conflictual material in a dream, which the patient claims to know nothing about. The analyst may identify the material, but if the patient offers no confirmation, then the analyst would do best to leave the material alone for the time being, not forgetting it, but not forcing the issue. Those who would insist on breaking through the patient's defenses at such points may find themselves with a rather empty couch. But if the analyst bides her time, the truth of the dream material will emerge eventually.

---

1. It may be argued that the disguising operation of the dream censor posited by Freud is not the same thing as lying, as usually conceptualized. Lying is ordinarily considered to be a deliberate act of deception. If the disguise of the truth is accomplished without will or consciousness, can it be considered lying? Freud's model of dream formation proposes a kind of intrapsychic lying—the dream censor disguises truths that would disturb sleep.

Almost always, the concrete images of the dream will have validity, even when a metaphoric interpretation also seems valid. Stephen Mitchell (1998) provides an excellent example of interpreting a dream metaphorically, but then discovering that the dream images also refer to a specific traumatic memory. His patient Robert dreams:

> I am climbing down a stone wall in my backyard; David (my son) is with me. I am lowering him down to the ground by holding onto his arm. He was about a foot from the ground when I let him go. It should have been safe, but he punched a hole in the ground and sank into some kind of chamber. He disappeared into the hole. There was some sort of light, as if there were a floor five or six feet below the ground. He bounced and rolled off to the side. I couldn't see him. I started screaming for my wife to call the police, an ambulance, something. I began digging frantically. I wasn't getting anywhere. There were sliding rocks. Then there were rescue workers, lots of people. There was a horrific feeling that David was dying. Then I noticed a piece of wood poking out of the dirt some distance away. It was moving. I dug down and uncovered a box like one of my filing boxes in which I keep all sorts of things I think I might need someday. I pulled the box up, and inside was David. He was alive and well.

Mitchell tells us about his interaction with Robert about the dream:

> I told Robert I thought the dream might be understood to suggest that there were places in his mind that he was not aware of, in which pieces of his own experience had been placed for safekeeping and future reference. I also suggested that his struggles with his son were in some measure reflective of struggles with a part of himself that had been long buried.
>
> Robert began the next session by complimenting me on my "creative" understanding of the dream, by which it soon became clear he meant farfetched. But he then told me another dream in which his wife (who has an interest in psychoanalysis and had encouraged him to enter treatment) disappeared into an elaborate system of underground pipes. In his associations to this image, he recalled that the house in which his family had lived during his childhood had a septic system underneath the backyard. The tank in this system would need to be drained

> periodically by a visiting truck, at considerable expense. To save money for the education of the children, his father undertook the massive project of digging trenches for lateral pipes to the tank which would increase the available drainage underground. The children would be enlisted in these massive digging projects. Robert remembered his mother's concern for his safety since the trenches were at times deeper than he was tall. There was one memory in which he struck at some rocks with his shovel, and water from an underground spring began to fill the trench. But he was pulled to safety before the trench filled with water[2] [pp. 22–23].

In working with dreams, I usually like to start with the most concrete implications of the dream. There is always time for a more metaphoric or symbolic interpretation. If the patient denies being aware of any connection to the concrete kinds of experience portrayed in the dream, my advice is: Wait. In time, the truth of the dream will probably come out.[3] I have experienced this phenomenon so often with so many patients that it almost seems like a rule of thumb.

For instance, a patient told me three dreams in her second session. There was a huge amount of material in the dreams, but I noted that in each dream she sustained a head injury. I asked, "Have you ever had a head injury?" She said, "No, nothing." The patient was comfortable with the more metaphoric interpretation, that she feared that her head, that is, her mind, would be damaged by the analysis.

The next session she returned, and said, "I can't believe I thought I had never had a head injury. After our last session, I remembered that

---

2. See Binswanger (1928) for a similar example (cited in Foucault, 1986, p. 58): the patient, who has not made much progress in treatment, dreams that she is crossing the frontier, and a customs agent makes her open her luggage. She takes out her things one by one, and finally takes out a silver goblet, wrapped in tissue paper; then he says, "Why do you bring me the most important thing last?" The dream can be easily seen as a metaphor for the analysis, in which she is saving the best for last. She is anxious for days after telling the dream; eventually she remembers a severe sexual trauma at the age of 5, which occurred in a room with a silver teapot wrapped in silver foil.

3. Otto Isakower (Reiser, 1997) is said to have developed this viewpoint into a dictum: "If in working with a dream you did not learn something new, by which he meant *relevant new historical information*, your work with that dream had not been successful" (p. 893). Like all generalizations, this one, too, is false, and may lead an analyst to feel obligated to find (or manufacture) historical information in a dream.

I was once working as a waitress, and another waitress carrying a tray full of dishes rammed the tray into my head, fracturing my eye socket."

In French, there is an expression, *l'esprit d'escalier*, literally, "staircase wit," which refers to the common experience of realizing the witty thing one could have said, or should have said, right after leaving (literally on the staircase). I think of this realization of my patient as *la connaissance d'escalier*, "staircase consciousness," in which a patient remembers something significant just after leaving a session, or shortly thereafter. It is a common phenomenon that patients remember something critical after leaving the session. Such insights often give the dream interpreter the sense that the dream has been "solved," but such "connaissance d'escalier" may not be the end of it. Much later, other memories of the dreamer, usually earlier ones, may be recalled which have had obvious bearing on the dream image. A year and a half after having the head injury dreams, the patient, in speaking about her early childhood, remembered how her mother used to slap her repeatedly on the head. Neither memory, of her injury as an adult waitress nor as a child being beaten by her mother, was available to her consciously when she first told me the dream.[4] When she spoke about the beating, I connected the memory to her dream from early in treatment, and she agreed.

Dreams are reliable in this way. If the dream portrays the patient doing something embarrassing, morally reprehensible, or something that would otherwise lead to social opprobrium, chances are that that experience is related to a real one. A man told me that he dreamt that he tied up a woman in a chair, gagged her, and then beat her cruelly. As he was doing so, he thought, "She doesn't really deserve this, but the last one did." And while having that thought, he realized in the dream that he had done it before. I asked him: "Have you ever done what you did in the dream or something like it?" (My question refers both to the manifest content and the latent content. The manifest content portrays the cruel act. But then the dream implicitly indicates that he has "done it before," since the last one deserved it.) The patient asked me, "What is this? Are you an adherent of the Alfred Hitchcock school

---

4. I would like to emphasize that while my patient could not *recall* either of these memories when she first told me the dream, she might have been able to *recognize* them. On the day she told me the dream, if I had asked her, "Did someone ever ram a tray into your eye socket?" Or "Did your mother ever hit you over the head?" I believe she probably would have answered "Yes" to either question. She would have recognized either fact, but she would probably not have been able to recall it unaided. This is quite different from memories "recovered" in therapy, which were previously not available either for recall or recognition.

of dream interpretation?" He then explained that in a Hitchcock movie, whose name he could not remember, a man has a repeated dream, which is ultimately used to solve a crime. In the previous week he had dreamt that he was having sex with one of his daughters. In that dream, too, I had first asked, had he done so? And he had also replied no, emphatically. But some time later in the treatment, he told me that as a teenager, he had forced a female relative into sexual play with him. Both dreams, taken together, were references to this teenage experience, about which he carried much guilt and shame.

I have many other examples of dreams whose details refer to actual experiences of the dreamer. A man, early in treatment, dreamt of having a sex change operation. As in the other examples, he seemed completely puzzled by the dream. He denied any actual fantasies of this sort. Eventually, we came to understand this early dream metaphorically as his fear that too much talk about feelings would be womanish, in his view. But several years later, conflictual homosexual and transvestite fantasies emerged, which connected more concretely with the dream.

That the concrete meaning of the manifest dream usually pans out does not invalidate the more metaphoric interpretation of the dream. This man truly was afraid of being "unmanned" by psychoanalysis. The concrete and the metaphoric can both be true. But it is of interest to me that the metaphoric interpretation is usually more acceptable to the patient than the concrete interpretation. Many psychoanalysts, finding the metaphoric interpretation more acceptable to the patient (and perhaps being proud of their creativity when they are the source of the metaphoric interpretation) may not go further. Ironically, the most powerful meaning of the dream may be right on the surface. Oscar Wilde once said, "Only superficial people look below the surface." While psychoanalysis is known as a "depth psychology," psychoanalysts do their best work looking not *below* the surface, but looking as deeply as possible *at* the surface.

In working with dreams, balance is important. If the dreamer is concrete, then the psychoanalyst may balance that concreteness with metaphoric interpretations. If the dreamer jumps over the detail of the dream into metaphor, then the psychoanalyst might do well to balance things by attending to concrete details, especially in situations where the metaphoric interpretation of the dream is functioning as a defense against a more concrete but conflict-ridden interpretation.

For example, a woman dreamt that she was a burglar. "The place I was burgling was a business building downtown. It had a marble lobby, brass elevators, and a guard. I had an accomplice, a man my age, I don't know who. It had a teenage quality. He and I are 'hanging' in the building. I know there is money in the basement. I will come back and steal it. We come there after midnight. I go down an elevator shaft. It is square. I climb down it, like a cat burglar. I get the money and I put it in my pocket and I don't get caught. I try to go back and do it again. I want to improve my technique. I have a flashlight around my neck, so I won't have to turn on the light. I take some more money. Like an idiot, I hang out there the next day. The guard notices and suspects me."

In the session in which she tells me the dream, she associates me to the accomplice and her husband to the guard. She then develops three metaphoric interpretations to the dream. She has the dream after increasing the number of her sessions. She wonders: Is she guilty about spending the extra money? Has she fully disclosed her decision to increase the number of sessions to her husband? Is she implicitly burgling money from him?

She also suggests a sexual interpretation of the dream. The flashlight is phallic, the elevator shaft is vaginal. The combination of the two, both in her control, could indicate masturbatory satisfaction. Finally, she connects the business building of the dream to a building in which she recently did some professional work in the building's basement, where the level of her "professional technique" was exposed. The building had a marble lobby, brass elevator and guard, although so does the building in which I have my office. She is extremely ambitious within her profession and competitive with me in that area.

All of these interpretations seemed valid. Yet I was struck by the burglary aspect of the dream, and, in my characteristic approach to dreams, I asked her if she had ever committed a burglary. She told me of two instances from her adolescence, in which she had stolen things, which fit in with the detail of the dream having a "teenage quality." She then reassured me emphatically, "I have never stolen anything since."

She entered the next session with an embarrassed look on her face. "I have to confess something, and I know it will be hard to do, but I might as well just get to it. It has to do with my cat-burglar dream. You asked me if I had ever stolen something. Well, last summer, you made an error in my bill. In July, I sent you a check for May. It was the same amount as my bill for June. You must have thought that that check was for the June sessions, and so your bill for the June sessions indicated that I had paid for them, when I knew I hadn't. I thought a lot about it, and I justified it to myself, that you made the mistake, so why should I pay it?" (Note that in the dream there is a male accomplice to her burglary.) "But after the dream, I realized that the burglary was my burglary, and I decided to tell you, so here is a check for that amount."

Freud believed that the dream thoughts are transformed by the dreamwork into the manifest dream elements, which are then organized into a coherent narrative by secondary revision. Freud argued that the overall narrative structure is not relevant to deciphering the underlying dream thoughts. Instead, we should analyze the dream elements via free association.

But we know that analyzing each individual dream element is no guarantee that some essential dream thoughts will not be overlooked. Freud's dream about his patient Irma, the first dream that he subjected to his system of analysis, is one of the best illustrations of the dream's truthfulness.

Freud dreamt that he was receiving numerous guests in a large hall. Among them was Irma, whom he had treated for hysteria. Freud took her aside to reproach her for not accepting his "solution" to her difficulties. She complained further of a somatic difficulty, and Freud became concerned he had missed an organic problem. He examined her, finding white patches in her mouth as well as scabs that were formed like the bones of the nose. Other medical colleagues then examined her, and it was determined that she had an infection. Freud remembered that his friend Otto had given her an injection and that probably the syringe had not been clean.

Freud interpreted the dream as a *wish* for self-justification. If Irma's illness were organically based, he could not be blamed for not curing her of hysterical ailments. But Freud's interpretation of the Irma dream, while deciphering the significance of various parts of the manifest content through his associations, turned out to be incomplete. He did not tell us of the clinical debacle that occurred with Irma, which was only clarified later by Max Schur (1972) and others. Schur had access to the Freud-Fliess letters at a time when they were not released to the general public. (This has since changed, since their publication in entirety [Masson, 1985].) Schur discovered that Fliess, the friend in Berlin to whom Freud associates in his interpretation, had operated on Irma, but that the operation had not gone smoothly. Rather, it was discovered that he had left a piece of gauze in the wound, which festered and nearly killed Irma.

In light of Schur's argument,[5] the manifest dream seems much closer to the essential dream thoughts than Freud acknowledged. Freud tells

5. There has been considerable debate, however, about the identity of Irma and the validity of Schur's interpretation. See Kramer (2000) for a summary.

us (1900): "*We were directly aware of the origin of the infection.* This direct knowledge in the dream was remarkable. Only just before we had no knowledge of it, for the infection was only revealed by Leopold" (p. 115; italics added). This is precisely what happened.

We could call Freud's technique "analysis of constituents without analysis of the whole." In my view, the piecemeal analysis of the different elements in the manifest dream can be helpful in understanding the dream. But unlike Freud, I would not dismiss the overall structure of the manifest dream narrative. On the contrary, I think that the best dream interpretations use piecemeal analysis as a means to clarifying the entirety of the *manifest* dream. I would go further and suggest that *if you analyze a dream piece by piece, and you arrive at an interpretation of the dream that fits into the totality of the manifest dream narrative, you are on the right track. If the associations contradict the manifest dream narrative or seem irrelevant to it, then they have not led you closer to the meaning of the dream* (see Erikson, 1954, and French and Fromm, 1964, for a related point of view). Associations, as Jung and others have pointed out, can clarify the dream, but they can also lead us astray from the dream.

The Irma dream demonstrates that the manifest dream does not lie. The manifest Irma dream tells us that something bad happened to Irma, that she has pains, for which she is being blamed, but that it is not just a question of her hysteria and her acceptance of Freud's interpretations. Instead, something organic that is not readily apparent is really troubling her. It is not just Freud's wish, but a fact. Freud's interpretation through his associations does not tell us this. His interpretation does not disclose Fliess' malfeasance and Freud's sense of guilt about this. His associations clarify various elements of the dream, but they contradict the fundamental fact of the dream, that Irma now has something physically wrong with her due to medical malpractice. We never lie in our dreams.

Stanley Palombo (1984) studied his own dream interpretation process with his patients. He found that when he asked patients specifically about whether they could connect an aspect of the dream with an actual experience, they did so 92% of the time. But if he did not ask specifically, they did so only 38% of the time. Thus, the connection of dreams to actual experience may be seriously underreported. Patients may tend not to tell their analyst about such connections, especially if they perceive that the analyst is not so interested in them.

I would like to make one modification to the strong statement with which I began this chapter. "We never lie in our dreams—but we can lie *about* our dreams." A dreamer may realize the implicit meaning of a dream, and alter her telling of the dream to try to disguise that meaning. Psychoanalysts value dreams because the dream itself seems to bypass the resistance, and it can tell us many things that the patient consciously resists telling. But in telling the dream, the dreamer's resistance may appear. Sometimes such resistance is blatant. For example, a woman dreamt of being addicted to heroin. She felt the meaning of the dream was that she was addicted to being a heroine, but she didn't consciously want to admit that. She found such wishes for grandeur more embarrassing than drug addiction. And so, in discussing the dream, she mispronounced the word "heroine" with a long "I" sound, as "herro eye n," hoping I would not notice that heroin is a homonym of heroine. Actually, the mispronunciation *directed* my attention exactly to what she consciously hoped I would not notice.

CHAPTER 6

CONDENSATION AND INTEROBJECTS

> The human mind is so constituted that it will insist on finding a resemblance between any two objects or forms presented for its inspection; and the more unlike the two objects, the more enjoyable is the challenge to discover the secret likeness.
>
> Goethe, *Wilhelm Meister*

THE CORE OF Freud's *The Interpretation of Dreams*, in my view, is his chapter on the dreamwork, and of this, the most brilliant part is his study of condensation. Here Freud is looking at how the mind can manipulate objects and features in the world, changing them at will. Freud's chapter on condensation is itself highly condensed. I would like to elaborate on the implications of the notion of condensation for a theory of dreams and a theory of thinking.

There are several kinds of condensation. They all have in common the fact that they condense several ideas or objects into a single dream element. Condensations can be distinguished both by *what* is condensed and *how* it is condensed (see Table 1 on p. 72). What is condensed can be words, natural objects of the world (including people), and ideas. These three kinds of condensation can be classified as follows:

1. *Lexical* condensation combines words or word fragments; for example, Freud's (1900, p. 296) "Norekdal," which condenses Ibsen's characters Nora and Ekdal; Blechner's (1997a) "prestyl dolby," which condenses the words "press the till, dough'll be [yours]."
2. *Formal* condensation involves the melding of two images into one, by combining their physical characteristics—in the manner of

Galton's composite photographs—or, we would say today, morphing. Formal condensation usually involves visual features, but it can involve other sense modalities.

3. *Ideational* condensation involves the mixing of two or more ideas into one dream formation. This type of condensation can include all aspects, including linguistic and visual. Since it is in the nature of dreams to be sensory, primarily visual, most ideational condensation partakes of sensory representation. Nevertheless, the condensation is ideational when the combination achieved by the dreamwork is not of the word or the image, but of the implied idea represented by the image. Identifying ideational condensation often requires the interpretation of symbols. It may not be apparent in the manifest dream itself, and hence one could argue that it is not a category equivalent to the other two.

In addition, condensations can be classified according to their *outcome*. They differ in terms of the nature of the product of the condensation—whether it is (1) an object that exists in waking life; (2) a new object never before seen in waking life, but which could exist in waking life; and (3) a new object never before seen in waking life, which could not exist in the waking world as we know it. I call these three kinds of condensation *simple overdetermined condensation, creative condensation*, and *partial condensation*, for reasons that I will now explain.

1. SIMPLE OVERDETERMINED CONDENSATION

In simple overdetermined condensation, the dreamwork condenses several ideas into one object. No new object or concept is created by the dreamer, but a single element may represent the convergence of several dream thoughts. That object is familiar to us from our waking life, but it signifies several underlying ideas, through the principle of overdetermination.

We see the object in the dream and have no evidence on the surface that it is a condensation. But when we ask the dreamer for associations, we begin to unravel the condensation. The evidence of the condensation comes from the various strands of associations that "show" the multiple sources of the manifest dream content. Thus, condensation occurs when multiple thoughts converge on a single object, much as in language, when multiple meanings can converge on a single word. For example, "bread" can mean a kind of food. Colloquially, bread also means "money." More figuratively, "bread" can also stand for any basic necessity. These multiple meanings of any word may converge on a single dream element. This may also occur with homonyms, where the written version of the word may differ while the spoken version is the same. "Read," as in "he has read a book," may be the past participle of reading. "Red," which has the same sound, can mean the color red. It can also imply coarseness ("redneck"), the emotion of embarrassment (to redden, i.e., blush), or communism ("Red China"). The record of such condensation can be found in the *radiations of meaning* that emanate from the dreamer's associations.

Of course, in this way, every element of a dream may be the product of condensation. If we ask for associations, we will find the sources of condensation. The problem here, though, is that we cannot tell if the associations tell us the true sources of the dream element, or if they provide an after-the-fact elaboration of the dream element.

As I noted above, one of my patients dreamt that she was addicted to heroin and had been put on methadone maintenance. She analyzed the dream in terms of her addiction to analysis and her erotic feelings toward me. In a subsequent session, she spoke of her need to accomplish great things to win people's love. She said, "I need to be a heroine" (mispronouncing the word with a long "i" sound). She then talked of needing to be a "hero." Later, it emerged that she had connected her thoughts of being a heroine with her addiction in the dream to heroin and tried to cover up this association by her mispronunciation of "heroine" (which became a sure giveaway that something was going on) and then switching to the masculine "hero." Thus, her "heroin" addiction in the dream was overdetermined. It condensed her erotic addiction to analysis and her addiction to being a heroine.

Here is another example of simple overdetermined condensation: While working on this chapter, I dreamt that I was using a locker in a gymnasium, but that I didn't know the combination for the locker. I realized on awakening that the "combination" in the dream was itself a condensation. The word "combination" is a synonym for condensation, although in the manifest content of the dream, its other meaning was apparent: combination being a set of numbers used to open a lock. The dream portrayed how I was looking for the right combination of meanings of combination (condensation), that is, how I was seeking a solution to the problem of condensation and was unraveling its many meanings, as I am trying to do in this chapter.

A telling sign of overdetermination is unusual or redundant use of words in a dream. For example, a woman dreamt: "I was taking a bath and the water was really black. Later, someone poured milk into the tub."

Note that the word "really" is not necessary; its redundancy may indicate that it is overdetermined. The woman was of mixed race. As she told the dream, she had no awareness of the dream's reference to mixed race and her concerns about whether she herself was really black. The liquid in the bath condensed the issues of race, cleanliness, and nurturance.

2. CREATIVE CONDENSATION

In creative condensation, features of two different objects are combined to create a new object. The manifest dream content contains a new person, or object, or concept that is not part of the dreamer's waking world. The new creation of the dream is fully formed, yet the evidence that condensation has occurred is discernible in the manifest dream content. Associations may reveal the source of the condensation, but even without associations, we know that it has occurred.

The combined features may come from the same modality, such as two visual elements. In the nineteenth century, Galton was known for merging two photographs together into one composite image. In the twentieth century, this process was achieved with computers and came to be known as "morphing." One example of such condensation is Freud's dream (1900) in which "My friend R. was my uncle. [He was not in reality.] I saw before me his face, somewhat changed. It was as though it had been drawn out lengthways. A yellow beard that surrounded it stood out especially clearly" (p. 137). The features of various people are drawn together by Freud's dream into one new person, never seen before this dream. The assembled physical characteristics radiate out in meaning to people with different personal characteristics, but related to one another by the question, "How guilty of crime are they?"—Freud's yellow-bearded Uncle Joseph, who had been convicted of illegal financial transactions, is combined with R., whose unblemished character is marred by one small crime.

The work of condensation is apparent from the manifest content without any associations, although associations may clarify the source of condensation. If someone dreams of a woman who looks like Judy Garland, but is blond and tall, you know that there is condensation at work, although you may need the dreamer's associations to know what blondness and tallness mean to the dreamer and how they combine with the dreamer's associations to Judy Garland.

The condensation of two identities in a single dream figure can be especially useful to clinicians. Sometimes such dreams help the dreamer become aware of unconscious connections between people that help clarify mysteriously strong feelings. For example, a woman was having trouble in her marriage. Her husband's sexual advances left her cold or repulsed her. While trying to decide whether to divorce, she had a scary dream. She was in the house in which she grew up, and Saddam Hussein was living in the house. Another man was there, either David (her husband) or Bruce (her brother). Then they were in an apartment, and they tried to escape. The dream continued with their escape maneuvers.

In thinking about the dream, the patient was surprised by the male figure who was "either David or Bruce." They do not look alike and she wasn't sure how a person could be either, but that was her experience in the dream. It led her to wonder if they were connected psychologically for her. I noted that she seemed terrified in the dream. She started crying and recalled being persistently physically abused by her brother during her childhood. Most people who knew her then had no idea of the abuse and assumed that she and her brother were perfectly close (just as in her adulthood, most people thought her marriage to be a good one). The dream raised the fundamental question of which ways, rationally or not, her husband seemed similar to her brother and how that connection could be frightening her and contributing to her marital difficulties.

3. PARTIAL CONDENSATION: "INTEROBJECTS"

Sometimes condensation occurs differently. Instead of the dream thoughts converging on a single element in the manifest dream, they converge and create a new object that does not occur in waking life and could not occur in waking life. It may have a vague structure that is described as "something between an X and a Y." Hobson dreamt of "a piece of hardware, something like the lock of a door or perhaps a pair of paint-frozen hinges." In dreams we accept these sorts of intermediate structures. Hobson calls them "incomplete cognitions" and Freud calls them "intermediate and composite structures." I would prefer to call them partial condensations or, to use a neologism, *interobjects*. Rather than focus on what they are not (not complete condensations), I would prefer to focus on what they are (new creations derived from blends of other objects).

The combination is not fully formed into a new object with a complete "gestalt," but rather remains incompletely fused. With partial condensations, the evidence of condensation is much more obvious from the manifest content than in the other two types. The created object is not easily describable in the terms of the waking world of objects. The dreamer may say (Meltzer, 1984), "It was something between a phonograph and a balance" (p. 45). It is unclear whether, in the dream itself, the object's characteristics were vague, or merely hard to describe. An artist could probably draw a single object that was something between a phonograph and a balance, perhaps incorporating familiar parts from each object. But it is also possible that in the dream experience, the object so described was either a stable double image, or an image that shifted between two objects, or something else. An inquiry into the dreamer's experience may clarify this. Can the dreamer elaborate on how the object in the dream was "between" two objects?

In conducting such an inquiry, the interpreter should tread carefully. Secondary revision and the reality principle are always ready to smooth out incongruous perceptions that are unacceptable in the waking world. For this reason *it is important, in studying dreams, to transcribe verbatim the wording first used by the dreamer to describe the dream.* Otherwise, the details are easily glossed over or "regularized."

Some interobjects are symbolic of a question being unconsciously considered by the dreamer: Is it X or Y? There is a fine example of this in Ferenczi's *Clinical Diary* (1932):

> Patient B.:
>
> 26 April 1932
>
> "Dream, with an almost certain pre-history of infantile-genital violence: She sees a row of soldiers or gymnasts all without heads, lined up stiffly; on the left side (shoulder) of each one there is an upright, fleshy appendage sticking up. The association shifts to a bowling alley (ninepins). The single thrusts are signified by individual soldiers; the idea of orgasm, perhaps, by all nine. Simultaneously their headlessness represents pure emotionality, all intellectual control being absent: L'amour est un taureau acéphale. [Love is a headless bull.] But at the same time the patient's psychic state is also represented: it occurs to her that it must be difficult for the ninepins to keep their balance, since they are weighted down unilaterally on their left side" [p. 90].

The interobject is the "soldiers or gymnasts," and the dreamer provides associations necessary to clarify the meaning.[1] Both the soldiers and gymnasts are headless; their main function is bodily, not mental. The dreamer, having experienced infantile-genital violence, identifies sexuality, at least that of her abuse history, with mindlessness. The focal question of the dream may be: What are men like for me—soldiers or gymnasts? Is their physicality and aggression dangerous or merely sport?

Sometimes interobjects are created from words. A patient of Erikson reported a dream with such a lexical interobject, in which she saw a novel word S[E]INE, which turned out to be a condensation of the words seine ("his" in German), sine ("without" in Latin), Seine (the French river), and the letter "E" which was the initial of Erikson's name.

Freud (1900) seemed not to think highly of interobjects. He wrote: "But it is obvious that condensations of ideas, as well as intermediate and compromise structures, must obstruct the attainment of the identity aimed at. Since they substitute one idea for another, they cause a deviation from the path which would have led on from the first idea. Processes of this kind are therefore scrupulously avoided in secondary thinking" (p. 602).

Freud is right that in communicating waking thoughts, we avoid intermediate and compromise structures, lest we be thought psychotic. Yet if they are socially unacceptable, that does not mean that they have no use. These intermediate and compromise structures, these interobjects, may have an elementary function in human thought that has barely been explored. There are constructive aspects of extralinguistic formations, like interobjects, that can be crucial in the formation of really new ideas that would be harder to come by using only fully formed, secondary process formations.

CONDENSATION AND CATEGORIES

Which are the most salient dimensions by which we classify our environment, and which ones can be condensed? When I teach a course on dreams, I teach my students the "Condensation Game." I tell them: "Let us try deliberately to simulate dream condensation. Imagine, for instance: What is between a tree and a horse?" When I ask my students

1. It may be questioned whether "soldiers or gymnasts" is a true interobject. Further inquiry (which is no longer possible with Ferenczi's patient) might clarify whether the dreamer's percept involved something between soldiers and gymnasts, or whether the dreamer simply couldn't tell which they were.

this question, I am always astonished at the range of answers they produce; each answer highlights a different dimension of "horse-ness" and "tree-ness."

One answer is "a wooden horse." Another answer is "a tree with short hair and the texture and warmth of a horse's body." Both of these are a condensation of materials and form. In the first, the wood of the tree has been combined with the shape of the horse (probably this answer was inspired by the Trojan example). In the second, the materials of the horse's body have been reshaped into a tree.

Another strategy of condensation is to combine features. Thus, we could get a horse with branches coming out of it. Or a tree trunk that culminates in a horse's head. Or a tree with a mane.

One can also combine actions: hence, a tree that neighs. Or a horse that sheds in winter.

Another condensation is a giraffe. Here, the height of a tree is grafted onto the neck of the horse.

Another strategy is to combine words, a lexical condensation. In this manner, we arrive at a tree-house (a loose distortion of tree and horse) or a sawhorse (this one is more complex in origin, perhaps, combining the conception of woodwork with horse) or the German actor, Horst Buchholz. Here the condensation plays with the similarity in sound of "horse" and "Horst" and "Holz," which is the German word for "wood."

And one smart aleck, answering the question "what is between a tree and a horse," responded "grass." But that, too, involves a kind of dreamwork; it takes the word "between" and focuses on its spatial meaning rather than its conceptual meaning. It involves imagining a horse and a tree in a real location, and between them, grass.

In summary, the many possible condensations make us aware of how we categorize our world. We can create condensations using the materials, forms, or features of objects, or we can use words themselves as objects to condense. The Condensation Game makes us very aware of how we think about any one object or person, and how differently other people may encode the same object or person.

CATEGORY TRANSGRESSIONS

The Condensation Game also invites us to relax our normal sense of categories, as we all do in our dreams. Category transgressions are unacceptable in daytime communication, except perhaps to poets and madmen, but they are acceptable to most of us in our dreams.

Dreams can transgress category boundaries with impunity. Suzanne Langer (1967) wrote: "When new unexploited possibilities of thought crowd in upon the human mind, the poverty of everyday language becomes acute" (p. 121). And so we dream. As Ullman (1969) has noted, "The task before the dreamer is to express relations he has never before experienced. The sensory effects streaming down to the arousal center employ the visual mode predominantly and as these generate further arousal new and relevant motivational systems or feelings are tapped" (p. 699).

Freud (1900, pp. 302–303) reported a dream in which he transgressed linguistic boundaries. His dream included the word "erzefilich," which does not exist in German. He analyzed that it was a condensation of several words, including "erzieherisch" (educational) and "syphilis."

Psychologists like Eleanor Rosch (1977) have studied the "natural categories" of our waking consciousness, but in dreams, myths, and art, we can be freed from these categories. It is not that they stop existing for us, but that they become "transgressable"; we can violate them without necessarily being considered mad.

Artists have been notorious for transgressing categories: Da Vinci's painting of John the Baptist in the Louvre is of a person who is between man and woman, or both man and woman. (The theory that the Mona Lisa is actually da Vinci's self-portrait as a woman works along similar lines, but the portrait of John the Baptist combines the genders even more smoothly.)

Picasso produced a well-known sculpture that is a car-monkey. He took a model car and showed how much it looked like a monkey face.

Category transgression occurs in music, too. Musical form creates its own categories, and then great composers write compositions that defy those categories, both falling within them and lying outside them. For example, Viennese classical composers established a relatively expectable sonata form, in which there usually was an exposition section with a first melodic theme in the tonic key, and a second melodic theme in the dominant key. Beethoven took this sonata form, and in some of his late work, created a musical structure that left the key-structure of sonata form intact, but had the change in keys occur within a unitary melodic element, blurring the distinction between first and second themes.

Arnold Schönberg did something similar, creating waltzes that are not danceable. He also created the new category of speech/song, that, when performed correctly, is not like anything heard before from the human voice. The very word speech/song, *Sprechgesang*, sounds like a dream creation.

Of course, these kinds of creations are familiar from mythology, and many have their counterparts there. The man who becomes a woman is incorporated in the story of Tiresias. There are many instances in which the human/animal distinction is transgressed: The Minotaur, for example, was half man, half bull. Snakes grew from the head of Medusa. Zeus transfigured himself into a swan, but as a swan he ravished the human Leda. The human/plant distinction is also transgressed in the story of Daphne, a woman who is transformed into a tree.

The Old Testament, too, has bushes that speak (the Burning Bush), animals that speak (Balaam's ass), and time that stops (the Sun and Moon stop for Joshua). All of our familiar parameters of dividing and organizing the world are up for grabs.

Transgressions of species, so common in mythology, are common in children's dreams. In the famous childhood dream of Freud's patient (p. 1918), the "Wolf Man," the wolves in the dream were "white and looked more like foxes or sheep-dogs, for they had big tails like foxes and they had their ears pricked like dogs when they pay attention to something" (p. 29).

Children are much more tolerant of interobjects than adults. The following anecdote captures the resistance of waking adults to interobjects and their wish to "correct" such thinking in children:

A nine-year-old boy reported a "scary and fun" dream. He dreamt that he and some of his friends had to escape from an island—it was a little like the island in the film *The Truman Show*.[2] They were crossing the channel and for some reason needed another boat. They were frightened, but then a seal swam up to them. They thought it was just a seal, but then they looked and under the water it was a whole boat, it was huge, so they climbed onto the seal/boat, and it brought them to the shore of the mainland.

When the boy told his father the dream in the morning, the father, speaking like an adult who cannot tolerate contradictions, said to him: "So really, it was a boat, a big, safe boat." The child, holding fast to the integrity of his dream, said, "It was a boat, but it was still a big, friendly seal." This child had not yet learned to regularize his perceptions to fit the way the world works (Schachtel, 1959; Foulkes, 1999).

---

2. *The Truman Show* was a film that dealt with fundamental questions about our perception of reality. In it, a man's entire life, which he experiences as real, is actually a made-for-television story, and all the people in his life are actors.

Psychotics also show freedom to transgress boundaries and categories, and the link between psychosis and dreams has long been noticed. Psychotics are also fond of neologisms that transgress linguistic boundaries. When one of my patients told me I was "consaring," he was, I discovered, combining "concerned" and "caring." Our waking sane consciousness might ask, "Why not say concerned and caring?" but he might ask, "Why not join them?" In doing so, he made his communication harder to fathom but avoided the humiliation that he feared from explicit statements of affection.

There may be some cultural differences in the way people organize categories and allow for their transgression. Consider the following: "I was standing in my home, holding something between a spear and a shield." How shall we interpret it? A spear is used for attack, a shield is used for defense. How do we understand the feeling state of this man?

In actuality, the above dream is made up. I do not know of anyone who has actually dreamt it. I have been told by my friend Catherine Ng that the Chinese word for ambivalence is composed of two words meaning literally "spear" and "shield." Was "spear-shield" first put together in a dream? If not, could it have been? And if a man had a dream in which he holds "something between a spear and a shield," could not such a dream signify his ambivalence?

The Chinese language is especially suited to produce such compound words. In Chinese, words and visual images are more closely linked than in Western languages, since the written Chinese language is composed of characters most of which are visually representative of an object or a set of objects. It is no accident that, in China, calligraphy is a highly sophisticated art form—for the characters have not only denotative meaning, but are themselves visually representative. So in the Chinese mind there might be a closer relation between word and image than for Westerners. Whether there is, then, a different relationship between word representations and thing representations for Chinese speakers, and whether their dreams create interobjects differently from Westerners, is a topic worth studying.

LIMITS OF CATEGORY TRANSGRESSION

There is a subtle form of boundary transgression that occurs in language, where words that ordinarily occur in one category transmigrate into another category. In late twentieth century North America, for example, it became a relatively common practice to force nouns into verbs by using them so. People came to accept "impact" as a verb, such as in the sentence, "How does the President's decision impact the economy?" But we do not yet accept all nouns as verbs. In our waking linguistic usage, we usually do not say, "The heavy rains greened the field," although poets can say such things and be understood.

By this principle, all colors could become verbs, yet some have done so to a greater degree than others. We speak easily of the "graying" of America, meaning the increase in the proportion of the population who are elderly. "Yellowing" is the process by which objects become yellow, that is, aged; this happens enough to white clothing in a natural process that we have created the verb "to yellow." The color red has received a special treatment. When things become red, we do not say that they have redded; we have a new verb form: to redden. The same form has been used for white: to whiten. We also whiten clothes, although white can also be used in a verb form: If we make a mistake in typing, we can "white it out." (That verb form may already be nearly as obsolete as the mechanical typewriter.) We also have "brownouts." But so far as I know, we do not yet have verb forms of orange or turquoise.

The Condensation Game shows how, given the right instructions, people can more freely transgress boundaries while awake. But there are limits. *The two objects to be condensed must have similarity along some dimension.* If you ask, what is halfway between a turkey and a theorem, or a banana and a theorem, you have a much harder time accomplishing any condensation. As Hillman (1979) has pointed out:

> Only *similars can be opposites.* Only those pairs having something material, essential in common can be sensibly opposed. A turkey cannot be opposed to a theorem, unless we can discover in what way they are like each other. Our psychological view is able to save the phenomenon of opposites by regarding opposition as an *extreme metaphor*, a radical way of saying one thing as though it were two violently differing things in sharp war with itself (Heraclitus again), which the valiant ego must imagine literally and meet as a challenge [p. 84].

What is halfway between a banana and a theorem? That is a tough riddle. They don't even have any letters in common. If you work on them long enough, of course, you will find something. For instance, they both have three syllables.

I have never actually heard a dream in which there was an object halfway between a banana and a theorem, and I would think it very unlikely (unless you are dreaming after reading this chapter). Even in the splendorously creative chaos of dreaming, there are rules for creating interobjects. What those rules are has never been specified. To address this question adequately, we need to consider some of the findings and theories of modern cognitive neuroscience.

It would seem from the present discussion that novel pairings can occur only between objects already linked in the mind along some dimension. One modern model of the mind, known as Parallel Distributed Processing or Connectionism (McClelland and Rumelhart, 1986), proposes that each object may be represented in several places in the brain, not in a single neuron, but in neuronal fields. Adopting this model of the mind, we might say that there are weighted links between the representations of objects in our neurons. When we are awake, certain rule systems, like day-logic and grammar, govern those linkages. At night some of those rule systems give way.

But are nighttime mental recombinations subject to total anomie and chaos? And if not, then which rules apply? We do not know. I have never heard a dream in which no object is recognizable from the waking world (although it must be admitted that if we ever had such a dream, it might be very hard to remember and report). If in dreaming, the rules of weighted connections take precedence over codified systems of day rules, then condensations may occur between objects stored in connected neuronal fields.

In this way, the interobjects produced in dreams may tell us something about the organization of the mind. In dreams, when the brain is *generating* stimuli rather than perceiving them, these internal organizational factors, of which we are usually unaware, can make their existence known. When the mind is producing percepts during dreaming, patterns of neural firing may bring together representations that are stored adjacent to one another, which allows the creation of new objects. Although aqueducts have very different functions from swimming pools, we may ignore that in dreaming. Instead, the dreaming brain "notices" the similarity of aqueducts and swimming pools—they are both manmade objects containing large amounts of water—and can condense them into "something between a swimming pool and an aqueduct," or an "aque-pool," as occurred in the dream of Bert States (1995).

If we could specify some guidelines for producing interobjects, would we be able to program a computer to produce them? And could we then come closer to enabling a computer to dream (Palombo, 1985)? This project has actually been achieved by a group of advertising researchers, Jacob Goldenberg, David Mazursky, and Sorin Solomon.

TABLE 1
TYPE OF CONDENSATION

		FORMAL	LEXICAL	IDEATIONAL
OUTCOME OF CONDENSATION	SIMPLE OVERDETERMINED	A cigar	The word "read"	A priest: condenses the image of father, Christianity, celibacy
	CREATIVE	Freud's "Yellow-bearded Uncle Joseph"	Freud's "erzefilisch"	A bathtub filled with black water and white milk, signifying mixed race
	PARTIAL	Hobson's "something between a lock and a hinge"	Erikson's S[E]INE	? See footnote 1

1. The contents of this cell are extremely hard to specify, since the condensations, being ideational, are not easily deciphered from the manifest content. This is the cell where the greatest inspirations are derived from dreams. It is the location where new conceptual combinations can occur: It is where Einstein might have conceived of the space-time continuum, condensing space and time into a new unity, space-time. It is where the composer Elliott Carter could condense modulation (traditionally a term applied to changes in harmony) and meter into "metric modulation."

They were interested in waking creativity, not dreaming, and designed a computer program that would produce creative advertising. The results were that the computer-conceived ads were judged more creative than those created by humans. But the rules by which the computer designed the ads, which they call the "replacement template," were essentially rules by which to create interobjects. Here are the instructions as described in their report (Goldenberg et al., 1999):

> Given a product (*P*) with a trait (*T*), the subject is asked to come up with a creative idea for an ad that conveys the message that *P* has *T*. In a visual format, an object *S* (symbol), which is universally identified with *T*, is replaced with *P*. The effect is enhanced if *S* is placed in a situation in which *T* is essential. Moreover, the replacement operation can be iterated: Rather than *P* one can use parts of it, or aspects of it, or objects associated with it, to replace the corresponding elements associated with *S* [p. 1495].

Thus, when asked to produce an ad for the World Tennis Cup tournament in Jerusalem, the computer generated a mosque with a dome that had a tennis ball texture. In advertising on-time performance for an airline, the computer generated a cuckoo clock in which a jumbo jet pops out of the clock instead of a cuckoo. Both of these creations—the mosque/tennis ball and the jumbo jet/cuckoo clock—are interobjects (although the authors do not use that term) and could have been generated by dreams.

It would be a worthwhile project to expand such computer modeling of cognitive processes in order to specify precisely the kinds of condensations that can and cannot occur during dreaming.

CHAPTER 7

ONEIRIC DARWINISM

> The relation of word to thought, and the creation of new concepts is a complex, delicate, and enigmatic process unfolding in our soul.
>
> Leo Tolstoy (in Vygotsky, 1934)

> In his last days, Satie dreamt: "Last night I dreamed I had two willies! You can't imagine how many things you can do with that thingamajig!"
>
> In: Volta (1989)

WHY DO WE dream? This question has been asked so often, we may take for granted that it is a worthwhile question. But the longer I think about and study dreams, the more the question seems outdated and too broad. It became outdated when dream researchers discovered that we dream throughout the night although we do not remember most of our dreams. That discovery changed our view of dreams from a relatively rare "minipathological" event to a regularly occurring mental function. With this knowledge, the question "Why do we dream?" became more similar to "Why do we think?"—a giant question with more than one answer.

The question of why we dream can be divided into two subquestions: (1) Why did humans evolve the capacity to dream? and (2) What use can we make of dreams through conscious reflection and analysis? In past times, the two questions have not always been kept distinct. Squier and Domhoff (1998) argue that we must differentiate between the functions of dreaming and the uses humans can put dreams to. "Dreams may be useful to waking consciousness in a variety of ways, which means they have 'functions' that were developed through cultural invention, but that does not mean dreaming has any psychological functions"[1] (p. 156).

The fact that we can find something useful in our dreams is not necessarily the same as the reason we humans have developed the ability to dream. We know that the layout of our ten fingers allows us to hold a steering wheel and direct a car while we are driving. Yet would that lead one to believe that our fingers evolved as they did so that we could drive? Or play the piano? Or type? Probably not. The distribution of our fingers evolved into its current configuration before there were cars or pianos or typewriters.

So it is with dreams. Over the centuries, dream interpreters have found many ways to make use of dreams. They used them to give the air of authority to prophecy as messages from divine beings. In the Western world over the last century, psychoanalysts and dream interpreters have vastly enlarged the repertoire of what can be derived from dreams. From many dreams we can discern a wish of the dreamer that is being fulfilled. We can also discern ideas and feelings that may be quite contrary to our conscious attitudes. Jung called this the "compensatory" function of dreams.

More recently, Benedetti (1989) showed how the dreams of schizophrenic patients and their therapists may outline new paths of cure, and I, in chapters 16 and 17, show how the dreams of a patient in psychoanalysis can suggest corrections or alternatives to the psychoanalyst. We can also discern from dreams the dreamer's current psychological concerns, traces of his early history, the ways he relates to other people, his feelings about his body, and many other things.

All of these are useful things that we can get from dreams. But are they *the reason* why our capacity to dream evolved? A person who remembers almost none of his dreams and who never tells them to anybody still dreams. *Our theory must incorporate the fact, which Freud did not know, that most of our dreams are never remembered, told, or analyzed.* Our explanation of why we dream would have to include a reason for these dreams—dreams, in fact, which may never be accessible to our conscious awareness. What use does our mind-brain make of dreams, whether or not we analyze or pay any conscious attention to our dreams? Do those dreams have a function in our mental life, and if so, what?

---

1. See also Domhoff, 1993, pp. 314–315.

Some of the hypotheses about why we dream include:

1. to maintain sleep in the presence of unacceptable wishes (Freud, 1900)
2. to compensate for excessively one-sided conscious attitudes held during the day (Jung, 1948)
3. if the dream is told, to communicate something to someone else that could not be said otherwise (Ferenczi, 1913; Kanzer, 1955; Blechner, 1983)
4. for no reason at all—dreaming is merely an epiphenomenon of periodic brain firing, with the mind "making the best of a bad job" (Hobson and McCarley, 1977)
5. a housecleaning of the mind—to rid the mind of parasitic connections and contents that are not functional (Robert, 1886; Evans and Newman, 1964; Crick and Mitchison, 1983)
6. to consolidate disparate areas of thinking and to integrate the information acquired during the day with other information acquired during the dreamer's lifetime (Winson, 1985, 1990; Fiss, 1991)
7. to remember emotionally-charged early experiences and to integrate them with current experiences (Reiser, 1993; C. Smith, 1995)
8. to regulate mood (Kramer, 1993)
9. to make connections "in a safe place" between dissociated areas of awareness, and thus to perform a kind of psychotherapy (Hartmann, 1995, 1998)
10. to formulate "extralinguistic thoughts" which could not be formulated in waking thinking (Blechner, 1998)

This is only a partial list of possible functions of dreaming.[2] I would like to suggest yet another purpose for dreaming. From an evolutionary standpoint, if something as complicated as dreaming has evolved in humans, it must be able to help the organism survive. What is the dream's contribution to the survival of man?

I propose one more reason that we dream—*to create new ideas, through partial random generation, which can then be retained if judged useful.* In Freud's view, the bizarreness of dreams is an epiphenomenon of the

---

2. See Moffitt, Kramer, and Hoffmann (1993) for others. Panksepp (1998, p. 128) has proposed that dreaming is an ancient form of waking consciousness that "may have come to be actively suppressed in order for higher brain evolution to proceed efficiently."

dreamwork's disguise of disturbing latent content. But in my theory, *the bizarreness of the dream is integral to its function*. Dreams introduce random variations into psychic life and internal narratives. They produce "thought mutations." Our minds can then select among these mutations and variations to produce new kinds of thought, imagination, self-awareness, and other psychic functions.

I call this the theory of Oneiric Darwinism. (Oneiros is the Greek word for "dream"; Darwinism refers to Darwin's model of mutation and selection.) Dreams allow a process of random (or, at least, relatively random) generation of psychic products, and mutations of memory traces, percepts, concepts, words, and any other mental contents. From among these new, mutated mental products, those that increase adaptability and usefulness are retained by the mind. Those that are useless or harmful are rejected.

In this way, psychic life could be seen to be isomorphic, to a certain degree, with selectionist processes in other aspects of human functioning. We all know Darwin's model for the evolution of man from earlier forms of life by means of mutation and natural selection. It has been said that Darwin's theory upset man's sense of himself in the universe because it proposed that we are not specially created by God, but descend from lower species. But the greater shock of Darwin's theories is that random processes are central to the design of the universe. The idea that chance processes are at the basis of the development of our grand universe of life flies in the face of the basic religious and ontological belief that God directs the universe with a grand purpose which man cannot understand. Did God, knowing what He or She was doing, create the world in a systematic fashion, or did evolution work in a random way, to create variation in organisms through random mutation, which then either survive or disappear?

Darwin (1859) himself was aware that such an idea would meet resistance. He wrote:

> To suppose that the eye with all its inimitable contrivances for adjusting the focus to different distances, for admitting different amounts of light, and for the correction of spherical and chromatic aberration, could have been formed by natural selection, seems, I freely confess, absurd in the highest degree. When it was first said that the sun stood still and the world turned round, the common sense of mankind declared the doctrine false; but the old saying of "Vox populi, vox Dei," as every philosopher knows, cannot be trusted in science [p. 186].

However, in the last few decades, similar models have been proposed for other biological processes. For example, the field of immunology was revolutionized by such a model. An earlier model of immunology proposed that when the body is threatened by an antigen (a foreign organism), the immune system produces an antibody that specifically fits the antigen and attacks it.

The older theory had assumed a purposiveness to the immune system, with a kind of "custom-fitting" of antibodies to elements that were threatening the organism. In 1973, Gerald Edelman proposed instead that the immune system produces a broad array of antibodies somewhat randomly, and that from this pool of antibodies, those that work against antigens are selected. For this work, he was awarded the Nobel prize. Edelman (1987) has since proposed a similar theory of neural development in the brain, applying a principal of random development and selection to the growth of individual neurons, which he calls "neural Darwinism."

Edelman (1987) has outlined three general requirements of any selection theory: (1) a source of diversification leading to variants; (2) a means for effective encounter with or sampling of an independent environment that is not initially categorized in any absolute or predetermined fashion; and (3) a means of differential amplification over some period of time of those variants in a population that have greater adaptive value (p. 17).

How are these three requirements satisfied by Oneiric Darwinism? The primary source of diversification is dreaming itself. The encounter with the environment can occur either in unconscious thinking or in waking conscious thought. And the differential amplification of those variants in the population that have greater adaptive value will come from the usefulness of the cognitive-emotional creations of dreams in waking life, although the individual may never be consciously aware of those mental creations or of their being tested.

Using this model, we can propose that such processes of random development and selection might operate not only on the cellular level, as Edelman (1987) proposed in *Neural Darwinism*, but also on the level of thoughts and percepts—that is, not only the brain/mind's hardware but also its software. In short, I am proposing that dreams are a process by which the mind introduces random variations and mutations into thinking. Some of these new thoughts turn out to be extremely useful and may be retained for use by the mind, consciously or unconsciously, in other contexts. Many of these new thoughts, however, may be useless, and can be rejected.

Oneiric Darwinism accounts for the value of unconscious dreams: New ideas and experiences can be generated in dreams that we never remember. If they are retained as useful, we may "rediscover" them while awake and never recognize their original source in our dreams, although sometimes we do. Sometimes, we may retain an inkling of the source of these thoughts or perceptions with a sense of "déjà vu"; we feel we have encountered these things before, but we cannot recollect where.

The theory of Oneiric Darwinism *does not require that dreams be consciously remembered for them to have their productive effect on waking thought.* Nevertheless, if the dream is remembered consciously, we may then work with it consciously and attribute our waking creation to the inspiration of a dream. There are many reports of this from scientists and artists.

For example, the chemist August Kekulé (1890) discovered the structure of the benzene ring in a dream. The "day residue" of the dream actually came fifteen years earlier, when Kekulé, still a student, had to testify during a trial concerning a neighbor's death. Among the dead person's belongings was a gold ring in the shape of two snakes biting their own tails. Kekulé was later considering how benzene arranged its six carbon and hydrogen atoms. Thinking about the problem, he dozed off, and dreamt of dancing atoms that fell into a snakelike pattern. As Kekulé wrote in his diary, "one of the snakes seized hold of its own tail, and the form whirled mockingly before my eyes. As if by a flash of lightning I awoke; and this time also I spent the rest of the night in working out the consequences of the hypothesis"[3] (p. 22).

Elias Howe, the inventor, learned from a dream how to perfect the sewing machine in 1846. He had been using a needle threaded through the middle of the shank, when he dreamt that he was chased by a tribe of cannibals who captured him, tied him to a stake, and threatened him with spears. As they got closer to killing him, he noticed that the spears all had an "eye hole" near the point. He woke with a start, remembered his dream, and realized that this would solve the problem he faced in trying to invent the sewing machine (Kaempffert, 1924).

On February 16, 1869, the Russian chemist Dmitri Mendeleyev was experimenting with a set of cards, as if he were playing solitaire, in order to find the arrangement of the elements. In his dream that night, he saw that his arrangement was on the right track but needed to be rotated 180 degrees. Upon awakening he did so and produced the periodic table.

---

3. The veracity of Kekulé's account has been challenged by Wotiz and Rudofsky (1984) but their arguments have been refuted by Ramsay and Rocke (1984) and Strunz (1993).

In all these examples, the dreamers were working on an intellectual problem in their waking lives, and the solution then was suggested by a dream. Was it purely by chance that the dream produced the solution, which the dreamer then recognized, or was the mind working out the solution unconsciously and then representing the solution in a dream? We do not know which is so. It would, of course, be good to know about the other dreams that were had by each dreamer during this time to see whether other, perhaps incorrect but relevant, solutions were being suggested by the dreams.

In each case, these innovators were able to trace their inspiration to a dream. But it is also possible that sometimes, when we are struck by inspiration in our waking life, the source of inspiration is a dream which we do not remember having, but whose contents have nevertheless made their way into waking consciousness.

Creative artists have also used their dreams as inspiration. Christopher Durang (1999) based his play, *The Actor's Nightmare*, on an actual nightmare that he had repeatedly and that he thinks is dreamt by about 80 percent of actors: They are acting in a play, suddenly realize they have not rehearsed it, and do not know what their next line is.

Charles Dodgson was a mathematician who also, under the pseudonym of Lewis Carroll, wrote poetry and literature, in which he cultivated a genius for the "nearly logical." Carroll has much to tell us about relinquishing rules of waking narrative, and he learned about this from his dreams. He wrote (Carroll, 1976):

> Sometimes one could trace to their source these random flashes of thought . . . but they had also a way of their own, occurring a propos of nothing—specimens of that hopelessly illogical phenomenon, "an effect without a cause." . . . such, again, have been passages which occurred in *dreams*, and which I cannot trace to any antecedent cause whatever [pp. 277–278].

One example is a passage in *Sylvie and Bruno* (Carroll, 1976):

> The Baron said, "My ancestors were all famous for military genius."
>
> My Lady smiled graciously. "It often runs in families," she remarked, "just as a love for pastry does" [p. 333].

This passage shows the genius of dreams, and their irony, too. The first clause of My Lady's remark suggests agreement with the idea of military genius running in families, but her second clause trivializes it in two ways: first, by comparing military genius (presumably important) with a love of pastry (presumably unimportant); second, the suggestion that love of pastry runs in families suggests, ironically, that a trait's running in families may be unprovable, and of no consequence in any case. Her statement is a kind of condensation; using those two mischievous words, "just as," My Lady puts together two seemingly unrelated traits, military genius and love of pastry, into a single conceptual grouping.

Lewis Carroll's phrase, "an effect without a cause," is not unlike a "subjectless predicate." Dreams often seem to be an effect without a cause, although dream interpretation sets out to elucidate the cause, or at least a possible cause. Much of Lewis Carroll's greatest work produces just this effect—seeming total nonsense that, on reexamination, proves to have a delicious near-meaning.

For example, again from *Sylvie and Bruno* (Carroll, 1976):

> He thought he saw an elephant, that practiced on a fife;
> He looked again, and found it was
> A letter from his wife.
> 'At length I realise,' he said,
> 'The bitterness of life.'
>
> [pp. 320–321]

This poem is like a resolved psychosis. First there is a set-up: what he thought he saw—a fanciful percept, perhaps frightening, perhaps delightful—and then, upon looking again, what he "actually" saw. At the end, the final couplet reflects back on this experience of corrected hallucination. The fanciful image of the elephant practicing on a fife turns out to be a letter from his wife, presumably more mundane, which makes him realize the bitterness of life. Also, the connection of his wife to an elephant may also contribute to his bitterness.

We can see how dreams could contribute to these creations. The experience of things suddenly changing is a common one in dreams. And comparing the situations before and after the transformation may lead one to an underlying content that is quite startling. Imagine you were told the following dream: "I dreamt of an elephant practicing on a fife. Suddenly, it became a letter from my wife, and I felt bitter." You could see in the dream a latent content, such as: If my wife is like an elephant, and I cannot make light of it, then I will feel bitter. As Freud noted in his chapters on the dreamwork, adjacency in a dream can signify an if-then relationship (Freud, 1900): "*Causation* is represented by *temporal sequence* . . . by the direct transformation of one image into another" (p. 316; italics added).

The manifest dream may be like an unusual percept or a hallucination. It can contain sudden shifts that at first seem meaningless, but which may yield insight and emotion upon reflection and analysis, as with Carroll's final couplet. When a dream is transformed into a poem by an artist like Lewis Carroll, however, the structure is often simplified and made more symmetric. The work of artistic transformation may be seen as one more level of dream revision.

ONEIRIC DARWINISM AND PSYCHIC DETERMINISM

The theory of Oneiric Darwinism flies in the face of a cherished axiom of psychoanalysis—the axiom of psychic determinism. In *The Psychopathology of Everyday Life* and other writings, Freud repeatedly argued that seemingly random and accidental errors, slips of the tongue and other parapraxes, are actually determined by unconscious motivation. "However, nothing in the mind is arbitrary or undetermined" (Freud, 1901, p. 242). "Psychoanalysts," says Freud (1910), "are marked by a particularly strict belief in the determination of mental life. For them there is nothing trivial, nothing arbitrary or haphazard. They expect in every case to find sufficient motives" (p. 38). He speaks repeatedly of "the strictness with which mental processes are determined" (1910, p. 29), of "a strict and universal application of determinism to mental life" (1910, p. 52), and of "a strong belief in the strict determination of mental events" (1923c, p. 238).

Many psychoanalysts since Freud have reaffirmed the postulate of extreme determinism. Charles Brenner (1955) writes:

> Let us start with the principle of psychic determinism. The sense of this principle is that in the mind, as in physical nature about us, nothing happens by chance, or in a random way. Each psychic event is determined by the ones that precede it. Events in our mental lives that may seem to be random and unrelated to what went on before are only apparently so. In fact, mental phenomena are no more capable of such a lack of causal connection with what preceded them than are physical ones. Discontinuity in this sense does not exist in mental life [pp. 1–2].

There is grandeur to such a theory, but it might not tell the whole story. I think we need a basic shift in psychoanalytic thinking—from strict psychic determinism, where seeming disorder comes from disguise and repression—to acknowledgment of some role of chance-processes in the sound functioning of an adaptive and creative mind. Every honest clinician would have to admit that not all slips of the tongue make sense psychodynamically, an idea that has been supported by modern psycholinguistic research (Fromkin, 1973; Baars et al., 1992; Motley, 1995). Of course, one could argue that they are all explainable and, that when they do not seem so, that reflects a lack of insight or resistance of the clinician. One could argue the opposite as well—that truly random or accidental events can be ascribed a meaning *post hoc* that seems to make sense, but is not truly causal.

We know that people are extremely adept at seeing order, meaning, and causation where none exists. Seligman and Yellen (1987) relate the following anecdote:

> Bernard Karmel put on a memorable demonstration in a colloquium at the University of Pennsylvania about a decade ago. He took a string of 50 or so Christmas light bulbs, wired to blink sequentially on and off and then crumpled the string up. The lights appeared to blink on and off in no discernible order. He then put on some Beatles music, and an irresistible illusion overtook the audience. The lights now appeared to pulsate in time with the music [p. 1].

There are other ways that researchers have documented the tendency for humans to ascribe meanings to stimuli where there are none. If you put people in a dark room and show them a stationary point of light, they tend to think it is moving. Rechtschaffen and Mednick (1955) put people in this situation and told them they would be seeing words written out by the pinpoint of light, and every person did, in fact, see words, even though the light remained stationary. One subject "saw" an entire paragraph written out.

Similarly, if you show people a video of two randomly moving dots, they tend to "perceive" that one dot is chasing the other. And we all know how easy it is to ascribe meaningful motivation to our pets. One of my favorite examples of this occurs in an interview between Bringuier (1989) and the great Swiss psychologist Piaget, when a cat arrives:

Piaget:	Here, Kitty.
Bringuier:	It's not very obedient.
Piaget:	It's uncertain [p. 2].

In this example, we have two intelligent men observing an animal's behavior and drawing different conclusions about the meaning of that behavior—but both men attribute some meaning to the behavior. In general, we humans tend to attribute meaning to our sense data.

Ian Hacking (1990) has traced changing attitudes toward chance in his book *The Taming of Chance*. Hacking writes:

> Throughout the Age of Reason, chance had been called the superstition of the vulgar. Chance, superstition, vulgarity, unreason were of one piece. The rational man, averting his eyes from such things, could cover chaos with a veil of inexorable laws. The world, it was said, might often look haphazard, but only because we do not know the inevitable workings of its inner springs. . . . Toward the end of the [nineteenth] century chance had attained the respectability of a Victorian valet, ready to be the loyal servant of the natural, biological and social sciences [pp. 1–2].

The Activation-Synthesis Hypothesis of Hobson and McCarley (1977) introduced one very important element into the theory of dreams that had been missing from the psychoanalytic viewpoint—the insertion of random processes into dream formation. I think we need a basic shift in psychoanalytic thinking—from strict determinism, where seeming disorder comes from disguise—to acknowledgment of some role of chance processes into the sound functioning of an adaptive and creative mind.

Hobson and McCarley proposed that the original source of the dream is a random visual stimulus generated by the pons. It is impossible to prove that such a stimulus is truly random, as Vogel (1978) pointed out. Hobson and McCarley posited that after the generation of this ostensibly random stimulus, the cortex tries to make a sensible narrative out it. They talked of this stage as the cortex "making the best of a bad job."

This negative view does not do justice to dreaming. These chance processes can lead to the freedom to create the new. This is just as in evolutionary theory, where random mutations are seen as the source of biological variation, and in modern artistic creation, where random processes have also been used to engender surprising creations—in music, by Cage, Boulez, and Stockhausen; in painting, by Jackson Pollock; and in improvisational theater, by Pirandello.

The mental images generated in a dream are not *completely* random. Even random selection involves choosing between a certain subset. After all, if a created percept were truly random, it might not have any recognizable features. Yet we know from experience that dreams are rarely, if ever, of something that is totally unrecognizable. We do not dream of shapeless masses of color. Our dreams tend to be of objects, people, places, and emotions. Details may be randomly altered, and there may be incongruous combinations. There are constraints to the randomness of our dreams.

In actual fact, very few dream images, in and of themselves, seem totally incomprehensible or out of the blue to the dreamer. Sometimes only their placement and their suddenness are bizarre. Thus a patient told me a dream in which he was a steward on an airplane, cheerily collecting laundry from the passengers and then doing the laundry on the airplane. The washing machine and the airplane were perfectly recognizable objects. That he would do laundry was not bizarre; he liked doing laundry. That he was a steward on an airplane was also not bizarre; it was once a career possibility for him. But to do the laundry on the airplane struck him as preposterous and hilarious. Two obvious facts from his life were put together in a way that waking reality testing would not allow.

Dennett (1991) has proposed a party game that illustrates one way that random factors could enter into the process of dream (and hallucination) production. In it, "one person, the dupe, is told that while he is out of the room, one member of the assembled party will be called upon to relate a recent dream. This will give everybody else in the room the story line so that when the dupe returns to the room and begins questioning the assembled party, the dreamer's identity will be hidden in the crowd of responders. The dupe's job is to ask yes/no questions of the assembled group until he has figured out the dream narrative to a suitable degree of detail, at which point the dupe is to psychoanalyze the dreamer, and use the analysis to identify him or her" (pp. 10–11).

But when the dupe is out of the room the host explains to everyone that they must answer the dupe's questions according to the following rule: if the last letter of the last word of the question is in the first half of the alphabet, answer "yes." If it is in the last half of the alphabet, answer "no." The process is said often to produce coherent dream narratives, which seem to be projections of the dupe. (It would be interesting to see how the resultant "dream" correlates with an actual dream of the dupe.)

Dennett relates this model of dream generation to the process of perception known as "analysis-by-synthesis," in which perceptions are built both of sensory input from the outside and of internal expectations of what can and should happen (Neisser, 1967). There are "generate-and-test" cycles, in which hypotheses about the percept are shaped by expectations and interests, and these are combined in a constantly oscillating process with actual sensory data.

Oneiric Darwinism holds that dreams allow the individual to break out of habitual modes of thought. Creative dreams are the opposite of what Donald Klein (1994) describes as:

> Iterative techniques for arriving at consensus among groups of experts. The best-known example is the Delphi technique. Each expert is presented with a series of questions and independently marks the answers along a gradient. The marks are averaged and a report then given to the experts concerning what the average answer was, as well as a measure of the spread around this average. Then the experts are asked to reconsider their vote. This procedure can be iterated until there is not further substantial movement in the average and the shrinkage of the spread of estimates has plateaued [pp. 364–365].

Such a process of moving towards a consistent average could be a process that occurs not only among groups, but within individuals. It reminds me of the definition of wisdom I once heard, which is doing the same thing over and over until you believe that it is the best way.

Collective wisdom is challenged when someone revolutionary comes along with a new idea that shakes things up and shifts the paradigm. Perhaps this goes on at an intra-individual level with dreams providing the shift from iterative thinking towards genuinely new thoughts. Instead of converging our thoughts centripetally towards what we already know, dreams allow our mind/brains to spin centrifugally toward outlying regions of new thoughts.

Some of these fanciful new thoughts may not reveal their utility for a long time. DaVinci imagined a flying machine centuries before the Wright brothers. Many creations of science fiction, thought to be preposterous in their time, have since been realized. Thus, when I hear a dream with an outlandish creation, I try to remain open-minded about its potential. Consider the following dream reported from Germany on the Internet by Burkard Sievers (2–15–99):

> I had received a parcel with a box in it on my fax machine. The box contained a delicious dish; some goulash with sauce etc. I was very disappointed that I could not eat it because it was in the fax. Then, still in the dream, I got a very clever idea of which I was very proud. I transferred the box from my fax into my e-mail. This allowed me to eat and enjoy it and it was very delicious.

This dream condenses very subtly. It contains the idea that when you have trouble receiving an electronic communication, transferring it from one medium to another sometimes makes it accessible. But in this dream, it is *food* that has been sent over the fax. It has actually been successfully transmitted, but it is *in* the fax. So transferring it out of the fax makes it edible.

A traditional psychoanalytic interpretation of this dream might see it as a triumph of wish fulfillment over the reality principle. The dreamer is hungry, finds the food that is inaccessible, and gets to it by cleverness. But viewed from the perspective of dream creativity, this dream envisions a kind of object transfer via technology that has long been the dream of science fiction and may very well become the fact of tomorrow. We have a choice: We could see the dream as an irrational wish fulfillment or as an attempt at technological creativity (or both). It shines forth as a product of Oneiric Darwinism—it is a mutation of our reality that may one day bear fruit or be tossed into the waste basket of useless ideas. Which is it—inspiration or ideational junk? Time will tell.

The theory of Oneiric Darwinism proposed here differs significantly from a group of dream theories which I call eliminationist or excretory theories of dreams. These propose that the main purpose of dreaming is to eliminate unwanted material from the brain (Robert, 1886; Crick and Mitchison, 1983). Excretion or elimination may indeed be one function of dreaming, but it only presents a part of the story. Dreaming is evolutionarily adaptive. It allows a relatively free creation of internally-generated percepts, recombined in many new configurations. Many of these will not be useful and will be tossed into the trash heap of forgotten dream images. Some of the new ideas and percepts, however, will be useful to the person, intellectually, creatively, artistically, socially, or along some other dimension. They may then be incorporated into the person's daytime thinking, either in a conscious process of incorporation, or else completely out of the conscious awareness of the person. In the latter case, the idea may be available to the person in waking without any awareness that its source was a dream. Some ideas may be useful, too, without ever reaching consciousness.

CHAPTER 8

DREAMS AND THE LANGUAGE OF THOUGHT

Dream: I have a manuscript. I need it translated. They don't translate it into English. They translate it into *meaning*.

WHAT IS THE language of thought? Is there a primary, primal language of thought? Does the brain use something like the machine language that computers use? For computers, basically all language is reducible to a code of 1s and 0s. People who are not computer scientists may deal with computers for decades, and never have direct contact with this system of binary code that underlies the most complex computer operation. But such a language exists. Similarly, there may be some underlying levels of brain language to which we so far have no direct access. Might dreams give us insight into this underlying brain language (Foulkes, 1985)?

The question of the language of thought has been addressed by philosophers for centuries. Socrates, in Plato's *Theaetetus*, argues that thinking is no more than silent speech. Here are his own words (Hamilton and Cairns, 1961):

> Socrates: And do you accept my description of the process of thinking?
>
> Theaetetus: How do you describe it?
>
> Socrates: As a discourse that the mind carries on with itself about any subject it is considering. You must take this explanation as coming from an ignoramus; but I have a notion that,

> when the mind is thinking, it is simply talking to itself, asking questions and answering them. . . . So I should describe thinking as a discourse, and judgment as a statement pronounced, not aloud to someone else, but silently to oneself.

Aristotle had a different view (McKeon, 1968):

> Spoken words are the symbols of mental experience and written words are the symbols of spoken words. Just as all men have not the same writing, so all men have not the same speech sounds, but the mental experiences, which these directly symbolize, are the same for all, as also are those things which our experiences are the images [p. 40].

So here we have two basic views: (1) that thought is silent speech and (2) that speech is a particular expression of thought, a translation of a basic underlying language in which all thoughts occur.

There are many reasons for each argument and the answer may ultimately not be entirely Aristotle's or Plato's view. The philosopher Gilbert Ryle (1949) made a small but significant adjustment to Plato's viewpoint, continuing to identify thought as silent speech, but also accompanied by visual imagery. He noted that:

> Much of our ordinary thinking is conducted in internal monologues or silent soliloquy, *usually accompanied by an internal cinematograph-show of visual imagery*. . . . The trick of talking to oneself in silence is acquired neither quickly nor without effort; and it is a necessary condition of our acquiring it that we should have previously learned to talk intelligently aloud and have heard and understood other people doing so. Keeping our thoughts to ourselves is a sophisticated accomplishment [p. 27; italics added].

The experimental psychologist B. F. Skinner argued that thinking was nothing more than silent "verbal behavior." In the cognitive psychology revolution that succeeded behaviorism, thinking came to be seen as potentially independent of speech. In a marvelous essay entitled "Wordless Thoughts," the philosopher Zeno Vendler (1977) argued that Socrates' view leads to preposterous conclusions. By contrast, at the most extreme end of the Aristotelian viewpoint, there are those who think that thought can be pure, unrelated to language, and that words distort thought. Thus Tiutchev said (Vygotsky, 1934): "A thought once uttered is a lie" (p. 254).

There are at least two possible points of view about the relation of dreams to the underlying language of thought: (1) that dreams, like waking speech, are a transformation of the underlying language of thought; and (2) that dreams *are* the language of thought.

In this regard, I am reminded of the exquisite brief dream which heads this chapter:

> I have a manuscript. I need it translated. They don't translate it into English. They translate it into *meaning.*

In this dream, there is a fundamental language called *meaning*. None of us speaks this language called "meaning." But do all of us understand it?

The question of what is the underlying language of thought is one of the most difficult in psychology. It was addressed most directly by the great Russian psychologist, Lev Vygotsky. Vygotsky (1934) studied the development of language and thinking in children, and asked profound questions such as: What is the basic language of thought? How does this basic language interrelate with communicative speech? How does the basic language of thought develop from childhood into adulthood? Is it a given, or does it develop out of social interactions? What are the overt manifestations of this underlying language of thought? Are there thoughts that cannot be expressed in language? If so, what happens to them?

Vygotsky paid special attention to what he called "inner speech," which he argued develops out of "egocentric speech" in children. As Piaget observed, young children in groups often speak in "collective monologues." Although very young children in groups may appear to be having a conversation, they are often speaking in a way that is not really communicative, but expresses private thoughts that are not understandable to other people. As children learn that society expects them to speak in a way that is communicative (usually between the ages of three and seven), the language of collective monologues disappears from their overt speech with one another, but, according to Vygotsky, it does not actually disappear. Instead, such language goes inward, becoming "inner speech," which bears the meaning of thought, without taking into consideration communicability to others.

What are the characteristics of inner speech? Its primary characteristic is, according to Vygotsky, the omission of the subject while preserving the predicate—which I call "subjectless predicates." There are some situations in our everyday speech in which we also use subjectless predicates. Vygotsky (1934) writes, "Pure predication occurs in external speech in two cases: either as an answer or when the subject of the sentence is known beforehand to all concerned. The answer to 'Would you like a cup of tea?' is not usually 'No, I don't want a cup of tea,' but a simple 'No.' Obviously, such a sentence is possible only because its subject is tacitly understood by both parties" (p. 236). If you merely hear someone saying "No," you will have no idea what he means, that is, what he is saying "No" about. But the situation is different if you hear the word "No" after hearing a preceding question. If the question is "Do you want a cup of tea?" then "No" means "No, I don't want a cup of tea." If the question is "Have the Russians invaded Afghanistan?" then "No" means "No, the Russians have not invaded Afghanistan." The same single word "No" can bear completely different meanings: "I don't want a cup of tea" vs. "The Russians have not invaded Afghanistan."

Vygotsky distinguishes between the "grammatical predicate" and the "psychological predicate." The grammatical predicate, as we learned in grade school, is the part of the sentence that follows the grammatical subject and gives information about it. In the sentence "John went to school," the grammatical predicate "went to school" gives us information about the subject "John."

The psychological predicate, by contrast, is the part of the sentence that gives new information, while the psychological subject is the information that is shared by the speaker and listener. The psychological subject and predicate may be the same as the grammatical subject and predicate, but they do not have to be. Vygotsky (1934) gives the following example:

> Suppose I notice that the clock has stopped and ask how this happened. The answer is, "The clock fell." Grammatical and psychological subject coincide: "The clock" is the first idea in my consciousness; "fell" is what is said about the clock. But if I hear a crash in the next room and inquire what happened, and get the same answer, subject and predicate are psychologically reversed. I knew something had fallen—that is what we are talking about. "The clock" completes the idea. The sentence could be changed to "What has fallen is the clock"; then the grammatical and the psychological subjects would coincide [p. 220].

The understanding of an implied subject is a very important aspect of communication. Two people, who share certain kinds of knowledge, can understand communications that would be incomprehensible to other people who do not share that knowledge. Couples in long relationships develop this sort of knowledge basis, so that their communications to each other can increasingly seem to resemble inner speech. I know a couple for whom it is normal to say, "Take the blue." To outside listeners, this is relatively meaningless. But if you know that they have two backpacks, one blue and one brown, and that the blue one has books in it and the brown one, food, then you know that "take the blue" means "bring the books" for this couple.

Sentences that seem meaningless or psychotic can often become meaningful when we learn the underlying knowledge base that they presume. The example of "Please sit in the apple-juice seat" described by George Lakoff and Mark Johnson is an excellent example of this; it seems like nonsense, but it makes sense if you know that the table has four place settings, three with orange juice and one with apple juice. Kraepelin (1906; see Heynick, 1993) described a similar dream-sentence: "Mr. N was awarded the prize for an article on dentistry though he was not working at the notary office" (p. 101). This sentence is virtually incomprehensible, unless you know that Mr. N did not belong to the officially recognized group of researchers, and the notary office referred to an authorized dental office and to being officially notarized (recognized as valid).

Gertrude Stein was particularly fond of such compound sentences, in which the connection between the two parts was not immediately apparent, such as (D. Smith, 1999): "It looked like a garden, but he had hurt himself by accident" (p. E4). Can you imagine a situation that would make this sentence understandable?

Another example is the quasi-telegraphic style that some people incorporate into letters. A letter from a friend may begin: "Glad to hear that you are well." While in English that sentence is not grammatical, it is easy to understand the implied subject: "*I am* glad to hear that you are well." The "I am" is virtually certain. Who but "I" wrote the letter? However, consider a letter that begins: "I saw our mutual friend Bill yesterday. Glad to hear that you are well." In this case, the second sentence would be much less clear. Who is glad? The writer of the letter or Bill?

Vygotsky's analysis of inner speech is brilliant. I find it disappointing, though, that he did not integrate dreams into his discussion of inner speech. At one point, he wrote (1934):

> Inner speech is to a large extent thinking in pure meanings. It is a dynamic, shifting, unstable thing, fluttering between word and thought, the two more or less stable, more or less firmly

> delineated components of verbal thought. Its pure nature and place can be understood only after examining the next plane of verbal thought, the one still more inward than inner speech [p. 249].

When I read that last sentence, I felt sure where Vygotsky would go next—to dreams, of course, which are more inward than inner speech. But I was wrong. Vygotsky continued:

> That plane is thought itself. As we have said, every thought creates a connection, fulfills a function, solves a problem. The flow of thought is not accompanied by a simultaneous unfolding of speech. The two processes are not identical, and there is no rigid correspondence between the units of thought and speech. This is especially obvious when a thought process miscarries—when, as Dostoyevsky put it, a thought "will not enter words" [p. 249].

Vygotsky did not continue his argument about inner speech, applying it to dreams.[1] But I would like to do so here. In my opinion, the "realm of thoughts that are incompatible with words" is precisely the province of the dream. For dreams can represent totally wordless thoughts. "A thought that will not enter words" can find expression in an image, or an emotion—all of which are prominent constituents of dreams. See the discussion, for example, of what I call the "negative dream screen" (chapter 15). No words can capture the terrifying emptiness of such dreams. For as soon as we use words, the void is already somewhat filled.

DREAMS AS SUBJECTLESS PREDICATES

In my view, Vygotsky's theory of inner speech provides the basis for a new understanding of dreaming and dream interpretation. Dreams are

---

1. I have not been able to find any references to dreaming in Vygotsky's work, and I have been told by James Wertsch, a preeminent Vygotsky scholar, that he also knows of no such reference. My colleague William Hirst suggests a reason that Vygotsky did not discuss dreams. It is that Vygotsky and his school were concerned with the development of higher mental processes through social interaction. Vygotsky proposed that higher mental functions are internalized social relations. Dreams, which appear to be the most asocial of mental phenomena, did not fit into their overall interest in the development of mind in a social context.

not primarily speech; they are comprised more of images and emotions. Nevertheless, with the exception of reliance on words, the properties of inner speech are close to the properties of dreams.

Vygotsky provides a theoretical underpinning to my view, expressed in chapter 2, that dream analysis is something like the game *Jeopardy*. You have to provide the question to which the dream is the answer. Or, in Vygotsky's terms, you have to provide the subject of which the dream is the psychological predicate. Then you will understand it. *In unconscious thought, subjects, being understood, are omitted.* In this sense, dreams are private and not meant for communication. *Dreams are subjectless predicates.*[2] They give the critical information without the explanatory context.

Vygotsky also writes:

> All our observations indicate that inner speech is an autonomous speech function. We can confidently regard it as a *distinct plane of verbal thought*. It is evident that the transition from inner speech to external speech is not a simple translation from one language into another. It cannot be achieved by merely vocalizing silent speech. It is a complex, dynamic process involving the transformation of the predicative, idiomatic structure of inner speech into syntactically articulated speech intelligible to others [p. 248].

This complex, dynamic process, the transformation of the predicative, idiomatic structure of inner speech into syntactically articulated speech, could easily be a description of dream analysis as well.

However strange its syntax and vocabulary, inner speech is made of words. Dreams by contrast are made mostly of images, emotions, and kinesthetic experiences. Dreaming is not identical with inner speech; dreaming is closer to what we might call *inner experience* or *inner representation*. It includes not only words, but images, experiences, and "virtual reality."[3] It is the representation of experience without the experience going on. *Just as inner speech is speech without interlocution, the inner representation of dreams is experience without event.*

We might conceive of dreams as being on the far end of a continuum, with inner speech somewhere in the middle of the continuum and

---

2. Lewis Carroll's term "an effect without a cause" is a variant of the subjectless predicate.

3. Recall here the definition of thinking proposed by Ryle, which included Plato's silent speech, but also added on an accompaniment of "an internal cinematograph-show of visual imagery."

intelligible speech on the opposite end. When we tell a dream, we are converting it from a primarily nonspeech experience into a verbal text. The dreamtext, which is different from the dream experience (Khan, 1976) is close in structure to inner speech, a plane of verbal thought that is primarily predicative. Good dream analysis then becomes the process of providing the subject of which the dreamtext is the predicate.

Dreams, like inner speech, are highly condensed. As Vygotsky writes: "A simplified syntax, condensation, and a greatly reduced number of words characterize the tendency to predication that appears in external speech when the partners know what is going on" (p. 238).

A fundamental difference between dreams and inner speech is that *dreams are often not understandable to the dreamer.* In dreams, the process of inner speech goes so far that the dreamer does not consciously have available the necessary understanding of the subject to grasp the predicate. The dreamer may stand in relation to his dream the way an unfamiliar person stands in relation to another person's inner speech. Dreams may be the extreme of inner speech, so private that they may paradoxically not be readily understandable to their producer, the dreamer.

The idea of inner speech not understandable to the self that produced it compels us to think of the dream not as a phenomenon of mind but of minds. We can see in our sleeping experience of dreams and our waking examination of them the dissociation between different mental states. We saw in chapter 4 that the dreamer who dreams the dream may be psychologically separable from the dreamer who understands the dream (Grotstein, 1979). The mind is divisible within itself, and the dream may portray aspects of thinking that are not accessible to parts of the waking self.

As I have already mentioned, Erikson (1954) described a dream that is the epitome of terseness and is rather like inner-speech. In it, there is only the image of a single word "S[E]INE," seen light against a dark background. It was dreamt by a woman whose difficulties were traced back to her seeing the painting of the Circumcision of Christ at the Louvre in Paris. The dreamer was multilingual, and she and Erikson analyze the dream image as a condensation of four elements: (1) the river SEINE in Paris, where the original trauma occurred; (2) SINE, which is "without" in Latin; (3) the German "SEINE," which means "his"; and (4) the bracketed E, which is the first initial of Erikson's name. So together this is "To see E without his . . . in Paris." (The ellipses are Erikson's.) In addition, according to Erikson's analysis, each aspect of the dream connected with an aspect of the patient's pathology. He tells us that the patient has a visual amnesia, and hence in the dream there are no images, only a single word. That the dream space is dark and completely motionless around a clear image was an inverted representation of the patient's memory of the trauma: an area with a dark spot in the center (the repressed picture) surrounded by bright and colorful halls. The lack of motion in the dream corresponds to the patient's symptoms: agoraphobia and immobilization.[4] There is no time dimension in the dream, just as there is now none in the patient's life.

We can see from Erikson's example how with even the most laconic of dreams, the associations of the dreamer can specify the context of the dream that will help make it understandable. The dreamer can also be helped by the associations of others, who propose contexts other than those immediately obvious to him. The discussion of a dream with one or several people opens the possibility of setting up the context for understanding—in Vygotsky's terms, for establishing the psychological subject for which the dream is a predicate.

Various procedures of dream interpretation, in which another person suggests a meaning of the dream to the dreamer, open up the possibility of the dreamer rediscovering the subject to the predicate which is the dream. If you will note, I am not suggesting that existing methods of dream interpretation are invalid because of this revised theory of dreaming. On the contrary, many different methods of dream interpretation can be *re-understood* within this theory to be valid. I would suggest, though, that we focus less on "dream interpretation," and focus more on "dream contextualization" and "dream clarification." Interpretation says: Dream *X* means *Y*. Contextualization and clarification say: Here is what the dreamer is concerned with and this is the question posed by the dream. When you know these things, the dreamtext *per se* is often understandable.

Free association, the linchpin of Freudian dream analysis, is one procedure that may help with contextualization and clarification. In my view, free associations do not take us back to the latent dream thoughts. They take us forward to them. By this I mean that the free associations do not reverse the process of dream formation. They can create, rather than uncover, the latent dream thoughts by creating contexts that make the dream self-explanatory, although they may also divert us from them.

Many techniques of dream interpretation aim for such contextualization, even Joseph's technique in the Old Testament. When Joseph interpreted Pharaoh's dream, he probably knew that one of Pharaoh's

4. This is an example of what Lakoff and Johnson (1999) were later to call "the embodied mind," in which the bodily experience of the world is transmuted metaphorically into the dream.

prominent concerns was: "How shall I run my country? How shall the crops turn out over the next years, and what can I, as the national leader, do about it?" Joseph figured out that these were the latent questions of Pharaoh's dream.

There is a close relationship not only between dreams and inner speech, but also between dreams and schizophrenic speech. That should come as no surprise, since the speech of schizophrenics has certain similarities to inner speech. One might characterize the speech of schizophrenics as inner speech made public, without the shame-induced regard for understandability. This has been my view (Blechner, 1995b), along with other psychoanalysts who have worked intensively with schizophrenics:

> Private thoughts are uttered pretty much as they are thought, without being formed to take into account the requisites of a listener for intelligibility. In this way, the schizophrenic achieves two aims: he emits his thoughts for public consumption but he assures himself that his communications will be accessible only to those who are truly interested in his experience and will take the trouble to decode his thoughts. The indifferent listener will hear only gibberish, and from him, the schizophrenic is safe [p. 379].

Frieda Fromm-Reichmann (1950) adopted the view that schizophrenic speech is close to inner speech; she claimed that the schizophrenic usually knows what he is saying, often better than his therapist, implying that he knows his unstated psychological subjects. For example, a schizophrenic man feels that his brain is receiving a broadcast from a distant planet with a Spanish name. You could usefully consider his delusion as a subjectless predicate. If you then find out that he lives in New York but was raised in the Spanish neighborhood of East Los Angeles, and that he has a strong ambivalence to that poverty-stricken but culture-rich background, then you have a much better idea what the delusion may mean. You know the subject of which his delusion is the predicate, and you can formulate an interpretation, such as: You are far from your Spanish-speaking home, but you have recurrent thoughts about your background and family that are disturbing.

If the text of the delusion—I am receiving a broadcast from a distant planet with a Spanish name, and it is very disturbing to me—were a dreamtext, you could use the same background material to help understand it. The provision of the background subject would not, in itself, be an interpretation. *But when you have enough of the subject, the dream-text (or delusion) itself no longer needs interpretation. It is understandable in its own words.* You might be able to derive that same meaning from associations to the dream. But when anxiety is high, as it surely is in hallucinating schizophrenics, the associations might as easily take you away from the meaning as toward it.

Dreams are different from inner speech, being mostly nonverbal, but when we awaken and think about a dream we just had, those thoughts about the dream are more like inner speech, as we convert the dream experience into a dream-text that we can tell other people. In fact, we can wake up from dreams thinking a sentence of inner speech that does not feel like a part of the dream, but seems intimately related to it. For example, one of my patients woke up from a dream and thought, "I come from a crime family." At first, she didn't understand what that sentence meant or what it had to do with her dream. We discussed it, and I encouraged her not to worry about the connection to the dream. I asked her merely to expand on that short sentence. She did so, somewhat reluctantly, and came up with: "The members of my family are as violent to me as criminals; they have their own internal system of rules like a Mafia family, and if you violate them, even though the outside world will think that you are behaving normally or even ethically, they will punish you for it." This thought, which might be called a post-dream thought, made the dream itself easy to understand.

RELATIONSHIP BETWEEN INNER SPEECH AND DREAM CONDENSATION

Vygotsky (1934) noted that another basic characteristic of inner speech is what he called "agglutination."

> This leads us to the other semantic peculiarities of inner speech. Both concern word combination. One of them is rather like agglutination—a way of combining words fairly frequent in some languages and comparatively rare in others. German often forms one noun out of several words or phrases. In some primitive languages, such adhesion of words is a general rule. . . . The egocentric speech of the child displays some analogous phenomena. As egocentric speech approaches inner speech, the child uses agglutination more and more as a way of forming compound words to express complex ideas [p. 246].

Agglutination may be seen as a form of condensation, in which words are combined in ways that are not normally accepted. Lakoff and Johnson's "apple-juice-seat" is an example of such agglutination in English. But in English we tend to insert hyphens. German is not so cautious about agglutination, and words are more routinely joined together.

Thomas Mann entitled his novel *The Magic Mountain*, but in German, "Magic Mountain" becomes one word, "*Zauberberg*." Gustav Mahler's song cycle "Songs on the Death of Children" becomes one word in German, "*Kindertotenlieder*."

How do such agglutinations relate to dream condensation? In chapter 6, we identified three basic kinds of dream condensation, which could have lexical analogues. The first, *simple overdetermined condensation*, already exists in normal language, in the form of homonyms or words with multiple meanings. But in dream overdetermination, words can also acquire unusual and unexpected meanings, and the meanings may blend and interact in ways that are more fecund than normal daytime thinking. There is a striking parallel with inner speech. Vygotsky (1934) states:

> Basic semantic peculiarity of inner speech is the way in which senses of words combine and unite—a process governed by different laws from those governing combinations of meanings. . . . 'influx of sense.' The senses of different words flow into one another—literally 'influence' one another—so that the earlier ones are contained in and modify the later ones. . . . In inner speech, the phenomenon reaches its peak. A single word is so saturated with sense that, like the title *Dead Souls*,[5] it becomes a concentrate of sense. To unfold it into overt speech, one would need a multitude of words [pp. 246–247].

Our second type of condensation, *creative condensation*, has its analogue in normal agglutination. As I am writing this book, I have been tempted several times to write the word "dreamtext." My word processor's spell-checker has cautioned me not to do so, but anyone seeing the word would understand its meaning.

---

5. Vygotsky (1934, p. 247) explains that the title of Gogol's *Dead Souls* initially refers "to dead serfs whose names had not yet been removed from the official lists and who could still be bought and sold as if they were alive. . . . When we reach the end of the book, 'dead souls' means to us not so much the defunct serfs as all the characters in the story who are alive physically but dead spiritually."

Our third type of condensation, *partial condensation*, has its analogue in the neologisms of inner speech, in which the source words are not kept intact, or in which the new word is a virtually new creation. Children sometimes make up secret languages with such new words. The writer Lewis Carroll, who, as already noted, used material from his dreams in his writing, was particularly adept at such word creation: Consider his "Jabberwocky." This word has no precise meaning, but it is "language-like" and is suggestive of something to most people. To me, "Jabber" suggests silly wordiness and the "wocky" suggests wackiness, so that I have always understood Jabberwocky as "wacky wordiness." Such terms can function as lexical Rorschach tests.

I will shift here in my discussion of dreams. I have examined Freud's theory of dreams and compared it with other psychoanalytic theories, like those of Jung and Levenson, and the theories of cognitive neuroscience, such as Hobson and McCarley's activation-synthesis theory and Crick and Mitchison's theory of elimination of parasitic nodes. I have specified the way that dreams condense and reorganize information, creating interobjects and other novel dream creations. Based on such phenomena, I have proposed an additional function of dreams in human thought called Oneiric Darwinism, in which the mind creates thought mutations which can be retained and developed if useful. I have proposed a new approach to understanding dreams as subjectless predicates, grounded in Vygotsky's theory of inner speech. This suggests a different way of working with dreams, one that involves contextualizing the dream more than interpreting it.

At this point, it makes sense for us to move more into the consulting room, to apply our understanding of dreams further to actual clinical work. Later (section IV) we will return to the theory of dreams and, with the help of clinical neurology, consider what dreams can tell us about the workings of the mind/brain.

PART III

CLINICAL WORK WITH DREAMS

CHAPTER 9

VECTORS OF DREAM INTERPRETATION

All generalizations, including this one, are false.

Mark Twain

WHEN WE LISTEN to a dream, we have choices about which information we will notice. What we find will be partly determined by what we look for. I call these choices in our approach to the dream "vectors of interpretation."

By vectors of interpretation, I mean an approach to looking at a dream from a number of particular perspectives, with each perspective yielding a different kind of information about the dream. I am borrowing the notion of a vector from physics and mathematics to capture the idea that I am thinking of, which is to look at the same object from different perspectives. My dictionary defines a vector as a line representing a physical quantity that has magnitude and direction in space as velocity, acceleration, and force. But I would like to use vector somewhat metaphorically. If you imagine running a line or a plane through something, you see it from a new perspective. For example, in three-dimensional geometry, let us take a look at a cone. If you take a cone-shape, and run a plane through it, parallel to the base, you get a circle. If you run a plane through it on any other angle to the base, you get an ellipse. If you run a plane through it perpendicular to the base and through the diameter, you get an isosceles triangle. If you run a plane through it, not perpendicular to the base, you get a parabola, shaped something like a woman's fingernail.

All those different shapes—an infinite number of circles, ellipses, triangles, parabolas—are latent in the cone. When you look at the cone, you may not see those shapes right off, but with the proper vector intersecting the cone, those shapes will appear.

That, in a nutshell, is my view of dream analysis. The dream has within it a huge amount of information about the dreamer. Exactly what information you will extract from the dream will depend on the vector of your dream analysis. The kinds of information that you can extract are all valid, but the dream will tell you different things depending on how you approach it. And so you, as the dream analyst, can choose the kind of information you will get out of the dream.

There are many different vectors of dream analysis. Freud's approach was to ask what is the unconscious wish expressed in the dream. While Freud may have been wrong in saying that wish fulfillment is the cause of all dreams, it is still a magnificent way to approach dreams. Freud has often been called a pessimist, but the theory of dreams as wish fulfillment is an extremely optimistic viewpoint. If every dream has encoded in it a fundamental desire, then the process of dream analysis can, when properly carried out, reveal to the dreamer what he truly desires in life. This is one very fruitful vector of dream analysis.

The dream interpreter should become familiar with many vectors of interpretation, including:

- What is the most prominent issue and the area of greatest conflict for the dreamer at the present time?
- What is the dreamer's personality like?
- What was the dreamer's childhood development like, down to some very specific facts of his history?
- What does the dreamer want?
- How does the dreamer experience herself in the physical world?
- How does she see her body?
- How does she see herself in relation to other people?
- What were some significant traumas in the dreamer's history?
- If the dreamer is in psychoanalytic treatment, what is the nature of the transference and countertransference?
- What are the prominent emotional patterns of the dreamer?

Some other, more controversial aspects of the dream are whether it can also tell you something about the dreamer's physical health and about the future.

You can apply different vectors to a single dream, and derive different kinds of information. You can also apply a single vector to a *series* of dreams. Using the vector of change over time, you can listen to a series of one patient's dreams, and from them get an idea of how he or she is developing and changing (Blechner, 1983; Domhoff, 1996). You can also look for themes of bodily issues, early history, stance in life, ego psychological trends, emotional patterns, transference-countertransference configurations, Kleinian positions, etc. You can run a vector through all the dreams of the patients of one therapist, and from that get a good view of her countertransference. You can apply a vector through the dreams of patients who work with analysts from the same school; those who have done that think that Jungian analysts tend to get different kinds of dreams from their patients than Freudians do.

We could survey the entire history of psychoanalytic dream interpretation from the point of view of vectors of interpretation. I am going to outline here only some of the more important vectors of interpretation that have been identified. As I do so, I will refer back to Hobson's dream that we discussed in chapter 2.

DREAMS AS WISH FULFILLMENT

Freud proposed that all dreams represent the fulfillment of wishes. This generalization has been repeatedly attacked. As we noted above, even Freud backtracked on this generalization, claiming at times that dreams represented an attempt at fulfillment of wishes or that only some dreams represented wish fulfillments.

In my view, even if the wish-fulfillment hypothesis does not hold up for all dreams, we should not discard it. Instead, we should retain the idea of wish fulfillment in those circumstances where the dream indicates it. This can occur, for example, when the manifest content of the dream indicates that the dreamer is trying to achieve something in the dream without acknowledging responsibility for it, suggesting that an unconscious wish is being fulfilled. For example, a man dreamt:

> I was outside in the driveway. My umbrella was in front of me on the driveway close to the curb. These two women came along. They were young types from my high school class, not educated. They were talking to each other. One was looking at the other. I knew she would step on my umbrella. My umbrella flew up and landed next to me. It clearly was broken. Then the two women were across the street. I went over to them and said, "You stepped on my umbrella." She denied it, somewhat hostilely. I was trying to be reasonable but forceful. I said, "This

> isn't about fault, it's about responsibility." There was tension there. I was pressing my point, but wasn't being hostile. Her friend took out a $25 bill. But then I thought it was too high. "You should pay something, at least $5." I searched for a $10 bill to give her. I only had 20s in my wallet. Also, a $1,500 and a $100 bill. I was trying to hide how much I had in my wallet.

At first he associated the umbrella to a penis; could the broken umbrella indicate castration? I acknowledged that as one possible meaning of the dream, but then I wondered, why is the penis symbolized by an umbrella? There are many other phallic shaped objects. The dreamer then started to talk about his financial dependency on his parents. He was employed in a job in which he often had to make financial negotiations. He was very good at it, but he was spending more money than he was making, and at this rate he would have to borrow money from his parents soon. I told him that his talk about money and the umbrella in the dream reminded me of the phrase: "Saving for a rainy day." I also noted that in the manifest dream, he leaves the umbrella on the ground. It looks like a set-up. He expects the women to damage the umbrella before it actually happens. So why should they be liable for stepping on it? It looks in the dream as if he wants them to step on it. Perhaps his unconscious wish is to have the umbrella broken. Then I wondered about his negotiating style in the dream. He is usually very skilled at getting his way in professional negotiations. The woman offers him $25. Having got that much, which is the real value of the umbrella, he starts to backtrack. What kind of negotiating is that?

He said, "That's just what I do when I negotiate something involving myself. If I am forceful and clear and feeling good, then I have to soften it and take it back some way. I'm weak."

I said to him that he is being unfair to himself. He is not weak, but conflicted. He negotiates well, but then he backs off.

He started to talk about his mother's ambivalent message to be successful, but not too successful. He said, "I feel like I have to get away from the influence of my mother, but then I think, I need her for money." He went on to describe obsessive calculations about how much money his parents have and how much money he can get from them.

I said, "In the dream, you say, 'This isn't about fault; it's about responsibility.' I wonder if by that, you mean that you can stop blaming your mother for your current situation, and instead take responsibility for yourself. If so, we could consider your dream to be a wish. It could be a wish to destroy the umbrella, destroy the protection that you have from your parents. Then, having done that, you look in your wallet and find that you have all this money. Perhaps when you free yourself from your psychological dependence on your parents, you will find yourself with more of your own money."

His associations then supported the interpretation. He thought of the television show *Rhoda* and said, "There was an episode in which Rhoda is talking to her mother, Ida. Ida wants to give Rhoda money. Rhoda says, 'I don't want your money.' I remember admiring it."[1]

DREAMS AS COMPENSATION

After Freud's approach of looking for the wish, the next major approach to dreams was Jung's idea of dreams as compensation. Jung's idea was *not* that the dream shows what the dreamer *really* thinks and wants. Instead, dreams show what, besides the dreamer's conscious thoughts, he *also* thinks and wants. As Jung (1934) wrote: "We must see to it that the values of the conscious personality remain intact, for unconscious compensation is only effective when it co-operates with an integral consciousness. Assimilation is never a question of 'this *or* that,' but always 'this *and* that'" (p. 104).

Hobson's dream may be an example of compensation. In his waking life, he has often attempted to undermine Freud and psychoanalysis. Not only has he attacked Freud's theory of dream formation (Hobson and McCarley, 1977), he has also criticized Freud's literature summary at the beginning of *The Interpretation of Dreams* for omitting much of the nineteenth-century dream literature that supported the idea of biological causation of dreams (Lavie and Hobson, 1986). Yet while Hobson is hostile to Freud and psychoanalysis in his waking life, the dream shows him as intimately engaged with and inseparable from Van (psychoanalysis).

Jung's theory of dreams as compensation is usually seen as separate from Freud's theory of wish fulfillment. Yet, in my view, compensation itself always implies a wish—a wish for balance in one's life. If

1. This is an abridged account of our work with the dream. We also then considered several other issues, including how the dream reflected the financial issues in the transference with regard to his fee (including the fact that $25 and $1500 bills do not exist in the waking world); how his sense of phallic competence and bodily integrity were related to his character; and how the motion of the umbrella, flying up and down, was related to fluctuations in a sense of potency, sexual and characterological.

a man is involved in violent and criminal action all the time, he may dream of spirituality. If a man's life is boring and passive, he may dream of adventure. In all of these dreams of compensation, the implicit wish is to bring to one's life that which one doesn't have.

One might argue that even if compensation dreams are expressions of wish fulfillment, they are not expressions of an infantile wish. But that may not be accurate, for one of the most basic infantile wishes is for homeostasis. From the very beginnings of life, our entire beings are set to seek a kind of balance[2] (Freud, 1920). If we are dehydrated, we feel thirsty and wish to drink. In our dreams, this thirst may be expressed at first symbolically, eventually leading to our waking up and needing to drink. (See, for example the dream of the cinerary urn [Freud, 1900, p. 123ff].)

A man who was a workaholic had greatly sacrificed his personal needs and the needs of his family and friends in order to pursue his ambitious career goals. He had a dream that he was driving through a hilly desert. He was driving much too fast, not stopping at intersections for other cars. It was exhausting and went on and on.

It was not hard to see the dream as compensation. At first the driving was thrilling, he said, but then it became too much. He was getting more and more exhausted, but he couldn't stop or slow down. From a compensation standpoint, his displeasure in the dream with the too rapid pace was a compensation to his conscious, waking attitude that he liked working all the time. In the dream, he kept getting into near accidents, although there were no actual accidents. This was also a compensation, at least in my view; he had gotten into interpersonal accidents because of the way he structured his life, but he had never recognized how much they affected him. The dream was a warning, as he realized himself; he said that if the dream kept on that way, eventually there would be a very serious accident and he might die.

INTERPRETATION ON THE SUBJECTIVE AND THE OBJECTIVE LEVELS

Another important vector proposed by Jung (1916–1948) is "interpretation on the subjective level." Freud (1900) had already asserted that the main character in a dream always represents the dreamer. By inter-

2. Freud (1920) argued that the mental apparatus tries to keep the quantity of excitation at a minimum. It is more likely that it tries to keep it at an optimal level.

pretation on the subjective level, Jung meant considering the dream from a perspective in which *all* the figures in a dream are seen as representative of aspects of the dreamer. He contrasted it with the "objective level," in which you interpret the people as representing either themselves or people other than the dreamer.

This notion was developed further by Fairbairn (1940), who suggested that the apparent interpersonal drama of dreams reflected the internal object relations of the dreamer, and was later adopted and expanded by Gestalt psychotherapists.

This vector raises one of the most basic questions about dreams: When they have several characters, are they representations of actual interpersonal situations with others, or do they represent different aspects of the dreamer's personality, portrayed as a drama among several people? Most psychoanalysts today would argue that both are true. The entire cast of characters in a dream represent different aspects of the dreamer; yet they may also represent the dreamer's view of his or her relationship with others.

The reason both can coexist reveals a deeper truth of psychoanalytic personality theory, which holds that the individual personality is composed of various aspects. These aspects are called "personifications" by Sullivan (1953) or "internal objects" by Klein (1946), Fairbairn (1944), and subsequent object relations theorists. There is a continual interaction between the actual beings in one's social situation and one's internal objects.

The person will tend to bring about the realization of his internal objects in a social situation. Thus, we find in clinical psychoanalysis the phenomenon of projective identification, whereby one person manages to get another to collaborate in living out his internal object relations (Ogden, 1982). Meanwhile, at least according to interpersonal theory, the internal objects will be shaped and modified by the actual persons in one's social environment. The tension between these two tendencies—the patient reenacting his internal object relations in the actual relationship with the analyst, and the real actions of the analyst who "resists transformation" (Levenson, 1972), modifying the patient's internal object relations—is the fundamental process of psychoanalytic treatment.

With this in mind, the psychoanalyst hearing a dream must ask two basic questions: (1) How does the dream reflect the entirety of the patient's personality? and (2) How does the dream represent actual interactions between the patient and other people, including myself, at least as far as these people are perceived by the patient?

How would "interpretation on the subjective level" apply to Hobson's dream? It would mean that Van, the psychoanalyst, would represent an aspect of Hobson himself. The interchange between Hobson and Van could then be seen as an internal struggle within Hobson. He is dealing with the conflict about whether he should "play along" with his own psychoanalytic interests or be dismissive of them, as with his statement in the dream: "That is why you have such beautiful buildings, and there is nothing in them."

One quirk of the objective and subjective levels of dream interpretation is that in most published dream interpretations, the "I" in the dream is assumed to be the dreamer. We rarely question whether the "I" is someone else. James Hillman (1979) is one of the few (along with Freud) to consider that "I" is not the dreamer:

> Here precisely is the inconsistency in most dream interpretation: all figures are taken on the subjective level, but the ego remains on the objective level. Although the interpreter may recognize that my car in my dream is not my actual car but images my "motoric driving," my "wheels," and that my sister in my dream is not my sister but the way her image affects my soul, still the "I" in the dream remains the I sitting in the client's chair of the consulting room. The "I" remains literal and intact, never truly resolved into its own image.
>
> So to reach the fully subjective, a dream-worker must reach into the last pocket of objectivity, the dream-ego, its behaviors and its feelings, keeping them within the image. The job becomes one of subjecting the ego to the dream, dissolving it in the dream, by showing that everything done and felt and said by the ego reflects its situation in the image, i.e., that this ego is wholly imaginal. Not an easy job, for the ego is archetypally an upperworld phenomenon, strong in its heroic attitudes until, by learning how to dream, it becomes an imaginal ego [p. 101].

We find in Freud (1900) one of the few published dream interpretations that I know of in which the dreamer is thought to represent someone else.[3] In the dream, Freud's patient wishes to give a dinner party but has only a little smoked salmon in the house and the cater-

---

3. Foucault (1986) says that Freud thought that "I" could be someone else, but gives no reference: "The subject of the dream, in Freud's sense, is always a lesser subjectivity, a delegate, so to speak, projected into an intermediate status, suspended somewhere in the play of the other, somewhere between the dreamer and what he dreams. *The proof is that for Freud this dreamplay may actually represent*

ers are closed, so she cannot give a dinner party. Freud analyzes that the dreamer has a friend who is often praised by the dreamer's husband. However, the friend is thin, and the dreamer's husband prefers a fuller figure. So the inability to give a dinner party is connected in Freud's interpretation with the wish not to give a dinner party, that is, not to fatten up her friend who will then attract the dreamer's husband.

But then Freud goes on to offer a second interpretation based on hysterical identification, in which the "I" in the dream represents the friend: "Her friend had also given expression to a wish—to become stouter—and it would not have been surprising if my patient had dreamt that her friend's wish was unfulfilled; for my patient's own wish was that her friend's wish (to put on weight) should not be fulfilled. Thus the dream will acquire a new interpretation if we suppose that the person indicated in the dream was not herself but her friend, that she had put herself in her friend's place, or, as we might say, that she had 'identified' herself with her friend" (p. 149).

But in this case, the dreamer's being a representation of somebody else is a secondary interpretation and follows the initial interpretation in which the dreamer represents herself. A dream interpretation in which the dreamer is not himself or herself at all is something I have not yet found.

To the vector of Jung and Fairbairn, of analyzing all characters in the dream as aspects of the dreamer, I would like to suggest a corollary vector—that, with dreams of a patient in psychoanalysis, the analyst consider all characters in the dreams as representations of the analyst. Although you may balk at such an idea, if you really try it out, you may find out some very interesting things about how you and your patient relate to one another.

Gestalt therapists have greatly expanded interpretation on the subjective level. They assume that *inanimate* objects in a dream are also aspects of the dreamer and ask the dreamer to imagine being those inanimate objects.

THE VECTORS OF EGO PSYCHOLOGY: THE FOUR W'S

Erik Erikson's important paper of 1946, "The Dream Specimen of Psychoanalysis," outlined a different set of dream-analysis vectors based on ego psychology. Erikson proposed that in dream analysis, you do a sentence-by-sentence analysis of the manifest dream with the four "W

---

someone else by an alienating identification; or another personage may, by a sort of heautoscopy, represent the dreamer himself" [p. 57].

questions": Who is there at that moment? What is the setting? What is the affect? And what is the sense of time? Using this kind of analysis, you often come up with a startling picture of the dreamer's interpersonal world, just from the manifest content. This method of analysis is especially good at telling you how consistent or haphazard is the dreamer's sense of the presence of other people in his life and what role they play.

For instance, Hobson's dream shows a great consistency, almost a fixed quality, in his object world, from the temporal and interpersonal aspects. Throughout the dream, it is Van and he. There are no other people, although Mary is mentioned. And always, it is in the present tense. But from an affective standpoint, there is much shifting and ambiguity, a kind of movement back and forth between casual playfulness and harsh interchanges. The back and forth in the affective structure of the whole dream is paralleled by the content, the throwing of the hinge back and forth. If the latent content of the dream concerns the interchange between psychoanalysis and empirical dream research, the manifest content reveals that the deeper issue is affective—how to move between anger and friendliness, between toughness and playfulness, and between rigidity and a ballet-like grace. And there is also a shift within the dream between action and dialogue. Hobson and Van begin the dream speaking about whether Hobson will be chosen for the invited lecture series. Then there follows a kind of ballet or mime. Hobson, in telling us the dream, says that when Van throws him the lock/hinge, it is "*as if to say*, 'Here, take this as recompense.'" This comment seems like secondary revision, a modification of the dream when the dream is recalled; the "as if to say" is not actually said in the dream. Much happens nonverbally between them that is very expressive and emotional, and, according to Hobson, understandable. The shift from nonverbal to verbal communication is subtle. In the dreamtext, Van says, "They chose Mary (or seems to say that, Hobson tells us)." This is one of those very special dream experiences. They have gone from speech to nonspeech to something in between—the dream experience is that Van *seems* to say something. Here we see another prominent issue of the dream—what do people say, how do you know when they say it, and can you understand it even if they just seem to say it?

THE VECTOR OF INFANTILE WISHES AND COMPLEXES

Other vectors of interpretation will yield different kinds of information from the dream. If you ask of a dream, as Freud recommended, what does it say of an infantile-sexual nature about the dreamer, you will probably find some important information. Hobson himself offers the association that his father lives in Williamstown, which he notes, dismissively, may suggest quixotically oedipal motives.

"Quixotically oedipal" is itself like a brilliant dream condensation. It mixes the myths of Don Quixote and Oedipus. Don Quixote was the wonderfully mad knight errant who fought windmills. He looks like he is combative, but his aggression is misplaced. Don Quixote's most intense real relationship is with Sancho Panza, a fact that aligns with another of Hobson's associations to the dance with Van: "itself a thinly veiled homosexual desire?" Hobson's associations highlight the aspects of the dream that are compensation. Despite the apparent sarcasm and hostility in the dream, there is also a loving aspect between Hobson and Van (psychoanalysis). He never admits it verbally, but it is implicit in all of his actions. Not only do they play catch with the lock/hinge; it is significant that Hobson is attached to Van from the beginning to the end of the dream. He never gets rid of him, and all of his attention and affect is focused on him.

THE VECTOR OF DREAM CHANGES OVER TIME

All the vectors we have examined so far have involved individual dreams. But there are also "longitudinal vectors," vectors that examine how dreams change over time. Anyone who keeps a dream log for many years will be fascinated by these changes, as well as by the aspects of an individual's dreams that do not change over time.

This vector is especially important in the clinical situation, where change is of the essence. How do the patient's dreams change over the course of therapy? The dream may be an indication of changes that have already happened in the person's life or it may augur changes that are imminent. The changes can be observed in many ways. Individual symbols may undergo transformation. Caligor and Caligor (1978; see also Caligor and May, 1968) report a series of dreams in which there is a progressive transformation of the common symbol of vehicles and their relation to the driver or passengers. The first dream in treatment is about a small car that drives into a gas station, where a friendly man fills up its tank. The car feels happy and strong, and flies off. Later in treatment, the dreamer is the passenger in a car. The driver keeps going faster, and the dreamer fears the car will get out of control. Still later in the treatment, the dreamer is driving a bus, which is also going increasingly faster and is getting out of control. The dreamer feels panicked, but there is a man standing nearby who is not panicked. The dreamer keeps control of the bus, though it nearly runs off the road. "In the progressive development of the vehicle image in these widely spaced dreams, we can see a symbolic development of this young man from childish, symbiotic relatedness, through gradual differentiation, to an assumption of his own autonomy despite its precariousness and the anxiety it engenders" (p. 123). There may be other dimensions to the progression of dreams. In the first dream the car goes off on its own. In the succeeding dreams, the patient takes on more and more responsibility, but he cannot do it alone. One cannot help wondering if the therapy, while enabling greater responsibility, is also engendering an increasing sense of dependence.

The changes in a patient's dreams can reflect not only changes in psychodynamics, but changes, too, in the level of waking reality testing. In psychotic patients, the contents of delusions and hallucinations may be incorporated into their dreams as symbols as they improve clinically (Arieti, 1963; Blechner, 1983, 2000a; Goode, 1999; Quinodoz, 1999; Williams, 1999). I will discuss this further in chapter 19, "The Reallocation of Madness."

THE VECTOR OF HYPERMNESIS: DREAMS THAT BRING UP TRACES OF EARLY MEMORIES

One of the more questionable issues about dreams has to do with the relationship between dreams and memory. There is a great deal of evidence that early memories can find their way into the content of a dream. At times, the memory will be accessible to the dreamer, but the dreamer may not realize how the memory shows up in the dream, although other people can.

I have seen this phenomenon often in my dream interpretation class. The class is taught to postgraduate students of psychoanalysis, so all of them are already experienced clinicians. A patient's dream will be read to the class with no background information. The class, with between six and 12 students, will register, sometimes with a sense of a great deal of confidence, that the dreamer was a victim of sexual abuse, or a war survivor, or physically beaten, or a victim of some other trauma; or that her family of origin involved divorce or was a single-parent family, or some other permutation. In one class, we checked for accuracy about these basic facts, and it appeared to be about 85%. There needs to be a more precise statistical test of this; without it, the debate about dreams and memory tends to bog down in polemics (e.g., Brenneis, 1994; Alpert, 1995). Because of the way dreams can also create new experiences, one could never use a dream as prima facie evidence of any historical fact about the dreamer; dreams can only function as signposts.

In many instances, the dream will condense an early memory with the current situation, including the experience of psychoanalysis. For example, a man had been born prematurely and spent the first two weeks of life in an incubator. When he was 35, he dreamt: "I am sitting on a bench with swimmers. There is a heat lamp to get heat from. There was a deal where you could get a raft, like a mattress, to go into water. It cost money, you got paid for it when you returned."

In this dream, he gets heat from the heat lamp. It is artificial heat, not human; but there are people all around. This dream image may be derived from his perinatal experience of being under a heat lamp in an incubator, with people around but no human contact, or from his fantasies about that experience.

One could also easily interpret the dream in terms of his experience of the analysis. The analyst is giving him a raft to go explore the waters. You pay for it at first, but by the end, when you return, you get paid back. (The dreamer was making a minimal wage at the start of treatment, but was doing well financially when he terminated.) Rafts save your life; they also resemble the couch. Thus the dream melded his very early experience with his current experience in treatment. For this man, the dream also predicted how the issue of body temperature would eventually be re-experienced in the transference. Later in treatment, he began to experience different temperatures in his body during sessions, with the side closer to the analyst being warmer.

Similarly, Niederland (1965) reports a schizophrenic man who dressed in very heavy clothes no matter what the weather was. They discovered the reason for this symptom through the following dream:

> I was near or at the North Pole in an arctic region. It was night and I was lying on an ice block or a refrigerator which was my bed or something. I was surrounded by ice and snow and it was totally dark. The night remained icy, cold, and dark for a long, long time, as if it would never end. Finally the dawn came and some people were walking in and out of the room where I was lying on the refrigerator which was also my bed [p. 567].

Niederland asked the patient if he had ever been actually frozen in something like what occurred in the dream. The patient mockingly told his parents about Niederland's question, but they were astonished. They told him that when he was less than a year old, they had left the window of his bedroom half open on an extremely cold night and had ignored his cries. Hospitalization for pneumonia ensued, and the patient remained an invalid for a long time. The analysis of the dream led to an abatement of the patient's symptoms. (For other examples of early memories recovered through dreams, see Rosen [1955], Pulver [1987], Williams [1987], and Share [1992].)

DREAMS AS INDICATORS OF HEALTH STATUS

One of the more controversial aspects of the dream is whether it can tell you something about the dreamer's physical health, both now and in the future. Freud (1900) considered the possible role of dreams in diagnosing medical illness. He noted that "Aristotle regarded it as quite possible that the beginnings of an illness might make themselves felt in dreams before anything could be noticed of it in waking life, owing to the magnifying effect produced upon impressions by dreams" (p. 33). He also cited other medical authorities, and considered the connection of physical illness and dream content as "established beyond a doubt" (p. 35).[4]

This point of view was applied to Freud's own dreams. Schavelzon (1983), an Argentine cancer surgeon who became a psychoanalyst, found the histological preparations of Freud's oral cancer from the period 1928 to 1939, and reproduced 26 of them in a book he published in 1983.

Schavelzon was probably the first to connect the Irma dream with Freud's cancer. In 1995, Hersh published a paper with the same view. The scabs and white patches in Irma's oral cavity are seen as predictions of Freud's illness. Irma's acting "like a woman with artificial dentures" has a seeming correspondence with the fact that Freud, later in life, had to wear an oral prosthesis because of his cancer surgery.

Following this line of thought, it is possible that another of Freud's dreams also refers to his oral cancer and the prosthesis. In it, Freud (1900) sees his son in a dream: "It seemed to me that his face or forehead was bandaged. He was adjusting something in his mouth, pushing something into it. And his hair was flecked with grey. I thought: 'Could he be as exhausted as all that? And has he got false teeth?'" (p. 559).

However, Jones (1957), in his biography of Freud, indicates that the first sign of the cancer appeared in February 1923, whereas the Irma

4. See also Jung (1934), Davie (1935), Sabini (1981), and Haskell (1985).

dream occurred in 1895, 28 years earlier, and the dream of his son also occurred before 1900. It would be quite extraordinary for a dream to predict a cancer so far in advance.

There are many other examples reported in the literature of dreams that predicted the onset of illness or that diagnosed an ongoing illness, with much less of a time lag between the dream and the illness. Oliver Sacks, in his book *Awakenings* (1973), describes a man who had a vivid dream that he was turning into a statue. He had viral encephalitis, which led him to become unable to talk and almost unable to move, much like a statue, until he was treated 40 years later with L-DOPA and was "awakened."

The problem with this literature is that it is mostly anecdotal. Examples of correct predictions and diagnoses seem very compelling, but we do not know how many times a dream has predicted something *incorrectly*. Those examples are usually not reported. I have had one dream in which a colleague with whom I work died, and another in which a relative contracted a certain illness. So far as I know, neither dream has come true after nearly a decade. Of course, eventually that colleague will die, as we all will, but I think the dream had more to do with my own psychodynamics than with predicting the future.

As another example, in 1963 Montague Ullman had a dream in which he had lost his focal vision and retained only peripheral vision (Ullman, 1973). He had to climb a staircase on his hands and knees. Ullman was interested in how his dream illustrated our need to ignore many of the violent things that we see in our society. But those who believe in dreams predicting illness would have to wonder if Ullman's dream predicted a future visual impairment. The answer is decidedly negative; 36 years after his dream, Ullman's vision is fine, and he has no need to find his way on his hands and feet.

OTHER PROPHETIC DREAMS

The belief that dreams are prophetic is extremely old. All of the dreams in the Old Testament of the Bible are prophetic, including Jacob's ladder dream, Joseph's dreams about his future relations with his family, Pharaoh's dreams that were interpreted by Joseph, and Nebuchadnezzar's dream that was interpreted by Daniel. In fact, God says in the Old Testament that Moses was the only prophet with whom He did not communicate through dreams or hallucinations, but rather "mouth to mouth" (Numbers 12:6–8).

The belief that dreams predict the future is held in many cultures. During a 1997 visit to China, I was told that many people believe that dreaming of blood brings good luck. Dreaming of money foretells tragedy. In Jamaica and in some Hispanic cultures, as well as in the Talmud, if you dream that teeth fall out, it means that someone will die. I have never been able to find out whether people in those cultures, knowing how their dreams will be used socially, can, even unconsciously, dream certain things to carry out personal wishes. For example, if you hate someone, you can dream something that will be interpreted to predict that person's death and be sure the person hears about your dream.

The belief that teeth falling out signifies an impending death seems to be quite widespread, in many disparate cultures. We know that the composer Richard Wagner and his wife Cosima considered it. Wagner dreamt of teeth falling out of his mouth in great numbers, and Cosima dreamt of a broken tooth and considered it an omen. Shortly thereafter, Wagner's friend Karl Tausig died (Wagner, 1978, p. 393).

A few days before his assassination, Abraham Lincoln told his wife he had had a dream in which he saw a coffin guarded by soldiers in the White House. After inquiring about who had died, he was told: "The President, killed by an assassin." While such reports may seem compelling, we do not hear about the times when presidents dreamt of their assassination and were *not* assassinated. Thus, the lore is accumulated of dream prophecies that have come true, and this tends to skew the evidence that dreams can be reliably prophetic.

A METAVECTOR: THE PROCESS OF THE DREAM INTERPRETATION AS A VECTOR

Besides all of these vectors, the dream interpreter should attend to a kind of metavector, which reflects back on the kinds of dream information and the kinds of interpersonal processes that have or have not been part of your dream interpretation. As part of your work of dream interpretation, you look at the vectors of dream interpretation that you and the patient have taken up, and use that to help explain the dream. As Levenson (1983) writes: "Unless one examines the method by which one arrives at the truth and treats that as having an independent validity, separate from the truth arrived at, then one simply is indoctrinating the patient" (p. 92).

What does this imply about dream interpretation? That whatever vector of interpretation you choose, you also ought to examine why you chose that vector.

There are other vectors of dream interpretation, and no one person can identify all of them. Each person who works with dreams can identify additional ones. You also may learn something about yourself if you notice which vectors you are most likely to use and which you avoid.

CHAPTER 10

HOW TO ANALYZE DREAMS

FUNDAMENTAL PRINCIPLES

Yea, and not only have we not explor'd
That wide and various world, the heart of others,
But even our own heart, that narrow world
Bounded in our own breast, we hardly know,
Of our own actions dimly trace the causes,
Whether a natural obscureness, hiding
That region in perpetual cloud,
Or our own want of effort, be the bar.

Matthew Arnold, *Merope*

THE ANALYSIS OF dreams remains one of the most vital aspects of psychotherapeutic work, yet some psychotherapists seem to have lost their enthusiasm for dreams and some hardly pay any attention to dreams at all. I hope in this section to revive interest in the dream and to familiarize the reader with the many possible approaches to understanding dreams.

All people dream at night. Some people rarely remember their dreams. Yet most people who claim not to remember their dreams find that this changes if they find someone to whom they like to tell their dreams and if they have good experiences exploring their dreams. We find over and over again that in psychotherapy, the analyst's degree of comfort and interest in dreams directly affects how much his patients remember and report their dreams. Some clinicians tell their patients at the start of therapy that dreams will assist their work. While such statements are helpful explanations, it is the experience of working with dreams that will convince the patient that dreams can be a fascinating source of self-knowledge.

When I teach courses on dream analysis to psychoanalytic students who already have substantial clinical experience, there are usually a few students who say that their patients never or hardly ever report dreams. I tell them that by the end of the course, when they will know more about dream analysis and feel more comfortable with it, their patients will report more dreams. It always turns out to be so.

What is essential to all work with dreams is the collaboration of the dreamer and the dream interpreter. In this chapter, I would like to describe a process of dream analysis that is collaborative in every sense of the word. It fosters the cooperation of the dreamer and the analyst; it recognizes that the dreamer has barriers to understanding his own dream, but that the analyst may have different barriers. It conceives of dream interpretation and dream clarification as a process between two people (or more—excellent dream analysis can also be done in a group [Ullman, 1996]) that will clarify many things about the dreamer. It may also clarify things about the dream interpreter and the relationship between the dreamer and dream interpreter.

OVERCOMING ONEIROPHOBIA

The first task of the dream interpreter is to develop an interest in dreams and a relative lack of fear of what dreams may tell. This is an achievement that may seem easier than it actually is. We all have areas of our personality that we would rather not know about, and we also know on some level that those dissociated areas of our personality are quite visible in our dreams. So some discomfort with dreams or fear of them, which I call *oneirophobia*, is normal.

The best way to become comfortable with dreams is to analyze your own. If you are in psychoanalysis, that is a good place to start (provided that your analyst is comfortable with dreams).

You can also work on dreams independently. Keep a log of all of your dreams. No matter how unforgettable a dream seems in the moment, the forces against remembering it may be high. If you do not remember your dreams, keep a pad of paper and a pen next to your bed. If you awaken from a dream, write it down immediately. Or find an alternative way of recording your dreams. Some people keep a small tape recorder or digital recording device near their bed. Some people, who have an answering machine at a different location, "call in" the dream and transcribe it later.

Keeping all your dreams in a computer file is a big help. It allows you to retrieve them easily, and if you ever have the feeling that something in one of your current dreams seems familiar but you cannot remember when you last dreamt it, you can use the "Find" function of your word processor to help you locate all previous occurrences of key words.

When you have recorded your dream, try analyzing it by yourself. One method, which was Freud's, is to write down every thought you have about your dream. This method of free association, which Freud himself used during his self-analysis, can be extremely productive—but you must write down everything that occurs to you, no matter how trivial or seemingly irrelevant.

When all of your associations are exhausted, start again at the beginning. Think about how you feel at each point in the dream, and jot it down. Give yourself time here to really think it through. If there are other people in the dream, imagine how they feel at each point in the dream. Finally, when that is all done, try imagining being every nonhuman or inanimate object in the dream. If you are taking a bath in the dream, imagine being the bathtub. What are you like? What do you feel? Are you new, shiny, clean, white, and hard? Or are you old, dull, grimy, and gray? Is the water cold, lukewarm, or hot?

Next, think about which aspects of your dream relate in any way to actual events in your life. Do this with all of your own actions in the dream, but do not stop there. Consider everything that everyone else does in the dream. If something strange or objectionable is done by anyone else in the dream, think about how you might have done something similar in your life. Or how you might have wanted to. Or you can consider, if you were going to do something like that, under what circumstances would you do it, and with whom?

Next, look through your dream for any resemblance to stories and myths. If you know classical mythology, think in those terms; but if you do not know much mythology, think in terms of stories you know from movies, fairy tales, novels, television shows, or from the news stories of the day. The most popular entertainers of the day usually capture some essential aspect of civilization that resonates with individual psychology. At the end of the twentieth century in the United States, a surprising number of my patients connected their dreams to the popular television show *Seinfeld*. They identified with the selfishness, alienation, sexual freedom, or meanness of the characters. In the idealistic 1960s, the Beatles provided dream models of gentle revolution and idealistic love. In the spirit of post-war capitalist expansion of the 1950s, there was Jack Benny, who mined the paradox between great wealth and cheapness. All of these are as valid when thinking about dreams as Zeus and Aphrodite.[1]

When you have done all this and taken your thinking about the dream as far as you think you can, it is time to tell the dream to someone else. It does not have to be a professional—it can be a friend or relative. The most important thing is that it be someone you are comfortable with. First tell that person your dreamtext only. Then let him tell you everything he can think of about the dream. Listen carefully and write notes about what he says. The parts that seem at first to have nothing to do with your dream may prove later on to be important things about which you have resistance, that is, things of which you would rather not be aware.

When your partner in dream analysis has said all he can, then ask him the same questions you have asked yourself concerning feelings, mythological references, and so on.

You will note that some of the things your dream-analysis partner says may strike you as off base. You may feel, "That is more true of him than of me." You may be right. The interpreter cannot help injecting some of his own psychology into the situation. There is no way around this, but try to withhold judgment for a while. Remember that almost everything he says, no matter how much it applies to him, may in part be insightful about you, too. And it may take some time for you to realize how.

This experience will make you appreciate the value of group interpretation of a dream. If you listen to the thoughts of several people about your dream, you will notice that each person brings something of his own psychology to his comments. But when you have, say, six people doing this, there emerges something common to everyone's reaction to the dream. That, which we might call the "dream precipitate," may be closer to the essence of your dream. And hearing so many different reactions allows you to pick and choose from them to find what seems most applicable to you.

When you have gotten relatively comfortable working with your own dreams, you can proceed to exploring the dreams of other people. You must never forget the anxiety that exploring your own dreams brings up, so that you can respect the same anxiety that others will experience in exploring their dreams.

---

1. Each has advantages. The advantage of older myths is that, having been in use for a longer period of time, they presumably have had a longer time to be stripped of their local detail and made more universally applicable. The advantage of the newer myths is that they are more resonant with the ongoing culture.

MUTUALITY AND COLLABORATION

It is worth learning several techniques of analyzing dreams, as long as you don't think about them too much in the clinical situation. They provide a framework for thinking about dreams, and they may give the dream interpreter a number of choices, especially when the dream analysis is bogged down. But the fundamental principle of dream analysis is that one must do what is necessary to get the dreamer engaged in the process. The more spontaneous this engagement is the better.

Jung emphasized the importance of mutuality in dream interpretation early in psychoanalytic history. He recognized that even if a psychoanalyst understands a patient's dream, it will not help the patient unless he, too, understands. He notes that the patient will probably fight him and not really hear him, if the analyst interprets the dream unilaterally. The best way to insure that both patient and analyst understand is for both to be actively involved in exploring the dream. In 1934, Jung wrote:

> When the understanding is all on my side, I say quite calmly that I do not understand, for in the end it makes very little difference whether the doctor understands or not, but it makes all the difference whether the patient understands. Understanding should therefore be understanding in the sense of an agreement which is the fruit of joint reflection [p. 94].

REIMAGINING THE DREAM

One of the primary necessities in working with another person's dream is to find out, as closely as possible, what the dream was really like. This is much more difficult than it sounds. We are all used to casual listening. But with dream analysis, you must listen to the dreamer's description of the dream in words and try to recreate the experience of the dream in your own mind.

You must ask yourself, "How did that actually happen in the dream, appear in the dream, feel in the dream?" The answer is not so obvious in many instances, and it may lead you to ask the dreamer some pointed questions that may help clarify what you do not understand. Thus, the first stage of dream analysis is careful listening. The analyst should *reimagine* the dream, inquiring about anything that is vague or unclear. You must try to get as close as possible to the dreamer's experience of the dream.

Sometimes patients cannot or will not associate to objects that seem central to the dream. Jung devised a very clever way to get associations. When his patient dreams of a "deal table" and then cannot come up with any associations to it, Jung says, "Suppose I had no idea what the words 'deal table' mean. Describe this object and give me its history in such a way that I cannot fail to understand what sort of a thing it is."[2]

When asked for clarification, the patient may provide much new material that was not included in the original dream report. There is an excellent example of this in Freud (1900): A patient told him:

> I dreamt that I arrived too late at the market and could get nothing either from the butcher or from the woman who sells vegetables.

Freud asks her to tell him the dream again, and he describes her second telling of the dream:

> She dreamt she was going to the market with her cook, who was carrying the basket. After she had asked for something, the butcher said to her: "That's not obtainable any longer," and offered her something else, adding "This is good, too." She rejected it and went on to the woman who sells vegetables, who tried to get her to buy a peculiar vegetable that was tied up in bundles but was of a black color. She said: "I don't recognize that; I won't take it" [p. 183].

This is quite a dramatic change from the first telling of the dream. In the first telling she seems to be alone; now she is accompanied by her cook. In the first telling she simply cannot get anything from the butcher or the woman who sells vegetables; now they each offer her something, try to convince her to buy it, but she rejects what they have to offer.

The first telling of the dream is a dramatic example of secondary revision, which we might in this case call "secondary pruning." As much as patients may add things to dreams to make them more sensible, they may also take things away to make the dream more acceptable.

If one interprets the dream within the transference, there is a great difference between the two versions of the dream. The first says, I cannot get anything from you. The second says, I don't like what you are offering to me, and I won't take it. The first sounds like privation; the

---

2. This technique of Jung's has since been popularized by Delaney (1991).

second, like disgust and rejection. A good psychoanalytic interpretation would recognize the validity of both tellings of the dream. Characterologically, they imply that she hides her active choices with the appearance of being a passively deprived person. Since Freud tells us that the woman was sexually abused as a child, the dreams revealed that she anticipated similar sexual advances from Freud, which she would have rejected. In the context of this sexual fantasy, the two versions of the dream, taken together, might imply: I don't want to have to undergo the trauma of unwelcome offers. I would rather that I just cannot have anything.

Some analysts make a principle of asking the patient to tell the dream twice. This, like almost any rote technique, may get you into trouble. Suspicious patients may think you were not listening carefully the first time around or may suspect you of some other motive. I think it is best to ask for the dream to be repeated only when it flows naturally from the dream interpretation process. For example, a patient brought in a dream that he had written down and asked whether I would like to hear the dream from memory or from the written text. In that case, I suggested that he first tell it from memory, and then consult his written text to see if there are any elements that he left out. This was proposed as a kind of collaborative experiment, and it proved important when every element in the dream having to do with money was omitted from the account of the dream told from memory.

In another instance, a gay man reported that he had a very erotic dream. He dreamt that he went to a sex club. At first he saw only heterosexual couples there. But then he saw four men together who he assumed were gay. One of them was very muscular, and he thought he wouldn't be interested. Then, one of the other men approached the dreamer. The dreamer thought he was okay and proceeded to perform fellatio on the man. He awoke from the dream extremely sexually excited.

The dreamer claimed that he had never been to a sex club. This interested me, for then I wondered, How did the sex club look in the dream? I asked for a detailed description. He told me he went in through a front door. Right in the entryway were two completely naked men who were entering in front of him. He found them extremely attractive, and it was actually to follow them that he entered the club.

I asked him why he had not mentioned this part of the dream in the first telling. It emerged that he felt genuine desire for the two men. He pursued them, unlike in the rest of the dream, in which other people pursued him. We had been discussing in analysis his lack of desire for his partner. Now, he was leaving out the objects of his desire from the telling of the dream, much as he avoided them in his life. He then recalled other incidents of feeling compelling desire in his life, and we analyzed further his fear and shame about his own desire.

This is also an example of the process of dream interpretation reenacting the content of the dream. One of the themes of the dream was his attempt to hide his real experience of desire, which is just what he tried to do in telling me the dream with parts of it omitted.

DO ASSOCIATIONS TO THE DREAM CLARIFY OR OBSCURE MEANING?

After you feel you have gotten as good an idea as possible of the patient's experience of the dream, you can move on to the heart of dream analysis.

What happens next?

Freud (1900) argued that the correct way to interpret dreams was to analyze each segment of the dream via the dreamer's associations to uncover the latent dream thoughts.

> The resolution of what are ostensibly acts of judgment in dreams may serve to remind us of the rules laid down at the beginning of this book for carrying out the work of interpretation: namely, that we should disregard the apparent coherence between a dream's constituents as an unessential illusion, and that we should trace back the origin of each of its elements on its own account. A dream is a conglomerate which, for purposes of investigation, must be broken up once more into fragments [p. 449].

We might call this approach piecemeal analysis of dreams or the "rebus technique"; in a rebus, visual images may represent each syllable or word in a phrase.[3]

Jung and Maeder were among the earliest and most vociferous critics of Freud's piecemeal analysis of dreams and his reliance on associations. Most psychoanalysts today, in their practice of dream interpretation, do not follow the rebus technique. They are not so

---

3. One of my favorite examples of a rebus shows pictures of (1) a tree branch; (2) a tiny lamb; (3) a bumblebee; (4) a railroad car filled with coal at the entrance to a tunnel; and (5) a heart. The solution to the rebus is: wood ewe bee mine valentine, that is, Would you be my valentine?

cavalier in dismissing the overall narrative structure of the dream as an "unessential illusion."

Freud's process of dream interpretation tends to ameliorate the "foreignness" of dreams. By studying our associations using Freud's technique, we anchor the dream products in our own conscious and waking thoughts, and thereby feel like the dream becomes more ours. Whether this brings us closer to the meaning of the dream per se, or to a simulacrum of the dream's meaning, is open to question. I would never abandon the use of associations totally. They are important in clarifying certain personal meanings and referents of the elements of a dream. But they should be used with caution. It is important to recognize that the dreamer's associations can take us closer to the meaning of the dream, but they can also divert us from the meaning of the dream. The longer I study my dreams and those of my patients, the more I am drawn away from Freud's procedure, toward an immersion in the dream itself.[4]

The analyst's associations are important, too, although here one must tread even more carefully than when considering the patient's associations. Every thought that the analyst has during the recounting of the dream may be important. Do not discard anything! It may prove spurious, but it may be essential to the understanding of the dream. You cannot know in advance.

I have had many such experiences. Interestingly, the value of my own associations stands out especially when I do supervisory consultations, that is, when other psychoanalysts come to me for help with their clinical work. In such cases, I am less concerned about contaminating the field of inquiry with my own associations than I would be when working with a patient directly. In one case of supervision, the patient dreamt that she was ascending a staircase in a strange manner, taking huge steps that were almost leaps. I had an image of a kangaroo, and it turned out that the dreamer had grown up in Australia and that the dream referred to an important event there. In another supervisory situation, the patient, a single woman, dreamt of a woman in a perfect white wedding dress. I no longer remember all the details, but I had a vivid image, not of a real woman, but of a Barbie doll. I mentioned it, and the supervisee, astonished, said that the patient had a lifelong obsession with Barbie.

---

4. There are interesting empirical data on the value of free associations to dreams. A dissertation done under Calvin Hall (Reis, 1951) showed that "free associations to dreams did not add to the understanding of a person's personality if the psychologist had access to a series of dreams from the individual" (Domhoff, 1991, p. 96).

Any experienced psychoanalyst could recount many such examples. It is not, in my view, a question of telepathy. We merely recognize many more things unconsciously than consciously, and sometimes our awareness appears to us in the form of a visual image whose source is unknown to us, at least at first. But a fundamental principle of work with dreams is to trust that most of those images are potential sources of valuable information about the dreamer. At the same time, one must guard against giving so much importance to the analyst's associations that the patient's dream is hijacked. The dividing line is delicate between using one's associations in a productive way and overwhelming the patient's dream with your own projections.[5]

FREUD'S FOUR APPROACHES TO DREAM INTERPRETATION

Freud (1923a) outlined four techniques of approaching the dream:

> (1) The Chronological Approach: Have the dreamer bring up associations to the elements of the dream in the order in which those elements occurred in his account of the dream. This is the original method of Freud's analysis of his own dreams. It allows for the most thoroughness. One is less likely to suppress any one element. On the other hand, it restricts the natural flow of associations, which often in itself sheds light on the dream. Another risk of this procedure, if followed slavishly, is that some patients may use it in the service of resistance, exhaustively spelling out associations and leaving no time for integration.
>
> (2) Start with the Most Salient Element of the Dream: The analyst can pick one element from the dream to work on, such as the most striking part, or the part with the most clarity or sensory intensity, or a spoken word. This method has the advantage of getting to the parts that empirically would seem to be related most to the latent dream thoughts. It relies the most on the analyst's expertise. It is also most subject to the analyst's countertransference and counterresistance. How does he choose what it most salient?

---

5. See my discussion of the "Lovely Dream" analyzed by Freud (chapter 16); see also Meltzer (1978).

(3) Start with the Day Residue: Disregard the manifest content and ask for the day residue. In other words, ask the dreamer what events of the previous day are associated in his mind with the dream he has just described. If this is done before procedure 2 (picking out one element of the dream that is most salient), establishing the day residue may give you more security in deciding which elements of the dream are most cogent. Also, for patients who are afraid of their dreams or of dream analysis, inquiry into day residue may lower anxiety by focusing away from the dream per se, although it may also foster resistance.

(4) The Free Approach: Give no instructions, and let the dreamer himself decide which associations he will start with. This method is the most "analytic" in that it allows the choice of associations to speak out freely. With new analysands, however, it runs the risk of their not knowing what to tell you, even if you think they should know from the basic rule that they should say everything that comes to mind. It also puts a larger burden on the analyst to hear with what Reik (1948) called the "third ear."

Each analyst should try all four of these procedures (as well as the other procedures outlined below) and accumulate experience as to which approaches suit him or her best. Also, different procedures may work better with different analysands. For example, asking for specific associations to each element of the dream may be thrilling to an exhibitionist, and he may yield much information. Some patients, on the other hand, who have been humiliated as youngsters and who have performance anxiety, may freeze with such a procedure, feeling it to be a test. The free approach may work better with them. Also, of course, the patient's experience of the approach to dream analysis can itself become material for analysis.

Another important factor in choosing the technique of analysis may be the level of resistance. Freud believes that a good sign is whether the associations converge onto a point (low resistance) or continually diverge (high resistance) which leaves the analyst at loose ends and unable to collaborate. At the highest level of resistance there may be no associations at all.[6]

---

6. Freud (1900) suggested that when there are no associations, the analyst consider translating the dream symbols directly: "The failure of the dreamer's associations gave us a right to attempt an interpretation by symbolic substitution" (p. 372).

But contemporary analysts view resistance as more complex and often interactional (e.g., Schafer, 1983). "Resistance to what?" we might ask. The analyst must consider whether the patient is resistant to exploring difficult material, or whether he is experiencing difficulty with the analyst's approach. This question ultimately takes us back to our guiding principle, that the best approach to dream analysis with any patient is one that engages him most spontaneously in the process.

HOW FREUD WORKED WITH DREAMS

It is worth examining in detail how Freud worked with dreams in the case studies he published. When I teach the case of Dora to my psychoanalytic students, they, especially the women students, are horrified by Freud's directive dream interpretation and what they see as his being coercive with her. Nevertheless, in my view, the case of Dora was not totally unsuccessful, despite the fact that Freud thought it was a failure.

When Dora came to Freud for treatment, she suffered from headaches, depression, suicidal ideation, *tussis nervosa*, leucorrhea, and occasional loss of voice. Dora's father was having an affair with a Frau K. On a vacation, Herr K, the husband of Dora's father's mistress, made a pass at Dora. Freud argued that Dora was sexually excited by the kiss, and her conflict centered around this, which was related to displaced oedipal feelings toward her father. Freud (1905) says to her: "The dream confirms once more what I had already told you before you dreamt it—that you are summoning up your old love of your father in order to protect yourself against your love for Herr K. But what do all these efforts show? Not only that you are afraid of yourself, and of the temptation you feel to yield to him. In short, these efforts prove once more how deeply you loved him" (p. 70).

Many modern readers are shocked and offended by Freud's interpretations. He ignores the fact that Dora's father has syphilis, which he contracted before his marriage and which he probably transmitted to his wife (and perhaps to Dora and Frau K). The agony and duplicity of the family complications seem, more than 100 years later, to be much more at the root of Dora's problems than conflict over sexual excitement. In our time, having your father's mistress' husband make a pass at you does not seem such a delicious invitation to an adolescent girl.

Dora's so-called first dream[7] starts: "A house was on fire." If we

---

7. I say "so-called" for the following reason: In his description of the case, Freud mentions that before the so-called First Dream, he and Dora had "previ-

see a house as symbolic of the family, Dora's house was indeed on fire, both with the father's affair and his syphilis. Later in the dream, as the family members are trying to save themselves, Dora's mother wants to stop and save her jewel-case. If one accepts Freud's translation of jewel-case for genitals, Dora's mother might indeed want to save her genitals (jewel-case) from the destructiveness of syphilitic infection (the fire). The behavior of Dora's father, both with respect to his syphilis and his infidelity, indicates that for him his wife's well being comes last; recognizing that, it does not require much interpretation, when in the dream he says, "I refuse to let myself and my two children be burnt for the sake of your jewel-case."

In her second dream, Dora's father has died. Dora goes into a thick wood, where a man she meets says to her: "Two and a half hours more." He offers to accompany her, but she refuses and goes alone. Freud did not realize that this dream was a warning that Dora would terminate the analysis in a couple of sessions, although he realized it after the fact, in his famous postscript to the case (where he develops the idea of transference).

Freud thought that Dora terminated the analysis prematurely and that the case was a failure. Yet when one examines the aftermath of the treatment, Dora seems to have made good use of the treatment, despite Freud, or, one might say, to spite Freud. Having been able to tell Freud off and assert herself against him, she then goes on to confront her father and Frau K about their affair. She is able to clear the air with them and to disengage herself from the fire (first dream) and deadliness (second dream) of her family. Her attacks diminish, and her depression lifts (p. 121). Freud notes that Dora acted out her feelings in the transference, rather than analyzing them, by leaving the treatment. She did, but sometimes acting out the transference can prepare a patient for resolving the problems in her life outside analysis. Freud, too, may have acted out the transference by trying to tell Dora that the main problem was her own conflict, not the internecine family situation. The Dora case offers a great lesson for psychotherapists: you may misunderstand the patient and give wrong interpretations, but if you act with genuine concern in trying to understand the situation, the patient may make good use of the therapeutic exploration anyway and get better.

---

ously analysed a few minor specimens." In my view, this is an example of tertiary revision. No dream is a minor specimen. The dismissal by the psychoanalyst of a dream's value, which Freud also did in the case of the "Lovely Dream" (see chapter 16), probably is a reflection of a countertransference reaction.

Foucault (1986) expressed a similar view:

> One could say that Dora got better, not despite the interruption of the psychoanalysis, but because, by deciding to break it off, she went the whole distance to that solitude toward which until then her existence had been only an indecisive moment. All the elements of the dream point to this resolution of hers as an active break no less than as an acceptance of solitude. Indeed, she saw herself in her dream as "going out without her parents' knowledge"; she learns of the death of her father; then she is in a forest where she meets a man but refuses to go with him; back home she learns from the chambermaid that her mother and the others are already at the cemetery; she does not feel sad at all, goes up to her bedroom, and proceeds to read a big book. Freud glimpsed this choice of solitude: beneath the explicit discourse and the dream did not Freud note the formula: "I am abandoning you and continuing my journey alone?" [pp. 56–57].

THE TECHNIQUE OF DREAM DISTILLATION

Another approach to working with dreams is to paraphrase the gist of the dream, stripping it of most detail, and then ask the dreamer for reactions. This is especially helpful in very long dreams. It helps both patient and analyst focus their attention on the basic structure and feeling of the dream. It is also helpful with patients who tend to get bogged down in detail and "miss the forest for the trees."

Jung (1948) was one of the first analysts to recommend this kind of *dream reduction* or *dream distillation*. He wrote: "Applying the causal point of view to the material associated with the dream, we reduce the manifest dream-content to certain fundamental tendencies or ideas exhibited by the material" (p. 27). Jung provides an excellent example of this procedure of dream distillation (1909): He tells of a patient who dreamt that "he was in a wild and desert place, and he saw, on a rock, a man dressed in black covering his face with both hands. Suddenly the man in the dream set out towards a precipice, when a woman, likewise clothed in black, appeared and tried to restrain him. He flung himself into the abyss, dragging her with him." The dreamer awoke with a cry of anguish (p. 8).

With this dream, Jung did not first ask for associations. He distilled from the dream a fundamental question: "Who was that man who put himself in a dangerous situation and dragged a woman to her doom?" The question moved the dreamer deeply, for that man was the dreamer himself. He related the dream situation to his prior suicidality and his former engagement to a woman. He lived in the tropics where conditions were harsh and felt that to marry her would have condemned her to almost certain death.[8]

The technique of dream distillation has been described by other psychoanalysts without attribution to Jung. Harry Stack Sullivan was scornful of Freud's theory of latent content, yet he was a master at unfolding it, even though he did not seem to think he was doing so, by means of the technique of dream distillation. The procedure matched Sullivan's general clinical approach, which was to strip away all detail and verbiage that was superfluous and get to the point (Sullivan, 1973). In his view, neurotics, especially obsessional neurotics, were expert at linguistic obfuscation, and the psychoanalyst needed to be equally expert at bypassing it.

Sullivan (1953) spelled out his technique of dream distillation, which is merely a special case of his general clinical approach:

> Thus the psychiatrist should treat reported dreams, I believe, in the same way that he treats everything else that seems to be extremely significant: the psychiatrist reflects back to the person what has seemed to him to be the significant statement, stripped of all the little personal details, confusions, and obscurities which often protect significant statements, and then sees if it provokes any thought in the mind of the patient.
>
> To give an example: An obsessional neurotic, who is reporting on a highly significant difficulty he is having in living, will usually tell the psychiatrist different instances of much the same thing for perhaps six weeks. The instances gradually become somewhat clearer to the psychiatrist—that is, he can finally guess what the devil's really being reported. He can't possibly do it the first time because the patient deletes, through security operations, everything that would improve the psychiatrist's grasping what's being reported. After the psychiatrist has delimited the area of the patient's careful deletions so that he can finally catch on to what's probably being reported, he can then say, 'Well, is it that you are telling me that you did so-and-so?' Whereupon, with considerable anxiety the patient says, "Yes,"

8. Stekel (1943) describes a similar technique as "simplification." Stekel advised his patients to "think in headlines like a journalist" (p. 387).

> and the psychiatrist has something to work on. I believe that it's the same with the dream, except that is doesn't take so long.[9] The psychiatrist clears up as much as he can of what is irrelevant and obscuring in the reported dream, presents what he seems to hear in terms of a dramatic picture of some important problem of the patient's, and then propounds the riddle: "What does that bring to mind?" And if the psychiatrist has been good at it, it often brings something very significant from the patient [p. 337].

In other words, the patient associates to the analyst's distillation of the dream. Sullivan (1953) provides a superb example of dream distillation:

> For example, for many, many months in working with a schizoid obsessional patient, I heard data of how vaguely annoying and depressing his mother had been for several years past. His father was a hellion, to put it mildly, and we didn't have so much difficulty understanding what father did. But about all mother did was somehow to depress and annoy him, discourage him vaguely. Now this patient dreamed of a Dutch windmill. It was a very beautiful scene, with a carefully cared-for lawn leading up to the horizon on which this beautiful Dutch windmill revolved in the breeze. Suddenly he was within the windmill. And there everything was wrack and ruin, with rust inches deep; it was perfectly obvious that the windmill hadn't moved in years. And when the patient had finished reporting his dream, I was able to pick out the significant details successfully—one of those occasional fortunate instances. I said, 'That is, beautiful, active on the outside—utterly dead and decayed within. Does it provoke anything?' He said, "My God, my mother." That was his trouble, you see. The mother had become a sort of zombi—unutterably crushed by the burdens that had been imposed on her. She was simply a sort of weary phonograph offering cultural platitudes, without any thought of what they did to anybody or what they meant. Though she was still showing signs

9. This is an instance in which Sullivan values highly the role of dreams in psychotherapy. Because of examples like this, I do not agree with Levenson (1983) when he writes: "Indeed, Sullivan had no use for the analysis of dreams as such, using them only to lead him back to the daytime residues, which could then be directly dealt with" (p. 133).

> of life, everything had died within. We made fairly rapid progress in getting some lucidity about the mother. You will note that I have not discussed the latent content of the dream; but in psychotherapy, as I've come to consider it, one is occupied chiefly in benefiting the patient [p. 338].

Actually, the mother's zombi-ness was precisely the latent content of the dream. But since, as Sullivan might say, in psychotherapy one is occupied chiefly in benefiting the patient, it matters little whether the truth that is uncovered is called latent content or something else.

THE TECHNIQUE OF GUIDED ASSOCIATION

An approach to dreams that combines Freud's method of free association and the detailed inquiry espoused by interpersonalists (Bonime, 1962; Levenson, 1983) might be called "guided association." This approach was often used by Jung, although he did not call it guided association. A good example appears in Jung's discussion of resistance in dream interpretation. He describes a man who dreamt (Jung, 1909):

> I found myself in a little room, seated at a table beside Pope Pius X, whose features were far more handsome than they are in reality, which surprised me. I saw on one side of our room a great apartment with a table sumptuously laid, and a crowd of ladies in evening-dress. Suddenly I felt a need to urinate, and I went out. On my return the need was repeated; I went out again, and this happened several times. Finally I woke up, wanting to urinate [p. 9].

The dreamer tells Jung that the dream was due to a bladder irritation and denies any psychological significance. Jung tells us:

> My first deduction was that the dreamer had a strong resistance because he put so much energy into protesting that the dream was meaningless. In consequence, I did not venture to put the indiscreet question: "Why did you compare yourself to the Pope?"[10] I only asked him what ideas he associated with "Pope" [p. 9].

10. Had he done so, it would have been a dream distillation.

The patient associates to the Pope and, gradually, ideas about celibacy and polygamy emerge which, for this man, are connected to urination, since when he was a child he was at a wedding ceremony that went on so long he wet his pants.

We can see Jung's tact in action. He identifies a point of resistance, and then pursues that point further by asking a somewhat general question. He either asks for associations about a detail that he suspects is important or poses an open-ended question like: "What happened then?" He pursues the inquiry but also respects the resistance.

We might call what Jung does the technique of "guided association." He does not leave association totally free, but, hearing signs of resistance, he guides the dreamer deeper into those spots. This approach is akin to what Sullivan and interpersonalists later call "detailed inquiry." Jung guides his inquiry closely by noting small signs of resistance, for example, a comment such as "Oh, nothing" or a pause in the associations.

The technique of guided association has been adapted by any number of psychoanalysts and other schools of psychotherapy. The analyst picks an area that seems particularly obscure and important, and asks the patient to fill in the detail. The idea is to clarify the dream, although it may also lead to secondary revision by the dreamer. It is truly a path to collaboration in creating dream meaning.

For example, a woman dreamt about a man who "cut off his penis and a nipple from my breast and we exchanged them. This was supposed to be temporary. And they were supposed to reattach themselves" (Fosshage and Loew, 1987, p. 12). Walter Bonime was asked to interpret the dream, or to describe how he would go about exploring the dream's meaning with the patient, and he wrote the following:

> "I'm confused about the cutting off of the penis and the nipple," I would say. "Did you watch him do it himself? And what were your sensations during the experience? You said it was not painful but you may have had some thoughts or emotions about his action. Say anything that flits through your mind as you recapture and describe how he cut off your nipple. Was it very bloody? Frightening? Casual? Perhaps there was no blood and it seemed weird, or even perfectly natural. What was your idea of how the nipple and penis would reattach? What do you think when you say they were 'supposed to'?" [p. 117].

The patient might answer all these questions, reconsidering her dream while awake. It is presumed that her thoughts will clarify the dream. But this may also be an example of the analyst and patient *creating* dream meaning. The dreamer may come up with details, but neither she nor the analyst can presume that those details were actually part of the dreaming experience. They may be akin to confabulation, in which people with memory loss fill in details by making them up. This does not mean that those details are irrelevant to the meaning of the dream—only that they are not of the dream. The psychoanalyst encourages secondary revision, and the dreamer cooperates.

A similar procedure is recommended by Rainette Fantz, a Gestalt therapist who was also asked to describe how she would go about interpreting the same dream. As I mentioned before, the Gestalt school has expanded Jung's subjective approach to dream interpretation, in which every character in the dream is an aspect of the dreamer. Gestalt therapists assume that *inanimate* objects in a dream are also aspects of the dreamer. They ask the dreamer to imagine being those inanimate objects. Fantz writes that she would ask the dreamer to imagine being the razor blade. The dreamer might then say: "I am sharp-edged, dangerous, cutting, steely—*I am not!* Well—I am slim, finely honed. Wait a minute—if I were thin and sharp, I would be dangerous! [The dreamer is overweight.] I could both elicit and cut off the responsiveness in others. That sounds pretty powerful. It might not be such a bad thing to be" (Fosshage and Loew, 1987, p. 235).

We have explored some basic procedures for engaging patients in the exploration of their dreams. In the next chapter, we will look more closely at special problems of work with dreams and different ways to approach them.

CHAPTER 11

HOW TO ANALYZE DREAMS

SPECIAL TOPICS

HOW MUCH DOES THE DREAM ANALYST'S THEORY SHAPE THE DREAM ANALYSIS?

Fosshage and Loew (1987) performed a clinical dream experiment. They took six dreams from different points in one person's analysis and showed them to six psychoanalysts from different schools of thought: Freudian, Jungian, Culturalist (Interpersonal), Object Relational, Phenomenological (Daseinsanalytic), and Gestalt. The analysts were asked to give their views of the meaning of the dreams and of how they would work with them. The book is compelling reading for anyone interested in dream analysis. I recommend not reading the book cover to cover; instead, read all six analyses of each dream together.

The study showed some tendencies that differentiate the analysts. The Freudian, Angel Garma, and the Object Relationist, John Padel, tended to see most images and symbols in sexual and bodily terms. "Down below" indicated the genitals; smoke and explosions indicated anal concerns. They illustrate Freud's belief (1900) that "a dream might be described as *a substitute for an infantile scene modified by being transferred on to a recent experience*. The infantile scene is unable to bring about its own revival and has to be content with returning as a dream" (p. 546). Some of their deductions seem inspired while others seem forced, what French and Fromm (1964) call the "Procrustean bed" approach to dream interpretation.

The Jungian, Edward Whitmont, brought in certain specialized concepts, like the animus. He also tended to refer to mythology more than the other analysts. When the dreamer feels she is outside of life for 20 years, he cites the story of the Lorelei (but other analysts bring up Rip van Winkle).

Despite such expectable differences, the conclusions drawn by these six different clinicians were remarkably similar. Not only did they all see the clinical issues of the patient relatively consistently, they even agreed about the significance of certain images. All the clinicians had a good basic sense of certain metaphors that guided their interpretation. The patient's first dream started on a rickety balcony, which all of the clinicians saw as indicating the dreamer's shaky sense of herself and her life situation. In my view, the best dream interpreters will learn all the prominent metapsychologies and use any or all of them when they seem applicable to a dream.

FINDING ALL THE THEMES

French and Fromm (1964) have outlined an approach to dreams in which intuitive guesses by the analyst are constantly tested and retested against other material produced by the patient, including the immediate associations, material from previous sessions, and the problems facing the dreamer in his life. Their work is an excellent example of painstaking examination of the different realms of the patient's material that Levenson outlines: the situation in the dream, the transference relationship with the analyst, the patient's historical past, and the situations in the life of the patient outside the analysis. They do an exhaustive examination of the patient's material, and their analysis is quite convincing. But there is probably no method of dream interpretation that does not risk missing important themes in the dream, and French and Fromm are no exception.

For instance, the first dream of the patient that they consider comes from the one-hundredth hour of analysis:

> In the dream, I was in the Army again. Went into the mess-hall with another guy. Had a little trouble getting food [vague]. Then I saw a couple of guys I recognized. A southerner called "the Colonel," actually a private, said: "Sit down, I'll take care of you. Will serve you like a king, on gold plates." I said: "Never mind the plates; just get good food."
>
> Then this guy's appearance changed—he now looked like Jack Benny. He said he was Jack Benny's brother. I said, "Are you related?" Everybody laughed.

> Then the scene changed. We were both being chased, going through a tunnel. I said, "This is ridiculous; if you are the brother of Jack Benny, who has millions, why doesn't he help you out?" [p. 10].

French and Fromm analyze the dream within the transference—in terms of the patient's conflict about idealizing the analyst while also feeling that a recent supportive comment of the analyst was "bullshit."

Nevertheless, their analysis of the dream ignores the theme of cheapness in the dream, even though it is in the manifest content, with the reference to Jack Benny's great wealth and the question of why he doesn't help his brother. Everybody who has seen Jack Benny perform knows that a constant theme of his humor is his incredible miserliness. The theme appears earlier in the dream, with the reference to gold plates. The dreamer both wants them (thus he puts them in the dream) but then disavows his wish for them. His associations also include concern about a lieutenant in the army who accused him of "goldbricking." (He accuses the analyst of bullshitting, but he worries that others think he is bullshitting.)

In another session, he talks of his wife's shame about his paltry contribution to the church (p. 56). In yet another session, he tells of his parents, on Christmas, giving him oranges, money, and coal "as reminder of a bad year" (p. 30). And a different dream describes a neighbor's house that is unkempt; when he looks at it, it becomes a beautiful mansion (p. 33). Yet with all this evidence, they do not identify the theme of money, generosity, and conflicts over wealth.

Later (p. 138) they graze along the edge of this theme when they report the dialogues that they originally had about the dreams. Erika Fromm noted the patient's aspiration for social status implied by the "beautiful mansion," which she felt was out of the patient's reach. But then she and Thomas French decided that that symbol indicated something more general—that the unreality of the patient's wish for the mansion symbolized the patient's wish for being cured without the analyst's help.

Of course, it is always easier for us to see the themes that another psychoanalyst misses, even while you or I miss themes in our own clinical work. In any dream analysis, you cannot help missing some of the themes because of your own counterresistance, which may be obvious to another person. But you can at least be warned that if you do not attend to the details of the symbol, you will likely miss something important about the dreamer.

There are also many possible pathways through different metapsychologies to a dream's meaning. For example, a more strictly Freudian analyst might have taken a different tack. He might have focused on the multiple "anal" images in this and in other dreams: for example, the *mess*-hall, bull-shit. These would be connected in traditional Freudian metapsychology with money, stinginess, and retention. When the same patient dreamt of "mixing concrete," a Freudian would see that as a potential anal reference as well, as Padel (1987) does concerning a different patient's dream: "Wet concrete has the homogeneous, mushy, gray-brown qualities which make it a fairly common symbol for feces; also, from the child's point of view, men get fascinatingly dirty as they lay concrete" (p. 137). This could then be linked to the patient's sense that he does not bathe enough and his wife's criticism that he donated the smallest possible amount to the church.

In my view, it is best to come to some kind of consensual interpretation of the dream with the patient, as far as you can go. Three primary factors in evaluating a dream interpretation are: (1) Does the interpretation make sense? Do all the dream details fit into the interpretation? Is it internally consistent? (2) Is there harmony between the deductions derived from the associations and the manifest content? and (3) Is there consensual agreement between you and the patient? If so, most analysts would say then you have done good interpretive work on the dream.[1]

But when you have gotten to this point, consider going further. I always want to know: What has this dream told us that we did not know before? What does it tell us that we could not have known any other way than through this dream? Ideally, a dream interpretation will offer something fresh and unique. When you and the patient feel satisfied with the interpretation, you can offer an inquiry into one further vector. It could be, for example, an inquiry into a concrete detail of the manifest content, and its connection with the patient's actual past experience. I am usually rewarded by such an inquiry, although often not immediately.

DREAMS REPORTED IN PSYCHOANALYSIS REFER IN SOME WAY TO THE PSYCHOANALYTIC RELATIONSHIP, WHATEVER OTHER SIGNIFICANCE THEY MAY HAVE

This assumption, in the years closing the twentieth century, became almost the Golden Rule of psychoanalytic dream interpretation. But it

---

1. The first two factors are also the criteria of French and Fromm (1964) for good interpretations. In my view, the third factor, which is fundamental to collaborative dream interpretation, is equally important.

was not always so. Freud came to consider this issue with difficulty and resisted it. When he was treating Dora, her so-called "Second Dream" (1905) includes the following: "I then saw a thick wood before me which I went into, and there I asked a man whom I met. He said to me: 'Two and a half hours more.' (When she repeated the dream, he said: 'Two hours.') He offered to accompany me. But I refused and went alone." If one were to look in the dream for a metaphor of the treatment, one might suspect that Dora is going to terminate in two hours. Her analyst will offer to continue, but she will refuse and go it alone.

Freud, in hearing the dream, had not yet discovered the transference (he would first describe it in his postscript to the Dora case; see Freud, 1905): "At the time she was telling me the dream I was still unaware (and did not learn until two days later) that we had only *two hours* more work before us" (p. 119).

In 1926, Otto Rank made the startling suggestion that when a patient tells a childhood dream in analysis, even then one should consider its transference implications. He raised this issue in reference to the famous dream that the "Wolf-Man" had at the age of four and which he, as an adult, reported to his psychoanalyst, Sigmund Freud. One could argue that since the dream predates the psychoanalysis, it is foolhardy to consider that it expresses the patient's view of the analyst or the analytic situation. But there are several opposing arguments:

1. Since the transference is presumed to reproduce early childhood attitudes, it is likely that the dream will reflect the nature of the transference. In other words, the childhood dream does not reflect back on the transference; it anticipates it.
2. Even though the dream predates the transference, the patient's decision to tell the dream at a particular point in the analysis may come from an unconscious awareness that it corresponds to the transference. The transference experience may be the precipitant for the patient remembering and telling the dream.
3. The memory of a childhood dream is subject to major revision in adulthood. The analyst cannot be sure that he is hearing a childhood dream, or a dream whose memory has been revised to fit the current situation.

Freud (1918) interpreted the Wolf-Man's dream solely in terms of his infantile sexuality, having to do with witnessing the primal scene, but Otto Rank (1926) argued that it was reflective of the transference and of actual details of Freud's office. The dream involves the Wolf-Man lying in his bed, facing a window. The window opens by itself, and outside the window is a tree with wolves sitting in it. According to Esther

Menaker (1981), Rank saw the dream as a communication to Freud. Menaker writes:

> In terms of the symbolic meaning of the elements of the dream, Rank interprets the tree outside the window as a family tree—Freud's family tree; and indeed there were chestnut trees outside Freud's office window which a patient lying on the couch would be looking at since the sofa faced the window. On the narrow strip of wall beside the window frame there hung photographs of Freud's disciples. These are the wolves sitting on the tree; they are the siblings whom the patient fears, envies and would like to replace. The dream as it reappears in the analysis under the pressure of the setting of a terminal date, is, in Rank's view, an expression of the wish on the part of the Wolf-Man to be re-born into Freud's family. In transference terms, Freud is a maternal figure, for the genealogical tree is the tree of life—the mother who gives birth to the siblings. . . . The sexual interpretation of the Wolf-Man's childhood dream may have some validity, but the therapeutic question is, how and in what way is it relevant to the current therapy. Rank's interpretation, which comes out of the present situation of the patient, addresses his need for growth of the self through processes of the internalization of new familial figures and new relationships. Ironically, the Wolf-Man, whose dream was never analyzed or understood in these terms, but was interpreted in accordance with Freud's theory of the Oedipal origins of the neurosis, did succeed in spite of serious mental disturbances, in maintaining some psychic balance by becoming part of Freud's family as one of his famous cases [p. 555].

And, indeed, as his life progressed, the Wolf-Man was emotionally supported by several psychoanalysts and financially aided by the Freud Archives (Gardiner, 1983).

After Rank reinterpreted the wolf dream, Freud wrote to the Wolf-Man for confirmation that the dream was indeed from his childhood.[2] The patient's answer, dated 6 June 1926, expressed certainty that it was just as he had "dreamed it in childhood and reported in the analysis and without any changes" (Wolf-Man, 1957, p. 449). Freud turned this

2. Freud seems to rely on the accuracy of childhood memory here, even though he frequently questioned such memory in other circumstances. Counterresistance can change any psychoanalyst's viewpoint.

letter over to Ferenczi who used it to refute Rank's criticism (Ferenczi, 1927).[3] Ernest Jones (1957) joined in by stating that at the time of the Wolf-Man's analysis only three pictures of followers were on the wall of Freud's office (p. 76).

To be sure, neither of these counterarguments is definitive. The Wolf-Man's memory that his dream was from childhood does not insure that he did not modify it as an adult. And Jones's argument that there were only three pictures on the wall is not so critical. After all, the Wolf-Man told Freud that in his dream there were six or seven wolves, but when he drew the scene for Freud, there were only five.

Setting aside the empirical question of how much or how often dreams reported in analysis refer to the analytic relationship, there is the practical clinical problem of how much importance to give to this aspect of dream analysis. There was once a time when analysts tended to give little attention to this fact and instead emphasized the intrapsychic aspects of the dream. At the beginning of the twenty-first century, the pendulum has swung in the other direction. With the so-called "two-person" psychology in ascendance, some practitioners tended to give primary or exclusive attention to the implications of the patient's dream for the analytic relationship. As in all clinical matters, balance is essential.

DREAM ANALYSIS USUALLY DOES NOT OCCUR IN ONE SESSION

I once had a student in my dream interpretation course who told me that she had learned from a previous professor that the psychoanalyst should never refer to a dream told in a previous session, unless the patient brings it up first. I strongly disagree with this point of view.

Dream interpretations can evolve over time. They are not limited to single presentations in single sessions. Psychoanalysts may refer back to particular dreams at different times in the analysis. Ideally, the patient and analyst will continually revise and re-revise their understandings of any dream as the analysis progresses. As new material arises, as certain

3. Yet two years before this publication, Ferenczi (1925) had stated: "I can only repeat here that for me and my analysis it is an advance that I take Rank's suggestion regarding the relation of patient to analyst as the cardinal point of the analytic material and regard *every* dream, *every* gesture, *every* parapraxis, *every* aggravation or improvement in the condition of the patient as above all an expression of transference and resistance" (p. 225).

resistances are dissolved, not only in the patient but also in the analyst, the dream may become more and more understandable. Interpretations of single dreams can be refined and expanded by attention to several dreams by the same dreamer that may converge on certain themes.

As we dream night after night, we may set up a separate life with its own continuity. Often it is the job of the psychoanalyst to perceive continuity within the patient's dream life. Eventually, one may wish to connect these trends with aspects of waking life, but that may take a long time. In the meantime, one can proceed totally in terms of the dream life.

The continuity of dreams may be seen in repeated themes that spread over several dreams. For example, in almost every dream of one of my male patients, there was a new building of some sort, described in quite elaborate detail. Many of the dream buildings had no referents in his real life. He was not an architect, nor were any of his relatives or friends. I wondered if these dreams were telling us about some unrealized professional potential. The dreams continued, with detailed descriptions of homes. I have actual visual images in my mind of many of the homes he described.

We were both puzzled by this panoply of architecture, but one day he recalled a fact of his past that helped explain it. His father, with whom he was not close, liked to do renovations in the house. There was one time that he and his father moved a wall in the house. It is one of his happiest memories. The good connection with his father, a sense of real collaboration, was revived in the transference and found expression in his dreams. We were building a new life together for him.

A refined and cultured woman, who had had a restrictive religious upbringing, had several violent and savage dreams. In one dream, she attended a picnic. A woman, whom the patient in real life found to be an annoying burden, had been killed and cooked for dinner, and the dish was enjoyed by the guests without their knowing they were eating human flesh. The dreamer knew it, but did not feel guilty because she had not cooked it. In another dream, she skinned her husband. In a very caring manner, she removed the outer layer of his flesh with a blade, which was supposed to have a beneficial effect. Each dream shows a psychological attempt to make aggressive feelings acceptable. In the first, they are acceptable because she is not overtly responsible for the violence. In the second, they are acceptable because the violence is done in a caring manner and for her husband's benefit.

Dream interpreters can follow continuous themes in a patient's dreams and notice significant milestones in how those themes develop.

Thus, in the case of Martha (Fosshage and Loew, 1987, p. 12), the first dream of her psychoanalysis described how she had spent 20 years, from age 30 to 50, sitting on a rickety balcony, watching other people's actions without actually taking part herself. (She was actually 33 when she dreamt this.) The dream captured her concern that she was not taking part in life, and that if she continued this way, she would miss the best years of her adulthood. Yet, at the start of her analysis, she was too constrained by her anxieties to do otherwise.

After two years of treatment, she dreamt of a rendezvous with a man that is supposed to take place on Friday night, but she would rather have joined him on Saturday. An astute dream interpreter might note that the theme of procrastination has reappeared, although things have improved. One day of procrastination is much less than 20 years.

ANAGOGIC AND ANALYTIC INTERPRETATION OF DREAMS

Freud distinguishes between dreams from below and dreams from above. A dream from below is primarily derived from an instinctual wish that has found a means of representation through the day's residues. A dream from above corresponds to waking thoughts that have achieved representation through energic relation to repressed material.

The distinction is related to the anagogic versus analytic distinction of Silberer (1914, cf. Freud, 1900, p. 524). Anagogic and analytic interpretation can be derived from any dream. The analytic interpretation[4] involves giving the dream a meaning of an infantile-sexual kind. The anagogic interpretation reveals "more serious thoughts," such as the visual representation of intellectual problems. Of course, they may be interrelated.

This dual approach to dream interpretation is shown by the following example: A Jewish woman was dating Eugene, a man from a Russian Orthodox Christian background. She dreamt:

"I'm being at dinner, and there is borscht. Carl is not eating it. I'm serving it. As I'm eating it, I realize that there is a purple condom wrapper in it. I run out of the room. My dog is there. She hasn't eaten. I realize whoever has been feeding her isn't feeding her. She is acting so hungry.

---

4. The word "analytic" here really signifies Freudian psychoanalysis; several contemporary psychoanalytic approaches would not assign such special importance to infantile sexuality in dream meaning.

"There is an earlier part of the dream in which there are all kinds of art posters in my kitchen, which I don't really own."

In the interpretation process, the dreamer gave the following associations: "A few days ago, Eugene and I were having dinner at Carl's house. Carl is a good cook. He is from a Christian background, and his family is very anti-Semitic, although he is not, and his wife is Jewish.

"Borscht reminds me of beets. I have beets wrapped in plastic in my refrigerator. I had forgotten they were there.

"The posters in the kitchen—I don't have them, but Eugene has them in his kitchen. I suppose the dream showed what I might feel if we joined kitchens, that is, got married or at least lived together.

"The condom wrapper—Eugene had thrown an empty condom wrapper into my trashcan the previous night. I did not want the housekeeper to see it, so I put it inside an envelope. That wrapper was green. Lambskin condoms have purple wrappers. I still have some, but I never use them. You could put lamb in borscht, although in this dream it only had beets and onions. Eugene and I actually cooked a borscht like that recently, but it didn't have a condom wrapper in it."

The analyst noted that borscht is usually Jewish. The patient said, "No, that's not really true. A lot of American Jews think that, but I think borscht is really an essentially Russian dish."

In the next session, the patient referred back to the dream. "I was thinking about what you said about borscht being Jewish. I still think that is wrong, but the vehemence with which I argued the point made me wonder. And after the session, I thought, my strong emotion was very much part of the tension that I am feeling about the Russian background of Eugene's family that showed up in the dream. I spent the weekend with Eugene at his family's house for the first time. There were subtle but definite signs of anti-Semitism over the weekend that I tried to ignore.

"Carl is in the dream because his family is from a town nearby to Eugene's, and I know they are extremely anti-Semitic. I think the dream had to do with that question, can borscht be Russian and Jewish? Can I feel comfortable with Eugene's family, and in a sexual relationship with Eugene? The condom wrapper was connected with sex and safety and shame."

The distinction between anagogic and Freudian psychoanalytic interpretations can be made with this dream, but the two aspects, here as in most dreams, need not be kept separate. The dream refers to adult feelings about religious differences that the dreamer had been dissociating. However, there is also a basic theme of hunger and deprivation, connected with the dreamer's very early childhood. (She nearly starved at the age of two.) The questions of sex, birth control, safety or danger (from sexually-transmitted disease, starvation, prejudice, and unwanted pregnancy), all interconnected for this dreamer, are condensed into the brief manifest content. The dream connects the themes with her current love interest, although the analysis of the dream elaborated how those issues were being expressed in the transference and in the dreamer's general defensiveness in all romantic relationships.

REEXAMINING SOME TRADITIONAL "RULES" OF DREAM INTERPRETATION

The psychoanalytic tradition of dream interpretation has accumulated a number of rules or traditions. Some of these have been proven to be more or less valid, and some, but not all, have good rationales.

NUMBERS IN DREAMS

One of these "rules" has to do with numbers in dreams: When there are particular numbers in a dream, they often refer to the age of the dreamer when something significant happened, an event or emotion to which the dream is referring.

There is a rational reason for this "rule," namely that for many of us, our first contact with numbers had to do with our own age. Before we could manipulate numbers as abstract entities, we could tell people that we were three years old. In this way, some of the "rules" of dream transposition derive from this "archaeology of language." The earliest uses of words are often the source of their function in transposition and symbolization.

This is the basis for the approach of Ella Freeman Sharpe to dreams. She wrote (1937): "The basis of language is implied metaphor and that we all learn our mother tongue phonetically" (p. 39). Because of these facts, dreams pun. They often refer words back to the first meaning that we heard in them. One of Sharpe's patients dreamt of Iona cathedral. His associations take him back to the fact that as a child, he heard the words "Iona Cathedral" as "I own a cathedral," which leads him toward the underlying meaning of the dream.

Such homonyms are the basis for the misunderstandings of many children of famous sayings and the texts of songs. I know a child who misunderstood the line from the *Star-Spangled Banner:* "Whose broad stripes and bright stars." She heard it as a question: "Who's brought stripes and bright stars?"

But of course all "rules" have their exceptions, and a skillful dream interpreter will know the rules and be ready to abandon them when the evidence is there. For example, numbers in dreams can refer to things other than age. A Jewish woman living in America had spent her childhood during the Second World War hiding in the home of a Christian family. Fifty years later, she returned to her native country, in the hope of revisiting her wartime hideout and recovering memories from that period. She went to the address that she remembered, but the house there was not the right one. That night, she had a dream that included a two-digit number. Upon awakening, she felt convinced that this must be the correct address, and independent sources later confirmed it. (Interestingly, after having the dream, and convinced that she now knew the correct address, she did not go there.) The dream, in this case, revived a fact that she had dissociated, probably because of great ambivalence about that period of her life.

THE ANALYST IN THE MANIFEST CONTENT

In the middle of the twentieth century, Maxwell Gitelson (1952) proposed the idea that if the analyst appears in the manifest content, it is an indication of problematic countertransference. When Gitelson wrote this, it was a time when most orthodox psychoanalysts were not so willing to consider the inevitable contributions of their own personality to the therapeutic process. So it was a good suggestion, whether or not it was correct, in that it led classical psychoanalysts to consider their countertransference more. In my view, Gitelson's suggestion was too restrictive; the countertransference may always be implicated in any patient's dream, whether or not the analyst is in the manifest dream content.[5]

IS THE FIRST DREAM IN THE ANALYSIS THE CLEAREST?

Another commonly accepted "rule" of clinical dream interpretation is that the first dream in the analysis is the clearest. As the analysis progresses and the patient's resistances are mobilized, the dreams become more difficult to understand. Jung believed this. He wrote (1934): "As

5. See chapters 16 and 17 for further discussion of this issue.

a rule, dreams get more and more opaque and blurred soon after the beginning of treatment, and this makes the interpretation increasingly difficult" (p. 93).

Other clinicians have repeated this maxim. Whitman, Kramer, and Baldridge (1969) claim: "It is a well-known fact that first dreams in an analysis are much more transparent and helpful in formulating the course and development of the transference neurosis than later dreams where defenses of various types have arisen to obscure the dynamics and ego coping mechanisms of the patient" (p. 706).

I have my doubts that this is correct. I think it is true that an individual analyst may have more trouble understanding his patient's dreams as the analysis progresses, but I am not so sure that this is because the dreams themselves become more opaque.

My evidence for this position is that if you bring a dream from later in an analysis to a group of clinicians who are not directly involved in the treatment, they will not find it particularly opaque. This is my impression from many years of teaching. My students and I do not have more trouble getting to the gist of dreams from the middle and late stages of treatment than from early stages.

An alternative explanation is that the difficulty in understanding the dream may be due to increases in the analyst's counterresistance and the complexity of the transference/countertransference relationship. The analyst has changed as much as the patient's dreams, and he may have trouble at various points in the treatment with the patient's material. Another possible explanation is that the early dreams are clearest because they are mostly *of the patient*, especially dreams that occurred before treatment. Once the treatment progresses, the dreams will reflect the psychologies of both the patient and the analyst and their interaction.

In each of the next eight chapters, we will examine closely a special aspect of approaching dreams. We will see how dreams are a frontier in the portrayal of how the mind works, as well as a clinical frontier, on the cutting edge of innovation in psychotherapy.

CHAPTER 12

HOMONYMS AND OTHER WORDPLAY IN DREAMS

IT IS VALUABLE FOR anyone who wishes to analyze dreams to become sensitized to wordplay, puns, and homonyms. Even if one has no special gift for punning, one should be ready to hear such material in the patient's associations. Some people who do not pun particularly well in waking life sometimes do so in their dreams.

Many American children delight in such wordplay through the riddle: "What is black and white and red all over?" The answer is "a newspaper," drawing on the homonym "read-red." The black and white set up the likelihood that the next words may also be colors. When we hear "red" we are likely to choose the color over the verb "read," but the joke breaks that expectation, as the answer is a newspaper that is "read all over." For many years, that joke thrived, but then a tasteless antijoke was set up against it: "What is black and white and red all over? A nun falling down the staircase." Here, the expectation of anyone who has heard the riddle is that of the two choices, red-read, the verb, "read" is the one to choose. And so the antijoke breaks *that* expectation: After being tricked into not hearing the color red, that is the homonym that applies.

The simplest words can have multiple meanings of which we might not ordinarily be aware. We all know the nursery rhyme that begins: "Mary had a little lamb." But consider what happens when we add: "Mary had a little lamb—and Jane a little pork." The sentence changes its meaning, and we suddenly become aware of two meanings of "had"—1) to possess; 2) to eat (see Vendler, 1977). The effect strikes us as comical; we thought of Mary as a sweet girl with her cute little lamb, and suddenly she is eating it. It may bring to mind the cannibalism of the song from Stephen Sondheim's *Sweeney Todd:* "Have a little priest . . ."

The sentence makes us aware not only of the two meanings of "had," but of another peculiar aspect of our language. If the sentence had been lengthened thus: "Mary had a little lamb—and Jane a little pig," the word "had" would not have been changed. The sentence highlights that, in English, we often use two versions of an animal name—the generic name versus the food label—such as pig versus pork, cow versus beef, sheep versus mutton, calf versus veal. With "lamb," the generic name and the food label are identical, which allows for the surprise effect of "Mary had a little lamb—and Jane a little pork."

Freud noted that wordplay was a basic element of Oriental dream interpretation. He added this footnote in 1909 to *The Interpretation of Dreams*:

> Dr. Alfred Robitsek has pointed out to me that the oriental "dream-books" (of which ours are wretched imitations) base the greater number of their interpretations of dream-elements upon similarity of sounds and resemblance between words. The fact that these connections inevitably disappear in translation accounts for the unintelligibility of the renderings of our own popular dream-books. The extraordinarily important part played by punning and verbal quibbles in the ancient civilizations of the East may be studied in the writings of Hugo Winckler [the famous archaeologist] [p. 99].

Freud (1900, p. 232) noted several homonyms in his patients' dreams. For instance, one of his patients discovered a special meaning when she dreamt of Italy (a place she had never been). In German, "gen Italien" (to Italy) sounds the same as "Genitalien" (genitals).

In another case, the Wolf-Man (Freud, 1918) dreamt "of a man tearing off the wings of an *Espe*." He thought that Espe was the German word for "wasp." Freud told him the correct word was "Wespe." But then the Wolf-Man (whose real name, we now know, was Sergei Pankejeff), said: "But Espe, why, that's myself: S. P."

There is also the well-known example of the French patient whose father had died of alcoholism and who dreamt of six roses (Malcolm, 1982). The French analyst said, "Six roses ou cirrhose? (pronounced: see-rose ou see-rose)" In French, the words for "six roses" and for "cirrhosis" are homonyms. Thus the dreamwork made a pictogram of a homonym of the latent content.

Proper names are a rich but often overlooked source of homonyms. When a patient dreams of her friend Eileen, the analyst John Padel sees dependency issues ("I lean") portrayed by the relationship with that dream character (Fosshage and Loew, 1987).

These examples make one wonder to what degree we hear all homonyms when we listen to language. Do our minds make those kinds of translations of words into all of their homonyms, and then allow representation of things by pictures of their homonyms?

Ella Sharpe thought so. In 1937, she wrote:

> Words have a history of displacement individually as well as racially from the first context in which we heard them, when they designated some definite sensible image. Words acquire a second meaning and convey abstract ideas, but they do not lose as far as the unconscious storehouse of our past is concerned the concrete significance the words possessed when we first heard and used them [p. 28].

She gives many dream examples, such as when the word "read" is connected with the "red" of menstruation.

We know from experimental research that when words are first heard, all homonyms are in fact considered. For example, the psycholinguist David Swinney (1979) has tested sentences like: "Rumor had it that, for years, the government building had been plagued with problems. The man was not surprised when he found several spiders, roaches, and other bugs in the corner of his room." He showed that both meanings of the word "bug" (an insect and a spy device) are mentally activated, at least for 200 to 500 milliseconds after hearing it. It is possible that the brain, in dreams, exercises this aural connectivity in an active rather than a passive way. Any word may be transposed to its homonym, especially if its homonym lends itself better to visual representation. It is much easier to form a definite image of six roses than of cirrhosis.

The range of such possible transformations can often be quite surprising and humorous. Stevens (1996, p. 41) reports a rather elaborate transformation:

He has a dream in Moscow in which he is observing a bee hovering at the entrance to a hole in a tree.

His associations are that the bee is operating in a cagey manner—hence, a cagey bee, a KGB! He had been warned about the KGB.

The knowledge of the role of homonyms in dream formation goes back to ancient times. According to Artemidorus (1990):

> Aristander also gave a most felicitous interpretation to Alexander of Macedonia when he had blockaded Tyre and was besieging

it. Alexander was feeling uneasy and disturbed because of the great loss of time and dreamt that he saw a satyr dancing on his shield. Artistander was in Tyre at the time, in attendance on the king while he was waging war against the Tyrians. By dividing the word Satyros into Sa and Tyros (Tyre is yours), he encouraged the king to wage the war more zealously with the result that he took the city [pp. 200–201].

DREAMS PERFORM AN ARCHAEOLOGY OF WORDS

Dreams sometimes make us aware of the many processes that we take for granted in language perception. Sometimes, in our dreams, we dissect words into components that we would not have noticed in our waking life. One of my patients, who suffered from excessive guilt feelings, had a dream in which a character's name was "Mr. Gill Tee." In another dream, a patient typed a memo which began, "Re: Ferral." A close friend had asked for a referral, and had been given my name, among others, which stirred many feelings in my patient, as well as leading her to wonder whether she needed a referral. In addition, "Ferral" was a homonym of "feral," and the dreamer's feral rage was something that needed further work.

Some dreams create neologisms, words that seem completely new, although analysis may reveal that they have roots in real words. The morphological groupings sometimes mislead the dreamer and the analyst. For example, a patient told me he had seen in his dream the words "Prestyl Dolby." Neither he nor I realized what this meant. The grouping of the "words" kept me from missing the hidden words: Prestyl looked like a new chemical, and dolby reminded me of the Dolby Sound Reduction system that is common in high fidelity systems. Homonymic interchanges are rife in dreams, and are very probably rife in our auditory processing, although this is accomplished mostly unconsciously for us. The "Dol" in dolby could have been "dole," but it is a harder stretch to notice the contraction "dough'll."

Several weeks later, he was talking about someone he knew who used to take cash from her father's cash register. In this context, helped by some other associations, we came to understand that the words, "Prestyl Dolby" meant "Press the till; dough'll be yours."[1]

1. See Blechner (1997a) for a more detailed account of this example. See Sharpe (1937) for a discussion of the relation between dream formation and poetic devices, including metaphor, simile, metalepsis, synechdoche, metonymy, and onomatopoeia.

PUNNING IN DREAMS AND DREAM INTERPRETATION

The day before his wedding, a patient asked me during a psychoanalytic session, "Is it possible to have an olfactory dream?"[2] The night before, in a dream, he had smelled something putrid, like "a smelly fart." When he woke up, there was no smell.

This patient had entered analysis concerned about his compulsive womanizing. He feared that he would never be able to commit himself to any one woman. This problem, we discovered, was multidetermined. First, there was much dissociated evidence that his father, whom he consciously idealized, had been quite a philanderer himself. In addition, there was a reaction formation against passive sexual submission to a protective but domineering brother. But perhaps the most potent cause of his compulsive infidelity was formulated a short while before this dream. It was that the patient dissociated from any negative affects toward his fiancée. When he felt aggression toward her, he would repress his hostility, but then retaliate by committing an infidelity. This occurred not only with his fiancée, but with anyone on whom he was dependent, including me. In the transference, when the patient felt judged by me, he resumed contact with his former analyst.

When I suggested we interpret the dream, the patient said, "I'm not sure it was really a dream, but I'm not sure what it was." Here he was doing with the dream precisely what he did with stinky feelings—he questioned whether they were real, but could not otherwise account for their presence. Thus the pattern of denial and confused anxiety was reenacted in his approach to the dream.

Later in the session, the patient spoke of a book by a Jewish author, and said, "I think it reeks of the shtetl." When I noticed his use of the word "reek," he replied that he meant only that it was characteristic of the shtetl and was not meant derogatorily. He said that he felt highly identified with Judaism, and affectionate toward Jewish traditions. Here, we see the same enactment—he denies his hostile feelings toward "shtetl Judaism" just like he questioned whether his fart dream was really a dream. His denial of the validity of his hostile associations is like his denial of the dream's existence. It is also like his denial of negative affects toward significant people in his life.

---

2. I have heard very few olfactory dreams. Reports of them in the literature are relatively sparse. See Fromm-Reichmann's comments in Bullard (1959, p. 165). Dreams involving the sense of taste are even rarer. For an example, see Seligman and Yellen (1987): "Then I saw an apple tree, with cold, wet, red, apples, but no leaves on the tree. I took one and ate it (it was so good, that I could even taste it after I woke up)" (p. 18).

In the previous session, he had been complaining to me about his bride-to-be's lavish spending, yet he had remained silent about it to her. So now, after hearing the fart dream, I told him that his questioning the dream's existence and his similar denial of the derogatory implications of his comment about reeking of the shtetl all seemed connected with his keeping his bad feelings about his fiancée's spending to himself. He replied, "I'm afraid if I tell her what's wrong, I'll wreak havoc on the relationship." I felt that he was punning unconsciously, and said, "You don't want to wreak anything. But what are you going to do when anything reeks?"

Once the process of punning had been established in the dream, I carried it over into the dream interpretation process.

MULTILINGUAL WORDPLAY

All of the examples of wordplay mentioned so far involve homonyms within a single language. People who are multilingual may draw homonyms between more than one language. Immanuel Velikovsky (1934), a psychoanalyst in Palestine who was fluent in both Hebrew and Arabic, heard the following dream of his patient, a farmer who had come to the city to be treated for impotence: "A man is running around asking and looking for a place to buy lime. I say to him, 'What are you worrying about? There is a pit full of lime right near your house.'"

Velikovsky asked the patient whether he was trying to have an affair with a lady in town. The patient acknowledged that it was true, but was amazed that the analyst knew. It had to do with the association of lime ("sid" in Hebrew) and lady ("sit" in Arabic). The patient then noted that the pit of lime near his house represented his wife, who was always available.

CHAPTER 13

DREAM ACTS

DREAMS IN ANALYSIS AS ACTIONS

DREAMS ARE MORE than their content. Every dream that is told in clinical psychoanalysis is also an action by the patient in treatment. In interpreting dreams, the psychoanalyst pays close attention not only to the dreamtext and the associations but also to how a patient tells or doesn't tell a dream. The telling (or nontelling) of dreams is a symbolic action within the treatment, and the content of the dream is often reenacted during the dream interpretation process. In 1997, Hobson and I participated in a conference on dreaming. I sent him my paper before the meeting, which included an exposition on his "Van" dream (see chapter 2), in which he and Van play catch with a piece of hardware. At the conference, before speaking, he tossed a copy of his latest book to me—a witty enactment of the dream, as if to say, "Here, take this as my latest viewpoint!"

Freud occasionally interpreted dreams as actions, usually when he saw them as resistance. One of the most famous examples of this occurred in relation to his theory of wish fulfillment, which was challenged both by Freud's patients as well as other psychoanalysts. One of his patients presented a dream that had no apparent wish in it. The patient had been resistant to Freud's theory of dreams as wish fulfillment, and so Freud interpreted the wishless dream as expressing the wish to disprove Freud's theory of wish fulfillment! Freud warns us of the same sort of psychodynamic if we provide dreams that are evidence against the wish-fulfillment hypothesis (Freud, 1900): "Indeed, it is to be expected that the same thing will happen to some of the readers of the present book: they will be quite ready to have one of their wishes frustrated in a dream if only their wish that I may be wrong can be fulfilled" (p. 168).

So if you come up with a dream that is counterevidential to this theory, that proves the theory. Many readers have understandably balked at this sort of circular argument (e.g., Grünbaum, 1984). But from a different standpoint, when Freud made this argument, it was a landmark in the interpretation of dreams. It was the first step toward an appreciation of the interpersonal dimension of dreams. Freud was suggesting that a person in an intense relationship, as most psychoanalytic patients are (unless the treatment is ineffectual), can use dreams to communicate with the other person.

In other words, dreaming is a process that is usually autistic, self-referential, and self-contained, but it can become interpersonal. Ella Sharpe was among the first to develop the idea of dreams as actions within the analysis. She wrote of dreams as resistance and as gifts to the analyst (Sharpe, 1937, 81ff).

How we tell a dream is often as important as the content. An analyst can begin the analysis of a dream by first analyzing the way the patient told the dream. After the resistance analysis is done, it is often possible to relate the resistance analysis to the dream content. Greenson (1967, p. 110) provides a fine example of this. A patient told him a dream in a very confusing manner, mixing the actual dream with associations to the dream and thoughts about things that actually happened in his real life. The account was so confusing that Greenson himself could not tell which parts were the actual dream.

Following the principle of analyzing resistance before content, Greenson asked the patient if he was aware of the fact that he couldn't simply tell a dream from beginning to end. At first the patient protested that he thought, following the principle of free association, that he should tell everything as it came into his mind. But then, thinking further on this, he noted that he often scrambled things when working on a task. He read books by starting in the middle, and then reading parts of it out of order. This tendency involved his defiant reactions to his father's being a well known academic and the whole family being renowned for their studiousness. It also represented a mixed reaction of attachment to his father and fear of that attachment.

THE NONTELLING OF DREAMS AS A DREAM ACT

We know that patients who are in psychotherapy vary greatly in their ability to remember and report their dreams. However, when the psychoanalyst tells a patient that he is interested in dreams and would find them useful to the therapy, the patient will usually remember more of his or her dreams. I have also observed something similar in teaching dream interpretation seminars. In these seminars, I ask therapists to report a dream of one of their patients, which we can study during the seminar. Invariably, at the beginning of such a seminar, there are a few therapists, and sometimes many, who say that none of their patients report dreams. They always find it to be startling, almost miraculous, that shortly after starting the seminar on dreaming, their patients start to report dreams. Again, there could be several variables: The most obvious is that the change is in the therapist. Now that she is interested in dreams, if her patient mentions anything related to dreams, she may perk up her ears, and she may better remember such material. But also, she is likely to say something in her sessions to her patients indicating an interest in dreams, which will encourage the patient to report dreams.

This is by no means a trivial fact. It implies that our ability to remember and report our dreams is under some conscious control. There are many studies of so-called "lucid dreaming," in which some people report that they can bring some aspects of their dreams, their progression and their content, under conscious control (Gackenbach and LaBerge, 1988). This phenomenon seems to me to be part of a subclass of dream phenomena under discussion here: the ways that conscious and unconscious intentions can affect the way a person remembers her dreams.

Sometimes, the remembering of dreams interacts with the character issues that a patient must deal with during psychoanalysis. For example, a patient who was profoundly dissatisfied with his life started analysis with me. His first marriage had been very troubled and ended in a bitter divorce. He initially reported that there were no problems in his second, current marriage. But he had had severe trouble sleeping for 20 years, and he wondered whether therapy could help that. I inquired about the disruptions in sleep. He often slept lightly, awakened in the middle of the night, and had great difficulty returning to sleep. I asked what his emotional state was when he awoke, and had he been dreaming? He said he didn't know, but would that be helpful? I replied that it might be, and suggested that when he awakened he should try to note whether he had been dreaming, and, if so, to write the dreams down.

In the next session, he reported that he noticed that the previous night, when he awakened, he had in fact been dreaming. He said, "Yes, I definitely am dreaming when I wake up. But I don't remember what I dreamt. I woke up, and thought I should write them down, but I didn't, and then I didn't remember them." I note that he is both cooperating with me and rebelling. He talks a good show of wanting to cooperate in the analysis, but then, in the night, makes a semiconscious decision not to write the dream down.

I class this sort of therapeutic interaction as a "dream act." At that point in the therapy, there had been no dreams. But in the act of waking up and not writing down his dream, he had acted in a way that suggested something of his character and his underlying difficulties. The task for the therapist in such a case is to explore the patient's action and its underlying meaning. Schimel (1969), Levenson (1983), Joseph (1985), and I (Blechner, 1995a) have noted the correspondence between the dream content and what the patient does in therapy. But here we have a dream act without any dreams.

I wondered if this sort of establishment of an alliance and then engaging in a covert rebellion was something he did in other areas of his life. He quickly answered affirmatively. He associated to his mother telling him to take out the garbage, and his saying, "I will later," and then not doing it.

It soon emerged that his pattern of establishing close ties and then secretly rebelling against them was a pervasive part of his life. It was constantly getting in the way of his working with clients in his business. He would set up a working plan with clients, and then privately become enraged at the way he felt entrapped by the client, which led to crippling inefficiency in his work.

Finally the patient did start bringing dreams into the analysis. His first dream went as follows:

> I needed an operation. I had no understanding why. To cover up the scars or deformities of the operation, they were going to give me breasts. I thought, "I'm going to talk to Lori [his wife] about this." She said, "Let me feel your chest. I can tell about these things." She started to feel my chest. It felt nice. Sexual. She said, "Let me see your breasts, if there is enough there for breasts." I said, "Hold on, you're the woman, not me. I don't want anything done to my penis." I kind of had a mixture of fear and fascination. I was turned on also.
>
> And then, I went back to sleep. I had another dream: I was in a board room. I was a new member of the board. I was kind of watching what was going on, instead of participating. I felt out of place. It was an internal feeling. Am I out of place before the breasts or after?

I asked him whether he had any conscious wishes of having a sex change operation. He claimed not to. But he had an interpretation of the dream that avoided the sex-change content of the dream. He said,

"I really like to play with my wife's breasts, and she hardly ever lets me do it to her as much as I would like. So if I could have my own breasts, then I could play with them whenever I liked, and not have to depend on her moods."

This was his first mention of there being any difficulty between him and his wife. That in itself was important. The scars and deformities could be the scars of his childhood and the deformities in his character that made it difficult for him to collaborate with anyone. He had already shown this to me in the transference, by his apparent compliance and underlying defiance of my suggestion to bring in his dreams.

Since he focused the dream on the issue of what his relationship with his wife was like, I noted to him that in the dream she seemed remarkably willing to help him out in whatever way she could. In the dream, she says, "Let me feel your chest. I can tell about these things. . . . Let me see your breasts, if there is enough there for breasts."

She is a woman. She knows about breasts. And if her husband wants his own breasts, she offers her expertise to help him. But then in the dream he panics. Accepting help may be feminizing.

There was a concern here with castration, which the patient noted himself: "I don't want anything done to my penis." In terms of the dream act, something else was happening. Note that he does not tell me directly that he was awakened by this dream, but implies it: "And then, I went back to sleep." So there is a subtle admission that he has now complied with my request that he record his dreams during his awakenings, but also an attempt to disguise that he has done so.

We can speculate that this is where some of the real action is going on, and where the content of the dream is related to the process of dream interpretation. Collaboration or asking for help is threatening to him. It threatens his masculinity, and so he reinforces his sense of masculinity by constantly sabotaging other people's attempts to help him. Such a dynamic is going to make for rough going in the analysis. What we call the therapeutic alliance is a source of anxiety to him, of his entire identity as a man, and so every vagary of the therapeutic alliance must be made explicit in the therapy and studied.

Four years later, however, another meaning of the dream became clear, which reinforced my conviction that every symbol is also itself. He was talking about his distrust of all people, especially women. He was experiencing claustrophobia and panic attacks, related to fears of death or of losing control, symptoms which were longstanding but which he had not revealed until recently. He connected them to his tonsillectomy when he was a child. His mother lied to him, as she often did when something was coming up that would cause anxiety. She told him they were going to an ice cream party after the doctor did a small procedure. When the doctor tied down his arms and forced the ether on him, he was terrified. Since that incident, whenever he has had surgery, he is afraid. After surgery he always has a period of panic, when he feels he must make sure he can get up and walk around.

As he told me this, I suddenly remembered his dream, which was about surgery. So surgery, whatever else it symbolizes, is also surgery. I wondered whether his dream was a reference to the tonsillectomy and to the trauma of surgery for him. Implicitly, the dream also contrasts his wife and mother. In real life he distrusts all women, but in his dream he recognizes that his wife is trustworthy and helpful to him. This is a good example, too, of the Jungian concept of compensation.

CHAPTER 14

SYMBOLS

> The most skillful interpreter of dreams is he who has the faculty of observing resemblances.
>
> Aristotle

IN THE PSYCHOANALYTIC history of dreams, symbols have become cheap currency. It was relatively easy for analysts to pile on symbol translations. As Freud (1900) revised *The Interpretation of Dreams*, the section on symbols was added. It eventually ballooned in size more than any other, as analysts pitched in and started identifying symbols. The process of expanding the chapter got so out of hand that eventually a whole section became repeated in the text on "Typical Dreams" (Freud, 1900, pp. 271 and 393).

Symbol translation is the easiest part of dream interpretation, but *good* symbol translation is the hardest part. People often ask for formulas and, in the simplest dream interpretation, you could look up various symbols in a book, find out what they supposedly mean, and go on from there. Of course, the task of the symbol-dictionary writer is never done, because there are always new things in the world. One of my patients began a session asking, "What do credit cards mean in dreams?" None of my books on dream symbols had credit cards listed, but new ones will. Credit cards can symbolize, most obviously, economic power, false financial security, and the temptation to indulge oneself beyond reasonable limits.

Dream symbolism touches on the fundamental question: How does our mind organize the world? What aspects of the organization of the world are intrinsic to it (Gibson, 1966, 1979) and to what degree are they imposed on the world by our mind/brains?[1] But symbolism brings

1. Readers interested in the intricacies of this question should consult Lakoff (1988) about whether Tuesdays have an external reality, and then consider Fodor's (1998) counterargument.

out an added aspect—how does the mind, in its transformative capacity, use one object to stand for another?

Our lives are drenched in symbolism. We do not necessarily think of words as symbols, so much is their usage overlearned, but language itself is nonstop symbolism. Words are used to stand for objects. Sometimes the prehistory of words shows a structural or physical connection between the word and the object, as in onomatopoeia. But most words and things are more arbitrarily connected.

Culture is built of symbols. But how? What aspects of our external world are brought into play in symbol construction? The answer is complex and multifold. We will consider some of the primary sources of relation between symbol and symbolized.

(1) Similarity of shape or form: Things that look alike can stand for one another. This is the source of much of classical Freudian sexual symbolism. The penis is oblong and cylindrical, so any object with a similar shape can symbolize a penis. This includes poles, brooms, cigars, hoses, spears, etc. The vagina and womb have internal space, and so, as topology meets psychoanalysis, any object with an internal space can symbolize the vagina or the womb. This includes rooms, houses, buckets, purses, boxes, etc.

(2) Linguistic connection: As we saw in Chapter 12, any object can stand for another object when their names are either homonyms or otherwise related linguistically. Thus, the bee that flew around strangely, the "cagey bee," can stand for the Soviet intelligence agency (KGB). A man who was feeling conflicted about commitment to marriage dreamt about a cantaloupe. He thought of the play by Edward Albee, *Who's Afraid of Virginia Woolf?* in which George says, "Here comes Martha with her melons bobbing!" drawing a connection between melons and breasts and also connecting with unhappy marriage. But he did not feel really convinced about the dream until he made the linguistic connection between "cantaloupe" and "can't elope," which came closest to the details of his concerns.

(3) Cultural references: These can involve any arbitrary representation of one thing by another through long-standing cultural association. Thus, anything in the shape of a cross can stand for Christianity. Stars, especially the six-pointed variety, can stand for Judaism. Stars and stripes stand for the United

States. These are so ingrained in us that when we hear them in a dream, we may not think of them as symbols. But they are.

(4) Similarity of associated materials: Such symbolism involves the connection of the symbol and the symbolized through a similarity of primary or accessory features. For example, pleasurable swimming dreams, which are common in enuretics, may symbolize bed-wetting. Fire may also symbolize enuresis, possibly through the unconscious connection of urination with the extinction of flames.

(5) Mythic references—the collective unconscious: Jung posited that certain symbols may be consciously unknown to us, but are part of our collective psychological heritage. These archetypal mythic characters may symbolize certain characteristics. Thus a clown may be connected with the mythic trickster, or a bearer of messages with the messenger, Hermes. Through these mythic connections, characters in dreams can stand for many of the attributes associated with the mythic character. Thus any Mary-like figure can symbolize the theme of virginity or motherhood.

(6) Idiosyncratic connections: Very personal symbols may be connected with their referents in a manner that is unique to the individual dreamer. A patient dreamt that the left side of his body was much warmer than the right side. His associations led to the strong emotional warmth that he felt from me, so that the side of him nearest to me was warmer. Another patient, wracked by an inordinate sense of guilt, dreamt of a man on a flying bicycle that made a buzzing sound warning of his approach. His name was "Mr. Gill Tee." She thus combined a punning name with an added wished-for feature of a warning sound that could prepare her for his guilt-laden onslaught.[2]

Dreams show the mind at work creating symbols. But what in a dream is a symbol? We decide that after the fact. Often our decision is based on the strangeness of the object. New creations in dreams are often thought of symbolically. Jung (1960) interpreted the combination crab-lizard of his patient as a symbol of the conflict between the cerebrospinal and the sympathetic nervous system.

---

2. This example was also discussed on p. 157.

But the decision of what constitutes a symbol may be a bit arbitrary. As already mentioned, the Gestalt psychologists have brought another principle into practical clinical work—that every entity in a dream, human, animal, or *inanimate*, is a symbol of some aspect of the dreamer. The dream interpreter can therefore explore the nature of anything in the dream, even the most common object, for symbolic significance. According to this approach, if you hear a dream that begins, "I was taking a bath" the bath is a symbol, and the implied bathtub is also a symbol.

What stands for what? The fact is that the potential number of symbols, of referents, and of connections between the two, is infinite. It makes life simpler for the dream interpreter if you posit that one area of human experience is of primary importance, although that strategy may not do full justice to the dream. When Freud identified bodily sexual experience as having special importance, his followers had an easier time with symbols. Their task became circumscribed—to find the symbols of body parts and body processes. In chapter 6 of *The Interpretation of Dreams*, there are lists of objects that stand for the penis, the vagina, sexual intercourse, urination, defecation, menstruation, and other bodily parts and processes. Even with such a limited focus, the lists are long (and became longer in revisions of the book). You can find other lists of symbols in such books as Stekel (1943), Gutheil (1951), and Garma (1940). Yet you should always be ready to learn that the dreamer may have reason to have a quite different meaning for the symbol. For example, Freud reasoned that tall, cylindrical objects often symbolized the male phallus, and this, of course, includes trees. But when his patient, the Wolf-Man (Freud, 1918), dreamt of a tree, it was also a symbol of a woman; he associated it to the legend of Tancred, whose beloved Clorinda was imprisoned in a tree; Tancred did not know this, slashed the tree with a sword, and blood flowed from the tree's wound.

The clinician's theoretical convictions about questions raised by symbols may profoundly affect the practical approach to working with them in dream interpretation. Is the best route to the symbol through the dreamer's associations, or is it better to bypass personal associations and consider accepted symbols of the culture? To what degree is the symbol acquired? Are we all born with a vocabulary of symbols? Are we born with certain innate rules of symbol formation? You may decide to use the patient's associations as the guidelines for which are the important symbols. Obviously, if you are looking for sexuality, or if you have another ax to grind (notice the symbolism in that phrase), your search for symbols will be directed accordingly.

As with most aspects of dream interpretation, it is not a question of either/or. Symbols are themselves condensations of various meanings. When hearing a symbol in a dream, the interpreter should consider at least three aspects of meaning: (1) the symbol's personal meaning to the dreamer as derived from associations, (2) the symbol's meaning as a universal symbol, and (3) the symbol's representation of itself (e.g. a cigar is a cigar).

The last principle could be restated as "every symbol is also itself." The most telling statement of this principle is the famous line of Gertrude Stein: "A rose is a rose is a rose." Stein's statement originated in her observation that as words get used and reused over centuries, they lose their power to evoke vivid sensory images of what they stand for. Word use leads to a kind of "meaning fatigue." By saying that a rose is a rose is a rose, Stein tried to bring back all the evocative qualities of the word rose. As she expressed it:

> Now listen! Can't you see that when the language was new—as it was with Chaucer and Homer—the poet could use the name of a thing and the thing was really there? He could say "O moon," "O sea," "O love," and the moon and the sea and love were really there. And can't you see that after hundreds of years had gone by and thousands of poems had been written, he could call on those words and find that they were just wornout literary words? No listen! I'm no fool. I know that in daily life we don't go around saying "is a . . . is a . . . is a . . ." Yes, I'm no fool; but I think that in that line the rose is red for the first time in English poetry for a hundred years.

The same thing may be said to have happened with psychoanalytic dream symbolism. For those in our psychoanalytic culture whose association of traditional sexual symbols is overlearned, it is a worthwhile exercise to try to consider them in non-sexual ways. When I teach dreams, I ask my students to try to hear a dream of a snake without thinking of the usual Freudian genital symbolism, which is not an easy task. It is like the old cartoon in *Mad Magazine*: A radio announcer says, "Now boys and girls, I am going to play you a great piece of music. Most of you will associate it with *The Lone Ranger*, but it is actually the overture to *William Tell*, a great opera by Rossini, about a Swiss hero. So I want you to listen to the music, and force yourselves to think about that story." The next panel shows the children squinting their eyes, trying to concentrate on the music. And the next panel shows their unshaven father running into the room, yelling, "Hi ho Silver!"

Equating a dream-snake with a penis has become almost automatic in Western, post-Freudian culture, but there are parts of the world where this symbol formula seems odd. A Chinese-born woman, Catherine Ng, was rather startled by the snake-symbol equation. She told me that for her and most other Chinese, snakes are considered food and popularly are turned into soup. Perhaps culture can shape any symbol system, and presumptions of universality are possible only if you stay home with your own.

Jung (1916–1948) also argued that so-called sexual symbols should not be the end-points of interpretation, but that overt sexual organs should also be considered as symbolizers:

> The sexual language of dreams is not always to be interpreted in a concretistic way—that it is, in fact an archaic language which naturally uses all the analogies readiest to hand without their necessarily coinciding with a real sexual content. It is therefore unjustifiable to take the sexual language of dreams literally under all circumstances, while other contents are explained as symbolical. But as soon as you take the sexual metaphors as symbols for something unknown, your conception of the nature of dreams at once deepens [pp. 49–50].

Erich Fromm (1951) cautioned us against cultural myopia and urged us to consider the context of the dreamer's life before assuming we understood his symbols. He noted that many people could agree that the sun symbolized mother, even life itself. But to the dweller in the Sahara desert, it might well symbolize thirst, evil, even death. So-called standard sexual symbols can also shift in cultures depending on the particular value system. In an ironic twist on Freudianism, for the Jivaro tribe of South America an erect penis in a dream is thought to stand for a snake, since for the Jivaro the subject matter of ultimate importance is hunting (Gregor, 1981). Theoretically, then, it follows that a penis could also symbolize a cigar, although I have not yet heard of such a dream.

The principle that sexuality in dreams may symbolize something nonsexual and vice versa was known to the scholars of the Talmud. According to the Talmud, if a man dreams of having sexual relations with his mother, it is seen as an indication that he will be rational; if he sleeps with his sister in a dream, he will be wise. But if he dreams of pouring oil on an olive tree, it was interpreted to indicate incestuous wishes (Berakhoth, 9:56b): "He who in a dream waters an olive tree with olive oil dreams of incest." Similarly, a man came to Rabbi Ishmael and said: "I dreamed that one of my eyes kissed the other eye." The Rabbi replied: "You should be dead; you slept with your sister." The implication is that incest is symbolized by the mingling of similar organic products.

EVERY SYMBOL IS ALSO ITSELF

Freud also was not averse to considering the symbol as itself, when he supposedly said, upon lighting a cigar, "Gentlemen, this may be the symbol of penis, but let us remember that it is also a cigar." This is often taken as an incident in which Freud was resistant to psychoanalytic interpretation applied to himself. But his statement has a much more profound implication—namely, that every object, no matter what it symbolizes, is also itself.

This may seem like a truism, unnecessary to state, but in the clinical practice of dream interpretation, it is often not given enough importance. Because of Freud's division of manifest and latent content, psychoanalysts have tended to feel that the symbol is less important than the symbolized. The approach that I have been proposing in this book is that they are of equal importance and interrelated. The meaning of a symbol should be considered in tandem with the specific features of the symbol itself.

Thus, when a person dreams of snakes, it is not enough to translate snake into penis. Why did the person dream of snakes rather than penises? The usual idea is that the sexual meaning is taboo, and therefore symbolism is required to disguise the "true" sexual meaning. But even in our modern times, when some people seem quite at ease in discussing penises and vaginas at social events, people still dream of snakes and spears and rooms and purses. It is an error to jump to the sexual symbol without considering the significance of the dream element for the dreamer. Does the person think of snakes, for example, as dangerous? Venomous? Sneaky? Slimy? Fast and treacherous? Something to be charmed? The source of beautiful leather?

Symbol interpretation requires the application of selective attention and then its renunciation. For example, to make the connection between the female genitals and its symbols, we have to focus on a particular dimension. Taking the topological point of view, we focus on the question of internal space. Anything with an internal space can symbolize the womb. But having thus achieved symbolization, we are left with the choice of symbol—why a room and not a purse? With enough attention, we start to notice other aspects of the symbol. A purse has internal space, but it also is meant to hold certain kinds of things and not others. It tends to be dry inside (unlike the female genitalia); it tends to hold money; it is portable; and so on. A room, like a purse, has internal space. But it also is larger; it has residential properties; it is not portable; and so on. So when we think of these two symbols of the female genitalia, we see broad differences in their implications about the genitalia—to what degree is it capacious, portable, moist or dry, easily opened or closed, simply constructed or elaborately constructed, related to money or shelter, and so on. *Symbols, then, are condensations of the symbol with the symbolized.* After we attend to the symbolized, we must reintegrate it with the properties of the symbol itself.

Very often, first dreams in treatment foretell the main themes, emotional concerns, and significant early memories that will emerge in the therapy (Caligor and May, 1968). Whatever happens to the patient in the dream may be either a fear or a wish of what might happen to the patient. The patient who dreamt of having her scalp pulled off was afraid of damage being done to her, although it may also have been a wish to have her defenses penetrated. But even if the dream is interpreted metaphorically and symbolically, one must not lose sight of the specificity of the symbol. This woman was afraid, but she also was referring in the dream to actual physical attacks to her head.

Similarly, consider the man whose first dream in analysis was that he needed surgery. It is easy to see surgery as a metaphor for psychoanalytic treatment: the patient is opened up, changes are made inside, and the hope is that he will function better after the treatment. But even as one considers such an interpretation, one has to wonder, Why has the dreamer chosen surgery? What is the experience of the dreamer with actual surgery? Is there a trauma associated with previous surgery? In this way, surgery is seen as symbolic of psychoanalytic treatment, and simultaneously, surgery represents itself. Surgery is psychoanalysis; surgery is surgery. Dream interpretation requires an analysis of both.

These two approaches to symbolism relate to Jung's distinction between the "causal" and the "final" approach to symbolism. The terms are a bit confusing, but the distinction is nevertheless an important one. The causal approach asks, "What does this symbol stand for?" The final approach asks, "Even if we are correct about what the symbol stands for, why did the dreamer pick this particular symbol and not another?" When dreams are analyzed, the analyst and the dreamer may be so delighted at answering the first question that they ignore the second.

One of my favorite examples of a multiple approach to dream symbolism that includes both the causal and the final approaches occurs in French and Fromm (1964). They analyze the following dream fragment, taken from an analysis conducted by Dr. David Hamburg:

> (He remembers only a fragment of a dream from a few nights ago:) Mixing cement.
>
> (Immediately on awakening, he felt as though he really knew exactly how to mix it, but really he does not.)
>
> (Only spontaneous association: recent tuckpointing. The patient was going to do it himself, but did not know how to mix concrete, so he hired somebody) [p. 42].

French and Fromm assume that "tuckpointing a house" is part of the forgotten dream, derived from the patient's association. They ask, "What is a house a symbol for?" They first give homage to the Freudian formula, that a house is a woman. But then they deduce from other material that the house stands for the patient's family, and that tuckpointing the house represents his attempt to hold his family together and make it better. Still later, in reference to another dream, they consider that a house may also represent the patient himself, in which case tuckpointing it would also represent trying to make his personality hold together better.

All of this, so far, is consideration of the house symbol from the causal standpoint. The house stands for the patient's family, but also himself, and perhaps, too, a woman. But then they turn to the final approach (although they do not use this term nor do they acknowledge Jung's contribution): "We have concluded that the patient was preoccupied with the problem of how to hold his family together. If so, we can now reverse the question. Why did he choose tuckpointing and mixing cement as symbols for trying to restore harmony to his family?" [p. 63].

Their answer revolves around examining the difference between the symbol and what is symbolized. Families are animate; houses are not. They thus see one function of the symbol as defensive. The patient resorts to the defense that they call "deanimation." By making the subject inanimate, he protects himself from many feelings toward the people involved and is able to focus more dispassionately on a task of improvement. He has thus taken the complex problem he is addressing in the analysis, of dealing with the members of his family, and restructured it into a more straightforward, workmanlike task. They see this as a strategy of the patient's ego to make his problem more manageable, so that he can continue to work on it without becoming discouraged.

A rose is a rose is a rose, and sometimes a bowel movement is a bowel movement. A woman in psychoanalysis dreamt:

"I'm in a public rest room, in a stall. It's a typical stall, with metal walls. I have to have a bowel movement. The toilet seat is so dirty, I can't sit down on it. I'm trying to find some position to have a bowel movement and not sit down on the toilet seat. I am really stressed out. I keep saying to myself, 'Just find another bathroom.' I'm holding onto the walls, trying to suspend myself over the toilet. I wake up."

Before reporting the dream to me, she had told this dream to a woman she worked with, who had interpreted that the bowel movement was something bad that she felt that she wanted to get out. Thus in the dream, she is trying to get rid of all "this shit I carry around with me," but she is trying to do it all alone and she doesn't succeed. The patient was finding it very difficult to tell me of the intensely painful feelings she was having and was considering changing analysts ("Just find another bathroom"). Her association to the dream right after telling it to me, that "I would have been able to if the dream had gone on longer," shows her confidence that she and I will be able to "work this out." And indeed, the dream helped her stay in treatment and work out the transference, rather than fleeing from it.

I felt that it was valid to interpret the shit as bad feelings that she cannot express in the transference, and which she has been discouraged from expressing in her family of origin and in her current family. But I also asked her if the events in the dream had ever happened to her. She could not remember. She had just recently moved into a new house, in which several of the bathrooms were broken. She then told me that for the last year, she has had periodic stomach trouble, in which she awakens early in the morning and has several painful bowel movements in a row. I asked when her last physical check-up had been. It had been before this symptom appeared. Then she added, "But it's probably nothing. I expect if I went to a doctor right now, I probably wouldn't even mention it [as she had not done with me]." The patient tended to deal with medical doctors transferentially, as people who don't want to be bothered with your complaints. The symbolic meaning of the dream, that she has some bad feelings to get out, was obvious to her before the dream. But she is also struggling alone with an actual bowel problem in the dream, as she is doing in real life. I noted that one message of the dream might be to rule out a medical problem and that she ought to mention the painful diarrhea to her physician.

CAN EMOTIONS BE SYMBOLIZED?

Dreams are characterized by their emotionality. Yet for some dreamers, emotions are not experienced, but rather they are symbolized. Freud changed his mind several times about whether emotions are ever changed in a dream. Sometimes he argued that emotions represent themselves, and the dreamwork leaves them intact. For example, Freud (1900) writes: "It will be noticed that the affect felt in the dream belongs to the latent content and not to its manifest content, and the dream's affective content has remained untouched by the distortion which has overtaken its ideational content." (p. 248; see also p. 323).

At other times (e.g., p. 467; see also Ferenczi, 1916), he raised the question of whether emotions could be transformed by the dreamwork. He felt it more likely that sometimes the dreamwork hides emotions. I would like to amplify that theory, and note that sometimes the emotions are suppressed experientially in the dream but are nevertheless symbolized in the manifest content.

For example, one of my patients was a woman who was very successful in her career. She had been raised in a very traditional manner. Her mother was a housewife, and her father seemed to enjoy being the main financial support and the clear leader in a patriarchal family. My patient did not consciously experience guilt about her success. But she kept having dreams in which she was punished. Her first such dream went as follows: "I was being prepared for execution. I was wearing an orange jumpsuit, like the one worn by the Unabomber.[3] There were people I know around. My husband was helping prepare me to be electrocuted. I was thinking about how embarrassing it would be to lose control of bladder and bowels in the chair."

She felt no conscious guilt, but the figure of the Unabomber allowed her to symbolize and condense guilt and a psychopathic denial of it; the dreamer felt that the Unabomber was definitely guilty of premeditated murder, although she noted that he did not feel guilty. In this way, she opened up a discussion of the standards of society as prescribed by her parents and how she felt about deviating from them. She noted that in the dream, she was worried about looking right, not losing control of her bodily functions, when she was being killed. She connected this to a diversion of her main emotions by a concern for looking right, which she eventually shifted in a way that seemed more attentive to her most serious emotions.

---

3. The Unabomber was a man who had sent letter bombs to various people around the United States, killing or seriously maiming them. He had been recently found and received much attention in the news.

CHAPTER 15

KLEINIAN POSITIONS AND DREAMS

> O God, I could be bounded in a nut-shell
> and count myself a king of infinite space,
> were it not that I have bad dreams.
>
> Hamlet

MELANIE KLEIN, one of the first psychoanalysts to develop the theory of object relations, worked out a series of psychological "positions" which have emerged as some of the most important and clinically useful psychoanalytic concepts. The Kleinian positions, however, have not to my knowledge been systematically applied to the understanding of dreams. I would like here to identify and discuss this very important vector for looking at dreams. The vector of Kleinian positions addresses the basic question: How does the dreamer experience himself in relation to the physical and interpersonal world?

Melanie Klein (1946, 1952) originally described two positions, the paranoid-schizoid and the depressive positions. Thomas Ogden (1989) revised Klein's psychology and added a third position, the autistic-contiguous position. Together, the three Kleinian positions form a series of dimensions along which one can experience oneself in relation to the world. They describe fundamental aspects of our relatedness to things and to people. This includes our relations to people as things and things as people, in all human functioning, not just psychosis per se.

In the paranoid-schizoid position, one feels oneself to be the focus of the universe, with other people as extensions of oneself or else as threats to the self. One feels no guilt, because all aggression makes one the victim. In the depressive position, other people are recognized as individuals in their own right, who can suffer from our own aggression. Therefore, we may feel guilt toward them, and try to make reparations to them if we have harmed them. In this light, the depressive position is seen as an achievement that is beyond the paranoid-schizoid position.[1]

Klein originally used the terms "paranoid-schizoid" and "depressive" about *intrapsychic* relations with internal objects. Ogden did something very interesting—he took Klein's metapsychology and put it in more interpersonal terms. In fact, by his account, the two original Kleinian positions *are* interpersonal, hence the need for an autistic-contiguous position, which is more exclusively intrapersonal. It deals with the questions: Can my body and self hold together? What is inside? What is outside? The paranoid-schizoid and depressive positions, as revised by Ogden, address the questions: What are the dangers to my body from others, and from my body to others? Do I use people? Do I care about them? Does everything they do matter primarily for how it affects me? Do they have an existence separate from me? Do I care what anyone else's experience is like for their own sake?

The original Kleinian positions have often been placed in a developmental hierarchy, where the paranoid-schizoid position is seen as more primitive than the depressive. Ogden made the Kleinian positions more complex. He argued that they are all stances in relation to the world, all in equipoise, balanced one against the other. An excess of any of the positions can lead to pathology. Thus, too much experience in the autistic-contiguous position leads to excessive bodily concerns, perhaps as hypochondria. Too much experience in the paranoid-schizoid position leads to excess self-involvement and the sadistic treatment of others as extensions of the self. Finally, too much experience in the depressive position can lead to excessive selflessness and masochistic suffering.

The autistic-contiguous position is an important dimension of much twentieth-century art. Consider Francis Bacon, who paints humans with varying gradations of their insides exposed. Bacon highlights the "meatness" of the human body. Some of his portrayals of the human figure look like carcasses. Inside is partly outside, and the distinction between

---

1. Jessica Benjamin (1988) deals with the shift from paranoid-schizoid to depressive. She highlights the importance, in a child's development, of recognizing the mother as an independent being with her own subjectivity, feelings, and private experience. This is one of the milestones of the development of the depressive position. Benjamin's views were an important correction to much previous psychological theory that saw the mother primarily as a need-provider to the child, rather than in the stance of an independent subject.

the human body and the inanimate world is blurred. Flesh is not just adjacent to the chair it sits on; it merges with it. In Bacon's triptych, "Scenes from a Crucifixion," the three panels show varying states of human flesh. The left panel is human, more or less, and the right panel is a butchered body; the middle panel shows an intermediate state between live organism and dead flesh.

Twentieth-century filmmakers also featured the autistic-contiguous position and its anxieties as a primary theme. The works of Jan Svankmajer,[2] the great Czech filmmaker, portray similar issues, often using the technique of claymation. The body, once whole, is dismembered, attacked, reassembled. Body parts that have been riven, one from the other, try to find each other. They struggle to regain their interconnection, their proper use, their existence within a bodily gestalt rather than as mere parts.

The works of Bacon and Svankmajer, along with those of many other artists (e.g., de Kooning, Picasso) could be derived from dreams. They are like dreams in which a frightening subjective reality is portrayed. They make the boundary between our bodies and a carcass of meat seem fragile indeed. All of us could be butchered and turned into a carcass. What makes us human, what makes us a self, what differentiates us from a mere collection of bodily organs, what makes us different from the inanimate world, what differentiates us from other people—all these issues are described by the Kleinian positions, and are portrayed in dreams.

If we apply the vector of the three Kleinian positions to dreams, we raise many questions:

How do I experience myself as a physical body in a physical world (the autistic-contiguous position)? Am I a separate physical entity, with boundaries between myself and the rest of the physical objects in the world? What is the physical world of objects like? Is it full of hard, straight surfaces that I can lean on and which will support me? Is it a world of soft, liquid, changing features that is enveloping, protective, or engulfing?

How do I experience myself as a person among other persons? Are all people significant primarily for how they affect me (the paranoid-schizoid position)? Are other people important as separate experiencers, on whom I have an impact (the depressive position)?

There is much to be learned from analyzing dreams according to the Kleinian positions. There are two basic approaches. We can ask:

---

2. See, for example, Svankmajer's *Scenes from the Surreal* and *Faust*.

(1) Which Kleinian position predominates in the dream? An alternative approach is to ask: (2) What is this dream like from each of the positions?

If we take the first approach, we may ask: What proportion of dreams are primarily focused on the autistic-contiguous position? The paranoid-schizoid? The depressive? My own impression is that very few dreams, at least those I hear from clinical situations, are really in the depressive position. Most are focused primarily within the autistic-contiguous and the paranoid-schizoid. This is another way of saying that our dreams are mainly self-absorbed, with our own bodily concerns and ourselves as centers of the human universe. (We could say, however, that this fact is somewhat iatrogenic; the psychoanalytic tradition of interpreting everyone in a dream as an aspect of the dreamer *forces* the dream into the paranoid-schizoid position.)

Freud's "Irma" dream, however, is at least partly located in the depressive position. Freud examines Irma, and he registers her suffering. She says, "If only you knew what pains I've got now in my throat and stomach and abdomen—it's choking me." And Freud is alarmed and looks at her. "She looked pale and puffy." As the dream progresses and the other doctors join in the examination of Irma, her subjective feeling fades into the background. She becomes a medical "specimen."

Although the manifest Irma dream seems to be in the depressive position, once Freud starts associating to it, his focus becomes more paranoid-schizoid—toward a concern with what Irma's medical status would mean about him—about his standing as a physician, his competence, his ability relative to his colleagues. But as I have already mentioned, subsequent re-analyses of the dream (e.g., Schur, 1972) have revealed that Irma was referred by Freud to Fliess for a nasal operation to treat her hysteria. Fliess left a piece of gauze in the wound, which led to serious postoperative complications. It would seem likely that Freud felt guilt at her suffering. His associations lead away from such depressive concerns, but the manifest dream makes them abundantly clear.

Let us apply the second approach, of examining the Irma dream from each of the Kleinian positions. First, considering the autistic-contiguous position, we would ask: Where is the dream taking place physically? What is the physical world like in this dream? What are the surfaces and spaces of the world like in the dream? Hard or soft? Sharp and dangerous or curved and gradual? Smooth or rough? What is this dreamer's sense of the world like, and what is his sense of his body in relation to the world? Does it fit in smoothly or is there physical conflict?

The dream starts in a large hall with numerous guests. It is a big, relatively public space. But it moves quickly into a much more restricted space. Freud takes Irma to one side, and is soon looking into her mouth and observing a white patch and whitish scabs. We can feel a movement from the public to the private, from the open space of a large hall into a confined, inner cavity of the mouth. If Freud were our patient, we would want to know more about this shift from public to private. Nevertheless, we can speculate, from the autistic-contiguous position, that the dream shows a special concern with the oral cavity.

From the perspective of the autistic-contiguous position, the Irma dream also shows Freud's (or someone's) sense of his physical body in the physical world: there is intrusion, resistance, embarrassment, false body parts, and disease.

From the paranoid-schizoid position, there is the supposedly helpful doctor who sees in the patient a threat to his self-esteem. Is the doctor concerned for the patient or for himself? Is he more taken up with the needs of the patient, or of his competitive feelings and his need to maintain his status?

From the perspective of the depressive position, the dream has separate people who express subjective states. Irma's reply about her suffering enlists the depressive position. I am suffering, you don't realize how much, do you care? Who comes first, you or I? Do you appreciate my whole person-ness, do you appreciate my suffering, my embarrassment, and so on? As I noted above, the manifest dream per se, which starts with such a vivid expression of Irma's suffering, is more in the depressive position than Freud's analysis of it, which focuses primarily on his wish for self-justification before his colleagues.

Using the vector of Kleinian positions, let us examine another dream, the dream of "Martha," from Fosshage and Loew's (1987) book, *Dream Interpretation: A Comparative Study*. One of Martha's dreams is a beautiful example of a shift from the paranoid-schizoid to the depressive position. Martha has a cockroach phobia, and she dreams:

> I was in the bathtub and a cockroach was there. It was half dead. It got on my leg. I didn't panic. I got out. It crawled onto the wall near my bed. A girl was there and she went over to kill it, but it was too big and wouldn't quit. I took a can of spray and gave it one long spray. As I sprayed, it got bigger, turned into a chicken, then into a dog. I stopped spraying since I didn't want to kill a dog. It had some human characteristics, too. It asked to leave. I opened the door and apologized for spraying [p. 12].

The dream starts deep in the paranoid-schizoid position. The dreamer sees the cockroach as an enemy, a disgusting intruder. But as she tries to kill it, it becomes transformed into more evolved species, finally turning into a dog with some human characteristics. As it evolves, so too does the dreamer's feeling toward it. She comes to feel concern for it, even guilt, a prerequisite of the depressive position, according to Klein. She takes care of it by opening the door and even apologizes; reparation is another hallmark of the depressive position, according to Klein.

The dream can be seen as the evolution of the patient's feelings towards the people in her world—her mother, whom she perceives as intrusive and unpleasant at the beginning of treatment; her father, whom she considers disgusting; the analyst; herself; and perhaps others. Her paranoid-schizoid position defines her attitude to nearly everyone.

The dream is a milestone in her treatment. It marks a transition for her into accepting other people as humans toward whom she has concern, care, and guilt.

THE DREAM SCREEN AND THE AUTISTIC-CONTIGUOUS POSITION

Bertram Lewin (1973), with his notion of the "dream screen," focused particularly well on what I would call the aspect of dreams having to do with the autistic-contiguous position. Thinking of the dream as a film, Lewin focused attention on the background setting of the dream, and related that background to early, sensual experiences of the dreamer.[3] Lewin drew our attention particularly to the transformation of early bodily experience into dream images. Because those early experiences are prelinguistic, they are best remembered in the nonlinguistic format of dreams. Isakower, in his 1938 paper on the pathopsychology of falling asleep, had already identified such experiences in the imagery we have when we are falling asleep, which he thought was related to the image of the breast.

Lewin suggested an added vector of looking at dreams: What is the textural experience of the perceived dream? A dream may be just a static image, as opposed to a moving, changing scenario. Is the dream a story with words? Is it just a feeling? The dream screen may revive

3. An even earlier discussion of dreams as a filmlike dramatization can be found in Ella Freeman Sharpe's book *Dream Analysis* (1937, 58ff.).

early experiences of body and feeling states that we could not remember any other way.

In my view, Lewin's idea was a good one and can be understood in terms of the autistic-contiguous position. However, Lewin's work needs to be expanded. The analogy of dreams with film is a common one, yet I think it is somewhat inaccurate. We rarely dream in two dimensions. Although our dreams are often primarily visual, they occur in three-dimensional space. If they are films, they are IMAX films or what Aldous Huxley called "feelies" in his book *Brave New World*. In our dreams we usually feel in the midst of the imagery, we experience the space kinesthetically as well as visually, and our emotions are usually prominent.

THE NEGATIVE DREAM SCREEN

I have observed a rare version of the dream screen, which I call the "negative dream screen," that especially captures the immediacy of early traumatic experience and its subsequent elaboration in the Kleinian positions. A patient dreamt that he was holding his nephew: "He wasn't a person. He was a circle with a hole in the middle. A dangerous, devouring circle. The more open and open this hole, the more I was afraid it would get me. Someone said, 'You can't drop your nephew like that.' It was devouring and unpleasant."

The dreamer had nearly starved during the first two weeks of his life. This left an "imprinting" of potential starvation that felt to him like an immediate and constant danger during his adult life. He illustrated well what Winnicott wrote (1988):

> Chaos first arrives in the history of the emotional development of the individual through reactive interruptions of being, especially when such interruptions last too long. Chaos is at first a broken line of being . . . if the disturbance is beyond a degree that is tolerable . . . then . . . chaos enters into the individual's constitution.

Chaos had indeed entered this man's constitution. He experienced many aspects of the psychoanalytic relationship as putting him on the brink of destruction. Any break in the regular scheduling of daily sessions felt life threatening to him. It did not threaten him only with hunger; it threatened annihilation. He could be turned into that hole portrayed in his dream that opened wider and wider until it became nothing—a powerful image of hunger ("open your mouth wide") turning into a self-destructive nothingness.

For this man, existence could turn into emptiness and nothingness, which was tersely portrayed by the blunt imagery of the dream. If one examines almost any dream from the perspective of Kleinian positions, one can grasp how the dreamer experiences the physical and social world. And if the clinical work is effective, this basic patterning of experience can shift.

CHAPTER 16

THE PATIENT'S DREAMS AND THE COUNTER-TRANSFERENCE

The Mind is so near itself—it cannot see, distinctly—and I have none to ask—

Emily Dickinson

WHEN FREUD WROTE that dreams are the royal road to the unconscious, he meant the unconscious of the dreamer. They are indeed that, but in clinical psychoanalysis the dreams of the patient may provide a road to the unconscious of the analyst, too—a road perhaps less royal than rocky and perilous. In this chapter, we will consider how the analyst may use the dreams of the patient to better understand his own unconscious, as activated in the psychoanalytic relationship, with the hope that as the analyst becomes clearer about the contributions of his own unconscious countertransference, counterresistance, and counter-anxiety, he may be better able to help the patient with his transference, resistance, and anxiety. In short, we will consider how an analyst may use his patient's dreams as supervision.

The idea that patients may consciously or unconsciously supervise the analyst is not a new one. Langs (1978) outlined many ways that the patient may unconsciously communicate to the analyst that there are violations of the frame of psychoanalysis. Casement (1991) has expanded Langs' work and has shown how the analyst can continually adjust his approach by carefully learning from the patient what the patient needs, without recourse to Langs' fixed and arbitrary vision of psychoanalytic conduct. Probably the most daring innovator in this area was Ferenczi (1988), whose research into mutual analysis in the 1930s, only recently published, allowed the patient access to the analyst's associations in the interest of removing countertransference blocks and thereby helping the patient.

Ferenczi was a pioneer in exploring the potential of a patient's dreams to clarify the countertransference. His experiments with mutual analysis included the understanding of his patient's dreams in terms of both the transference and countertransference. He wrote in his diary on January 19, 1932: "R.N.'s dream. Former patient Dr. Gx. forces her withered breast into R.N.'s mouth. 'It isn't what I need; too big, empty—no milk.' The patient feels that this dream fragment is a combination of the unconscious contents of the psyches of the analysand and the analyst" (Ferenczi, 1932, p. 13). Ferenczi connected her dream to an episode from his own infancy, which he recalled for the first time with emotion, and which freed him to be more empathic with the patient's traumatic history.

The idea of dreams as supervision implies a theoretical postulate—namely, that dreams are not just a reflection of intrapsychic process, but can instead be used by the dreamer for interpersonal communication. This was not Freud's view. In *The Interpretation of Dreams* he wrote: "The productions of the dreamwork, which, it must be remembered, are not made with the intention of being understood, present no greater difficulties to their translators than do the ancient hieroglyphic scripts to those who seek to read them" (p. 341). In 1933, Freud returned to this question: "dreams are not in themselves social utterances, not a means of giving information" (p. 9). Freud conceived of the dreamwork as a disguiser, as a flawed attempt at hiding the dream's meaning from the analyst and patient, which the analyst, through his skill, triumphs over. Ferenczi took a different approach; he may have been one of the first psychoanalysts to view some dreams as communications by one person of his views about another person. In 1913 he stated, "one feels impelled to relate one's dreams to the very person to whom the content relates" (p. 349).

Today, many analysts see the intention of dreams as ambivalent. Dreams can function as both disguisers and communicators, especially those dreams that are told to another person. We know from experimental dream studies that many more dreams are dreamt than are remembered (Aserinsky and Kleitman, 1953); most of us know from personal experience, too, that more dreams are remembered than are told to someone. Thus, when a dream is remembered and told, there may be an intent not to hide, but to communicate something. That which is expressed may be some aspect of the patient's personality, but it may also be a communication to the analyst about his or her personality, at least as perceived by the patient, that for any number of reasons cannot be expressed overtly by the patient. It may also be a plea for a change in the analyst, or in the relatedness between patient and analyst.

In chapter 19, I will discuss a subset of such dreams: those of borderline and schizophrenic patients expressing a simple message to the analyst that cannot be stated by the patient in direct, waking speech. These include communications that are the opposite of the stated words of the patient: one patient, for example, expressed only caution and distrust of the analyst in her waking words, but expressed confidence and a sense of warmth about the analyst's manner in her dream.

To that view of dreams, I would like now to propose an expanded view of dreams as commentaries on the analyst's personality and functioning that either cannot be said by the patient, or if they can, are not being heard by the analyst. Dreams, when communicated by a patient to the analyst, can be a form of unconscious supervision. This function of dreams is not meant to supplant the more usual considerations of dream functions in psychoanalysis—as expressions of wishes, as expressions of childhood traumas, as expressions of psychic conflict, as a kind of play space, as expressive of the transference, as indices of bodily and psychic states, etc. These functions of the dream are well documented and discussed in the psychoanalytic literature. Nevertheless, dreams can also function as a kind of supervision of the analyst—as a commentary on the analyst's countertransference, or the flaws of his approach in treating the particular patient, or the expression of appreciation for an analytic intervention, even one that, in waking life, the patient has met with protest and resistance. These are only some of the aims that the patient's dream supervision can have.

Kanzer (1955), in his seminal paper on the communicative function of the dream, describes a number of ways that the dream can be used by the analyst as supervision. He discusses how the patient's dream may communicate not only the patient's dynamics, but also the possible countertransference interferences of the analyst. For example, a woman dreams: "I am lying on the couch and you are sitting at the other end of the room. I rise up to come to you but find that there is freshly laid concrete between us. This hardens rapidly as I put my feet in it. I am caught in a vise, am terrified and scream" (p. 262). She awakens with an asthma attack. Kanzer sees the dream and the subsequent asthma attack as an attack on herself and the analyst, seeking to have him abandon his neutrality. But he also questions the analyst's own involvement: "whether his own interpretations were 'too freshly laid,' too 'concrete,' and posed the threat of holding her 'in a vise'" (p. 262). This double consideration of the meaning of the dream, as reflecting both the patient's and the analyst's involvement in the analysis, is the first step in the process of interactive dream interpretation that will be further explored in this chapter.

Similarly, another patient described by Kanzer dreams that he is standing behind his brother, who is trying to replace a door that has come off its hinges. He is bungling the job, but the patient decides to say nothing. Kanzer considers how the saying nothing refers to the highly obsessional patient, who talks much and says nothing. But he also considers the dream as an attempted corrective to the analyst, who reacts to the patient's obsessiveness with disapproving silence, while the patient bungles the job.

Dreams can, in this way, be transitional actions. They are actions midway between consciousness and unconsciousness, between repression and deliberate expression. They are communications with an option, to understand or not, for the dreamer and the analyst to whom the dream is told.

Understanding, however, is usually achieved neither quickly nor all at once, but rather, gradually and laboriously. When the dream contains a communication to the analyst about something about the analyst's personality or technique that troubles the patient, and the analyst, for reasons of personal anxiety or conviction, resists hearing this communication, then understanding will be slow, if it occurs at all. Levenson (1983) has shown that, in such cases, there is often an intermediate stage to understanding; the analyst enacts, in his process of dream interpretation, the very dynamic that the dream attempts to communicate. Greenson (1970) describes a superb example in which the dream interpretation process reflects the dream content, and in which the analyst reenacts the dream as he interprets the dream. He describes a case analyzed by Hans Thorner (1957) of a man with examination anxiety who felt he had a "black record," the nature or reality of which seemed unclear to the analyst. The patient reported a dream in which red spiders were crawling in and out of the patient's anus. A doctor examined him and told the patient that he was unable to see anything wrong with him. The patient replied, "Doctor, you may not see anything, but they are there just the same." The analyst interprets:

> Here the patient expresses his conviction that he harbours bad objects (red spiders) and even the doctor's opinion cannot shake this conviction. The associative link between "black record"

> and "red spiders" shows the anal significance of his "black record." He himself is afraid of these objects against which he, like the man in the dream, asks for help. This help must be based on a recognition of these objects and not on their denial—in other words he should be helped to control them. It is clear that we are dealing with a feeling of persecution by bad internal objects [p. 284 ff.].

Greenson (1970) criticizes Thorner's case as an example of interpreting from a theoretical position rather than from the patient's associations. He speculates that the patient's reproach to the physician combines a hostile transference and a possibly justifiable reproach to the analyst, and he wonders whether "the red spiders crawling in and out of the patient's anus are not the patient's reaction to his analyst's intrusive and painful interpretations" (p. 532). It is important to note that if Greenson's view is correct, then Thorner, in his one-sided, overriding interpretation of the dream, is recreating the dream in the session: the patient tells the analyst in the dream that the spiders are there whether he sees them or not, and the analyst, in the session, painfully reiterates his position that they are not.

Such clinical examples may at first seem discouraging. Lest anyone think that Thorner's case material is an unusual example of a countertransference blind spot, we should note that probably in every analysis a similar phenomenon occurs with some frequency. Take any reported dream interpretation, subject it to the scrutiny of several skilled analysts, and they will be able to find any number of countertransference trends portrayed in the patient's dream and reenacted by the analyst as he interprets the dream. But if such processes occur, then what value is knowing that to the analyst? Is there any hope that the analyst can become aware of his unconscious countertransference? Are there any means by which he can become more quickly aware of these developments by himself, and hence help the analysis to progress more productively?

My answer to this question will be in two parts. One will be to identify certain objective characteristics of the dream interpretation process, some common features of the interaction between patient and analyst, which might signal a strong countertransference, counterresistance, and counteranxiety (Wolstein, 1967). This may be called "the objective approach," which has much theoretical interest but certain limitations in clinical application. Although knowing such objective signs may be useful to the psychoanalyst, it is often not possible for the practitioner, in the heat of clinical struggles, to view the therapeutic process with such calm, objective reserve. The clinician may also find that certain blocks or gaps in his perception guard against his perceiving his own countertransference. When that happens, can anything be done? To consider this question, we shall have to switch perspective and take our second approach, the interactional, mutual approach to studying countertransference interference. This view holds that the analyst's blind spots may be portrayed by a patient's dream. The dream interpretation process itself may at first reenact the dream dynamics, so that the analyst will not see his own blind spots. But through a continual, circular, mutual process of revision and re-revision of the interpretation by both patient and analyst, the analyst may come to perceive his countertransference, and, having done so, may make great strides in understanding, clarifying, and resolving the patient's transference.

OBJECTIVE SIGNS

But first let us begin with the objective signs to the analyst, from his work as a dream interpreter, that his countertransference may be interfering with his ability to understand his patient. What follows is by no means an exhaustive list—on the contrary, it is only a tentative beginning, outlining some factors that I have observed in my own work and in reports of dream analyses by other analysts.

1. Breaking one's own rules of dream interpretation

The first sign is, by definition, relativistic. It is the breaking of rules by the analyst that are usual for his technique of dream interpretation. Thus, a procedure that is usual for one analyst may be part of an effective approach to dream interpretation, whereas another analyst, for whom the same procedure is anathema to his technique, may consider his use of such a procedure as a possible sign of countertransference.

Thus, no single procedure is a sign of countertransference for all analysts, but must be considered relative to his usual procedure. We all know that there are many codified formulas of the rules of dream interpretation. Grinstein (1983), Bonime (1962), and Altman (1975), among others, have compiled unified approaches. An analyst may subscribe fully to any one of these systems, although most analysts with experience eventually develop a standard of procedure that is quite personal.

Whatever that standard is, it must form the backdrop against which departures are defined, which can then be considered as possible signs of countertransference. (Of course, it may also be an inspired intervention and an extension of the analyst's repertoire; the interface between creative analysis and countertransference is a complex one. See Meltzer, 1978.)

As an example, I would like to take a special look at one rule with which most Freudian analysts would agree—that is, the rule in interpreting dreams of giving primacy to the patient's associations. Freud repeatedly stressed the importance of this; even in the section on dream symbols in *The Interpretation of Dreams*, while providing many of the common meanings of certain symbols, Freud stressed that the individual's own associations may negate any meaning derived from formulas of symbol translation. Freud would have agreed, in theory, that ignoring the patient's associations, or the analyst's giving primacy to his own associations, is a sure danger signal. Many Freudians and analysts with other outlooks would agree, and if they find themselves overriding a patient's associations with their own, they ought to pause and consider their countertransference.

There are, however, analysts whose standard procedure does not give primacy to the patient's associations. Jung was one example. He felt that working primarily from the patient's associations leads one away from the true meaning of the dream, back to the patient's complexes which could be discerned without the dream. He felt that Freud's stated procedure of relying primarily on the patient's associations led to a reduction of the dream. Jung recommended instead a process that he called "amplification," in which the analyst provides his own associations to the dream. Jung (1944) writes:

> The amplification is always appropriate when dealing with some obscure experience which is so vaguely adumbrated that it must be enlarged and expanded by being set in a psychological context in order to be understood by all. That is why, in analytical psychology, we resort to amplification in the interpretation of dreams, for a dream is too slender a hint to be understood until it is enriched by the stuff of association and analogy and thus amplified to the point of intelligibility [p. 289].

Some Freudians, including, as we shall see below, Freud himself, agree at least in part with Jung. It is a rare analyst who today would never volunteer one of his own associations to a patient's dream.

However, I believe that while this procedure can be extremely productive, it must be done in combination with attention to the patient's associations. Otherwise, it leads to the converse of Jung's criticism of Freud's procedure—it leads to the enactment of the analyst's complexes, at least those stirred by the patient. Moreover, if it is the analyst's usual practice to give primary attention to his patient's associations, then he must consider his not doing so as an objective sign of possible countertransference interference.

2. The Leap into Latent Content

Another signal of countertransference interference is what I call a "leap into the latent content." By this I mean a too ready escape from the manifest material of the dream into an interpretation that seems arbitrarily derived from the manifest content. Especially common methods of leaping into latent content include: (1) a formulaic interpretation of dream symbols without reference to their specific meaning to the patient; (2) the interpretation of the dream through an arbitrary theoretical system of whatever kind; (3) the omission from the dream interpretation of certain sections of the dream; and (4) ignoring the persistent protest by the dreamer that the interpretation makes no sense.

Levenson has been a relentless critic of this sort of dream interpretation. He has often noted how a standardized "depth interpretation," such as of penis envy or oedipal conflict, can allow the analyst to deflect a more immediate reflection in the dream of the specific interaction of analyst and patient. (See, for example, Levenson, 1983, p. 95 ff., 1987, and 1991, passim.)

3. Ignoring the Transference and Countertransference Aspects of the Dream

In the interpretation of most dreams, the analyst should consider how the characters in the dream might refer to the patient and himself. This may include both particular details of each person in the dream as well as the relationship in the dream between people. When the analyst fails to perceive any correspondences between the dream and the analyst-patient dyad, some problematic countertransference may be at work.

There is no limit to the range of features of the analyst that can be included in the patient's dream, and the analyst should always be ready to discover new ones. One of the most common, however, is a reference to the analyst's name. An analyst with many years of experience will have accumulated a large number of references to his name. Yet even the most proficient dream interpreters have missed a few. Ella Sharpe, for example, who was very attuned to such matters, seems not to have noticed the personal reference when a patient dreamt of "sharp cliffs" (1937, p. 103). Greenson, too, in his important paper on interactive dream analysis, did not interpret the "green" raincoats (1970, p. 541).

The analyst can never pick up all references to himself, but when he discovers an omission, he ought to consider the possible dynamics of his oversight. For example, a patient reported a dream to me early in the analysis in which a black prostitute was sitting behind him. Several years later, in referring back to the dream, I discovered that he thought that black was a direct reference to my name through its similarity to the letters Blech, which in any case, some people pronounce "Bleck." He said he thought the connection so obvious that he hadn't mentioned it. I first thought that I had missed it, because of the much more common association of my name to "bleach." But after such rationalization, I reconsidered whether I had resisted the patient's perception of me as a black prostitute.

OBJECTIVE SIGNS OF COUNTERTRANSFERENCE IN A DREAM ANALYSIS BY FREUD

I have identified three "objective" signs of countertransference interference in dream interpretation. I would like now to consider, from this perspective, a dream analysis reported by Freud (1900) in *The Interpretation of Dreams*. It is one of the relatively few examples from that book to report the details of the interaction between the analyst and patient during the analysis of the patient's dream. It is the so-called "Lovely Dream":

> He was driving with a large party to X Street, in which there was an unpretentious inn. (This is not the case.) There was a play being acted inside it. At one moment he was audience, at another actor. When it was over, they had to change their clothes so as to get back to town. Some of the company were shown into rooms on the ground floor and others into rooms on the first floor. Then a dispute broke out. The ones up above were angry because the ones down below were not ready, and they

> could not come downstairs. His brother was up above and he was down below and he was angry with his brother because they were so much pressed. (This part was obscure.) Moreover, it had been decided and arranged even when they first arrived who was to be up above and who was to be down below. Then he was walking by himself up the rise made by X Street in the direction of town. He walked with such difficulty and so laboriously that he seemed glued to the spot. An elderly gentleman came up to him and began abusing the King of Italy. At the top of the rise he was able to walk much more easily.
>
> His difficulty in walking up the rise was so distinct that after waking up he was for some time in doubt whether it was a dream or reality.
>
> We should not think very highly of this dream, judging by its manifest content. In defiance of the rules, I shall begin its interpretation with the portion which the dreamer described as being the most distinct [p. 285].

It is noteworthy how Freud comments on this dream. His first sentence is somewhat deprecatory: "We should not think very highly of this dream." This is an unusual association of the analyst; generally, we do not evaluate a patient's dreams, nor is it obvious what is less valuable about this dream. However, the fact that Freud does not think too highly of it can be connected with the high and the low levels of the dream. That he starts the dream analysis with his own evaluation of the dream is a sign that some sort of countertransference, perhaps competitive and evaluative, may be at work, and that observations of this countertransference and its interactions with the patient's personality may be part of the latent content of the patient's dream.

Freud then associates the climb that starts with difficulty and ends easily to the introduction to Daudet's *Sappho*, describing a young man who carries his mistress upstairs in his arms, at first with ease, but then with difficulty. This is the opposite of the situation in the dream, but the patient finds that it fits some of the day residue, a play he had seen the night before.

We may note here another aspect of Freud's first comments on the dream: "In defiance of the rules . . ." In this dream interpretation Freud breaks a number of his own rules, including the rule of following primarily the patient's associations. Instead, he starts the interpretation with his own association to Daudet's *Sappho*. While the patient finds this relevant to the day residue, Freud seems involved with his own association to the detriment of his attention to the patient's. The patient's association is to lines from Uhland: "I was lately a guest at an inn with a most gentle host;" And then to Goethe's *Faust*:

Faust (dancing with the young witch):

> A lovely dream once came to me,
> And I beheld an apple-tree,
> On which two lovely apples shone;
> They charmed me so, I climbed thereon.
>
> The Lovely Witch:
>
> Apples have been desired by you,
> Since first in Paradise they grew;
> And I am moved with joy to know
> That such within my garden grow.

To grasp fully the transference significance of this association, we must examine the last two lines in the original German:

> Von Freuden fühl'ich mich bewegt,
> Dass auch mein Garten solche trägt.

The speaker is moved with joy, with "Freuden," which seems a clear reference to his analyst's name. In other contexts, Freud was aware of this typical play on his name, yet here he overlooks it (see Freud, 1900, p. 207, n. 2). One can speculate that the patient feels joy (Freuden) in his analysis—that there is a strong positive transference.

Freud does not interpret the dream within the transference[1]; yet several factors in the manifest content suggest that the dream refers to the experience of analysis. At one moment the dreamer is the audience; at another, he is an actor, suggesting the dual roles of an analysand. Secondly, the obscure part of the patient's dream, which Freud (1900) stated is usually of greater importance, is his anger with his "brother" who is up above, while he is down below. Moreover, it had been decided and arranged even when they first arrived (i.e., even when the analysis

---

1. Bass (1995) has commented that in 1900, Freud had not yet developed the notion of the transference, so that he can hardly be expected to have interpreted this dream within the transference. In 1914, however, when Freud had published a good deal about transference, he still tended not to attend to it in interpreting dreams. The now famous dream of the Wolf-Man is a good example.

was started) who was to be up above and who was to be down below—the initial contract between analyst and patient. That this is part of the transference-countertransference interaction is signaled by the dream interpretation interaction: the subservience of the patient's associations to Freud's. We can see from this dream, by the way, that the questions of asymmetry and mutuality, which received much attention in the 1990s (Blechner, 1992; Burke, 1992), have been ongoing since the beginning of psychoanalysis. Although Freud was alarmed by Ferenczi's experiments in technique, the problems addressed by Ferenczi seem to have been relevant to Freud's own clinical work.

There is something important about how the analysis of this patient started. This is probably within Freud's conscious or unconscious awareness; his association is to the beginning of *Sappho*, in which a man carries a lady he has just met up several flights of stairs. At first, she seems light and he is full of energy. By the last flight, she seems an intolerably heavy burden. One point of this passage is that the drama of an entire relationship can be foretold by a very early interaction between two people. This is often true in psychoanalysis. The course of the entire analysis is often adumbrated by the first session, the first dream, even by the first contact before the first session.

In the second part of the dream, the dreamer comes across an elderly gentleman, and after their encounter, he is able to walk more easily. (Who would not welcome such an outcome of analytic treatment?) Yet some powerful countertransference is at work, so much so, that later Freud speaks of his own association to *Sappho* as if it were the patient's: "The wet-nurse, as well as Daudet's *Sappho*, seem to have been allusions to the mistress whom the patient had recently dropped" (p. 287).

What is the source and nature of Freud's countertransference? We can only speculate. When Freud concludes that the dream alludes to the patient's wet-nurse, we may wonder whether the intensity of the maternal positive transference is interfering with Freud's acknowledging his own representation in the dream. Many years later, Freud (1931, pp. 226–227) described his difficulties with preoedipal transferences, which he thought might be better handled by female analysts than male analysts, an issue that has been examined further by Lasky (1989).

The exact nature of the transference and countertransference must remain a subject of speculation. It ought not, in any case, deter us from our main concern, which is to study how the process of dream interpretation reenacts the dream themes and to discover if there are any techniques by which the analyst can deepen his understanding of the patient's dream and his own countertransference involvement as reflected in both the manifest dream and the subsequent interaction during the dream interpretation.

Freud's analysis of the "Lovely Dream" contains at least two of the objective signs of countertransference interference that we have identified: he breaks his own rules and he ignores overt references to himself and to the analysis. Freud even goes so far as to consider that his own association of Sappho is the "prototype in the dream-thoughts" of the patient. This seems like an overvaluation of his own associations. While it is true that the analyst often can derive the most inspired interpretations from the way his own associations resonate with the patient's material, such inspiration often teeters on the edge of counterresistance and requires extra caution.

RECIPROCAL PROCESSES OF DREAM INTERPRETATION

While the objective signs we have identified may be useful for signaling countertransference intrusion, they must be taken with measured skepticism. For example, while it is a danger signal if one ignores references to the transference, it is also possible to overattend to the transference implications of a dream. Khan (Curtis and Sachs, 1976) takes this position, asserting that since "analysts are addicted to being objects for their patients, it follows that they may not allow themselves to become non-objects, an essential requirement if patients are to experience themselves" (p. 349). In other words, there is danger in too much transference interpretation, in what we might call "hypertransference" approaches, where the focus on the references to the analyst can squeeze out any other possibilities.[2]

How can the analyst know when she is too focused on transference interpretation or not focused enough? There is no sure way; one must simply continue to listen to subsequent dreams and other material for constant correction of one's analytic course. The likelihood is that, in the first attempts at interpretation, the analyst and patient will replay the problematic process described in the dream. Levenson (1991) cites many cases in which a patient's dream portrays a dramatic situation which is paralleled by the interaction with the therapist; often, the analytic task, as outlined by Levenson, is to explore the parallel of the dream and the clinical interaction, and then for the analyst to consider how

2. A similar debate occurred in the 1920s, when Rank argued that the Wolf-Man's dream, which Freud had interpreted in terms of infantile sexuality, also referred to the transference and the real details of Freud's office.

he can extract himself from the neurotic interaction, leading the patient to find a new way of dealing with his world. In this chapter, I would like to expand on this area of study. Some of the best examples of the parallels between dream material and subsequent enactments in the dream interpretation process have been identified by analysts examining the dreams of other analysts. It is surely easier to identify the countertransference and counterresistance of other analysts than one's own. While such "Monday-morning quarterbacking" of other analysts' work is interesting theoretically, it may lead one to the question, "Are there ways the analyst and patient can articulate the countertransference and counterresistance illustrated by the dream without the help of an outsider?"

Joseph (1985), like Levenson, discusses "the way in which a dream can reveal its meaning in a fairly precise way by being lived out in the session" (p. 451). This is one of the reasons that attention to a single dream and its implications for the analysis should not be confined to the session in which it is presented. Rather, it is only through the continuous reciprocal, interactive interpretation that its meaning will become clear. The analyst will likely see the transference implications of the dream more clearly; the countertransference implications will be less within his awareness, so that he may at first reenact them rather than see them. But then, gradually, he can get insight into the countertransference implications. This can occur either through his self-analysis and continued attention to the patient's associations, or through the patient's becoming more bold and spelling out his view of the countertransference more explicitly, or through some other mutual process. A breakthrough is more likely to occur if there are continual revisions of the interpretation by both patient and analyst.

For example, a young woman undertook psychoanalysis because of a troubling involvement in sexual masochism. One year into the analysis, she had the following dream:

> The dream doesn't really take place in my parents' apartment. There is a bookcase there in what used to be my bedroom. What next occurs is a realization that the book that perfectly captures the situation is *As You Like It.* Then we are in the dining area. Both my father and I end up sitting at the dining room table, which is oval. I sit at my father's place. My father is in my mother's place. My father also had the same thought, that *Macbeth* accurately reflects the situation. I think he must think of the correct play himself. He then says: "It's not *Macbeth*, it's *As You Like It*." Then, in the dream, I told you the dream.

She associated the dream to James Thurber's story, "The Macbeth Murder Mystery," which is hilarious and makes "Who committed the murder?" the central question.

The patient was extremely intelligent and witty, but used intellectual games as a defense. The form of her participation in the dream interpretation was much as in the content of the dream itself. In the first session after she had the dream, she told me, "I had a strange dream, and in the dream, I told you the dream. But now, I am not ready to tell it to you." In the next session, she made reference to the content of the dream: "Well, of course, it was about incest, as I told you." Actually, she had not told me (at least not according to my memory), although she had done so in the dream. On the one hand, this shows one function of the dream telling within the dream—it allows a persistent avoidance of actually telling the dream. But it also indicates the parallel between the dreamtext and the process of dream analysis. Just as in the dream, where she expects or hopes that her father will realize what she is thinking without her having to say it, so too does she expect or hope that her analyst will know the content of her dream without her having to say it. This had been a continual event in the analysis. The patient had actually stopped working with a prior therapist when she had concealed some very important information and that therapist had failed to notice it. The patient claimed that she had continued working with me because she had not been able to fool me. (Of course, in telling me this, she did not tell me how she had tried to fool me, and how I had seen through it. Probably, as in the dream, she hoped I would know this; and I certainly had my ideas, although, as always with her, I had some doubt.)

You can see, here, from my description of the dream, the nature of the transference and countertransference. (As I write this, I realize that I am talking to you, reader, as the patient talks to me in the dream and the sessions—as if: "Of course you know."[3]) By itself, the dream could be interpreted as indicating, on one hand, a romanticized transference within an oedipal constellation—mother is out of the picture, father sits in her chair, alone with his daughter, and the daughter wants him to

---

3. This may be an example of parallel process different from that usually discussed in the literature. Searles (1955), Ekstein and Wallerstein (1958), Caligor (1981), and others have discussed parallel processes that occur in psychoanalytic supervision. Perhaps parallel processes can occur, too, in a psychoanalytic book, where the relationship between the writer and the reader parallels the relationship between analyst and patient described in this book.

think of romance and seductiveness (*As You Like It*), not violence and guilt (*Macbeth*). Intellectual games had, in fact, been the favorite means of sexual seductiveness between her and her father. Moreover, the way they played them had a distinctly sadomasochistic cast. However, her manner of reporting the dream added several dimensions to this interpretation; she had a wish for me to have total empathy with her that bordered on mindreading. At the same time, there was a dread of overt self-assertion and a kind of covert control that was achieved through these sorts of intellectual games, in which the rules alternatingly adhered to and broke stereotyped gender roles. (Note that in the dream, the patient sits in the father's chair and he in the mother's, reminiscent of the switches in gender roles, clearly in *As You Like It* and more subtly in *Macbeth*.)

The dream itself succeeded in engaging me in a sort of mind game. I was intrigued by a startling coincidence that seemed like telepathy. The patient spoke fluent French, and I remembered that during the session in which she told me that she had had the dream, without telling me the content of the dream, I had thought to myself, "À votre guise," which in French means essentially, "As you wish," or, one might say, "As You Like It!" But the experience that this was telepathy seemed to me to reflect the nature of the transference wishes, with which I was complying.

Then, in the next week, I discovered how my deep and convoluted attempts to understand the dream, as I have just described them, were in themselves part of the transference-countertransference matrix. The patient told me at the start of a session that she was very angry with me. "Do you know why?" she asked. [I was here already bracing for a new game in the Olympics of empathy.] I confessed that I did not. But instead of games, she told me, quite simply, that she was angry that I interpreted too much about her. Some things she told me were simple conversation, ice-breakers, and she felt I was overinterpreting and overpathologizing her. I then realized that the dream had, as well, been a simple message about this complaint. It was a wish-fulfillment transference dream. In it, the father [the analyst] is thinking *Macbeth* (i.e., tragedy, corruption, murder, greed, etc.) while she is thinking *As You Like It* (i.e., comedy, lighthearted, good-natured). She hopes that her father would understand this without her saying so in the dream, and he eventually did. But I did not, and my attempts at depth interpretation of the dream continued the pattern. Even her association to the "Macbeth Murder Mystery," which makes a delicious joke of a tragedy, had not stopped me. And so she had to tell me explicitly that my continued interpretation was too disturbing. This action on her part was itself a therapeutic breakthrough, since she tended, when angry, either to suppress her anger until there was an outbreak of violence, or to bind it in masochistic rituals. Of course, the grave, Macbeth-like issues of murderousness, deception, and conspiracy in crime were also potent issues in the patient's psychology and received further attention as the analysis progressed, but the dream alerted me to the need, at that time, to slow down and to temper the focus on those issues.

However, the meanings of the dream continued to unfold. I took the patient's request seriously, to focus less on what I saw as her pathology and destructiveness. I realized that I had been somewhat guarded in dealing with her, and wondered whether that was necessary. It turned out that my countertransference feeling with her was somewhat justified. In the ensuing months, the patient played a practical joke on me (the details of which I cannot relate for reasons of confidentiality). She had played this joke on other people, but it had a more serious outcome with me, in that it seriously embarrassed and humiliated me. It was a practical joke that her father had played on her, as well as on a number of his relatives and acquaintances. But the essence of the practical joke had been reflected in the dream: Is it a comedy or is it hostile? All practical jokes have this combination of motives: there is an aspect of fooling or humiliating the other person under the guise of humor and fun. The question raised by the dream of whether the play that describes the situation is *Macbeth* or *As You Like It* was very much to the point of the patient's psychology and her experiences with her father. He was someone who did things that were supposedly in good cheer but often conveyed a deep, underlying hostility, of which the practical joke was only one example. The patient was frequently the victim of these games from early childhood, when she was even less well equipped to handle them. They left her with the unconscious question, is what has happened with my father destructive or fun? Is this a destructive murderous tragedy (*Macbeth*) or a romantic comedy *(As You Like It)*?

Her association to Thurber's "The Macbeth Murder Mystery" set up the same dialectic: Can you make a comedy out of something that is full of underlying destructiveness? And the question of who did it, in the Thurber satire, was also relevant. When I was hurt by the patient's practical joke, her first reaction was of rather extreme nonempathy, as if it had been my doing and my problem that I got burned. From a great deal of analytic reflection on this, we were able to elaborate how my experience was like her own experience of her father's destructiveness. If he claimed no destructive intent, but she was hurt by him, then "Who done it?" The tension of this conflict lay at the root of her own masochistic sexual practices, which, by the way, she referred to as "The Game," but were quite sinister and lurid in their rituals of domination, pain, and control. In fact, the title of the play *As You Like It* contains within it the essence of her masochism, as if she were saying "Do with me *as you like it*, with no concern for my well-being, and I will act as a willing participant, but know that underneath this veneer of pleasure, there is great hurt to me."

FACILITATORS AND PITFALLS OF RECIPROCAL DREAM INTERPRETATION

As noted above, it often happens that, after a dream is presented by the patient, the transference-countertransference pattern described by the dream is enacted in the first effort at interpreting the dream. The countertransference implications of the dream will then become further clarified, either explicitly by the patient or by the analyst's self-analysis. Is there any way to enhance this process?

One possibility is suggested by the work of Gill (1982). He recommends attending explicitly to the implications of the dream for the "here-and-now" interaction between patient and analyst. This strategy may help, depending on how close the countertransference is to awareness. If it is relatively close to awareness, then speaking overtly about it could be useful. Unfortunately, if the countertransference tendency is strongly dissociated or if the analyst is not highly motivated to learn about it, or both, then the procedure will not work. Rather, what may then happen is that the way the analyst attends to the countertransference reenacts his problematic countertransference. This pattern is well illustrated in Gill and Hoffman's casebook (1982), an extremely valuable document of verbatim analytic sessions. It contains some examples of an analyst who intends to understand what the patient sees in him, but fails in that effort, and instead acts out the countertransference while ostensibly exploring it. For example, consider case D (pp. 69–90) in the casebook: an intimidating analyst engages in a democratic attempt to explore the patient's perception of his intimidation, but does so in such an overbearing manner that we are right back where we started—with the patient being intimidated into the study of the analyst's intimidation.

And in case B, this sort of circular process occurs in reference to a dream. The patient says:

> We saw the movie [*I Am Curious Yellow*] Saturday night and then Saturday night I had a dream that, um, was in a class situation. And I don't remember if there was anybody in particular who was running the class, but it was something we did do in a, in a way in the class I'm taking; because we were all, we'd all made puppets. And the part I recall now about the dream was my playing around with the puppet I made and feeling fairly free and yet always knowing that pretty soon I'd be asked to perform in front of others. And when this did happen in the dream and I had to make my puppet work in front of others, I completely lost control over it. I, I just sort of froze and I couldn't do anything.
>
> And then I think there was some awareness again of, um—because I had frozen and I wasn't handling my puppet, especially after having practiced much better or played with it beforehand—again of incurring disapproval. And in fact, there is a definite connection—because—with what was happening with F—because I think what I did with my puppet when I realized I was freezing and was going to get disapproval anyway since I wasn't going to be able to perform with it, I then—I can't remember now exactly how I did this—but in some way I turned it back on the class and asked them to tell them, tell my puppet about themselves. And somehow it ended up I and my puppet weren't doing anything and that I was making the class do it. And even though it was still a fiasco, somebody else was acting, it wasn't me. Somebody else was doing the work or, or expressing themselves, revealing themselves. And that is what I was doing with F. And it was the inability to feel free to really express myself and know what I liked and didn't like that I think was what was bothering me in that class. When I felt his disapproval, even if he really didn't give it, I assumed he was, because I knew I wasn't doing something that is a standard of his and that I wanted to be able to meet [pp. 33–34].

The dream is difficult to follow as it is reported; it could be stated as follows:

> I had a dream that was in a class situation. And I don't remember if there was anybody in particular who was running the class. We'd all made puppets. I was playing around with the puppet I made and feeling fairly free and yet always knowing

> that pretty soon I'd be asked to perform in front of others. And when I had to make my puppet work in front of others, I completely lost control over it. I just sort of froze and I couldn't do anything.
>
> And then I think there was some awareness again of incurring disapproval. I turned it back on the class and asked them to tell my puppet about themselves.

The patient says she is compliant to her father, and that he requires her to be so, but the interaction with the analyst suggests that she is compliant only on the surface; she is secretly and self-effacingly assertive. When the analyst starts to put forth his own ideas about the dream, it spurs her on to develop her own. He seems not very receptive to her ideas—after asking her about what the puppet was like, he virtually ignores her response—that at first the puppet had a definite character and face but then it is faceless. We can see her defensive pattern—to hide her identity behind a haze of obsessional facelessness. Her manner of speaking is so convoluted that it is extremely difficult to perceive what her ideas are; from the way she tells the dream, it is difficult just to get clear what happens in the dream.

The analyst seems to pursue a vague sexual interpretation rather single-mindedly. He thinks that her husband is the puppet, and that she is masturbating him in the dream, and that her pleasure in it is that she can treat her husband privately like a puppet, but not publicly. Is that also going on in the transference? She certainly is a lot more forceful and individualistic than she portrays herself. She tolerates the analyst's clumsiness, doesn't get overtly angry, and continues to formulate her own interpretation—which seems to be that she likes the idea of performing publicly but is afraid of disapproval.

The dream-interpretation process is an enactment of the dream—as we look over her associations, we realize that she has formulated her own interpretation of the dream. But she does so in a manner unobtrusive enough that the analyst can miss it. She has a clear face, but she shows it in a private and covert enough way that no one might notice; were she to have to be completely public and overt about it, she might freeze, so she lives out her wish to perform by turning the spotlight on others.

This process has gone one step further in this discussion; I realize that by summarizing her dream, by cleaning out its obsessional detail, I have also been presenting her dream for her, continuing to enact the dream message, that she cannot perform alone.

We do not know how this analysis continued; but let us imagine how it might continue, if the analyst did not seek outside supervision. The patient might continue to comply with the analyst's line of interpretation, and the deadlock might become even more fixed. If, however, the analyst were sincere in trying to understand his involvement in the dream, the patient might eventually summon the courage to express her own view of the dream, which she is close to doing anyway in the session reported in the transcript. It might take much longer for the patient and analyst themselves to clarify their interaction as reflected in the dream than for the analyst to do so with a supervisory consultation. But it might also be more useful and edifying to the patient if she and the analyst could themselves identify and analyze the parallel between the dream and their relationship, and work out a different way of interacting.

Circular reenactments happen with any analyst, no matter how skilled. None of us has all areas of our personality completely accessible to consciousness; on the contrary, every patient can perceive and describe specific areas of the analyst's personality that no one else can (Sandler, 1976; Wolstein, 1976; Levenson, 1983). Seeking objective signs of our countertransference involvement in dream interpretation may be some help. Consultation with colleagues may also provide an objective opinion about the transference-countertransference interaction. Ultimately, however, it is the continual attention to the reciprocal processes of dream interpretation, constantly evaluated and reevaluated by both patient and analyst, that allows an analysis of dreams to break through transference-countertransference deadlocks and become most productive for the patient's self-understanding in an interpersonal matrix. While the clarification of a dream's meaning through such a circular process may be slower than seeking a consultation, the solution of the dream within the analysis alone may have more value for the patient.

CHAPTER 17

DREAMS AS SUPERVISION, DREAMS IN SUPERVISION

He traverses—familiar—
As One should come to Town—
And tell you all your Dreams—were true—
He lived—where Dreams were born—

Emily Dickinson

EVERY ANALYST, over time, seeks the way to work through dreams with each patient in the most collaborative fashion.[1] There are many individual variations for making the best use of the circular processes that occur during dream interpretation. Ogden (1997a, b), for example, enhances his collaboration with patients by monitoring his own reverie processes throughout the session and connecting them to both the dream's manifest content and the patient's comments. Reverie processes include thoughts, both fully formulated and stray fragments, daydreams, emotional and bodily experiences in the session, as well as just prior to or just after the session. All such experiences are presumed to be potentially relevant to the patient's experience, no matter how disconnected they may first seem from the patient's experience.

As an example, Ogden (1997a) gives the following two dreams of a patient:

> I was watching a man take care of a baby in an outdoor place of some sort that might have been a park. He seemed to be doing a good job of attending to it. He carried the baby over to a steep set of concrete stairs and lifted the baby as if there were

1. See Bonime (1986).

> a slide to place it on, but there was no slide. He let go of the baby and let it hurtle down the stairs. I could see the baby's neck break as it hit the top step, and I noticed that its head and neck become floppy. When the baby landed at the bottom of the steps, the man picked up its motionless body. I was surprised that the baby was not crying. It looked directly into my eyes and smiled in an eerie way [p. 578].
>
> I've just had a baby and I'm looking at it in the bassinet. I don't see anything of me in its face which is dark, heart-shaped, Mediterranean. I don't recognize it as something that came out of me. I think, "How could I have given birth to such a thing." I pick it up and hold him and hold him and hold him, and he becomes a little boy with wild curly hair [p. 581].

I would ask the reader, if these dreams are new to you, please think about them on your own before reading further, for they are excellent illustrations of two principles set forth in this book: that dreams never lie, and that they can be examined through multiple vectors of interpretation.

I ask you now to consider:

- What were the conditions of this dreamer's birth and her earliest childhood?
- What were her parents' feelings toward her?
- What are the sexes of the characters in the dreams, and what does this tell you about the patient's relationship with each sex?
- What traumata, physical and emotional, have befallen her?
- What are the patient's primary defenses? How does she handle distress?
- What does the dream suggest about the patient from the objective viewpoint? From the subjective viewpoint?
- What is the analyst's countertransference from the patient's point of view?
- What is the patient implying might be most curative for her? What does she need?

Ogden follows his reveries. At the beginning of the session in which she recounts the first dream, he has a faint sense of nausea as he hears the patient racing up the stairs to his office. He has a basically irritated disposition toward her. He watches the second hand of his clock and feels that she is demanding a magical, transformative interpretation that will change her life.

The patient's mother was a very successful professional, and the patient is convinced that her pregnancy was an unwanted accident. She felt her mother hated her all her life and treated her with neglect and disgust. All of this is being realized in the countertransference, at first.

The patient's first dream shows the theme of neglect and seemingly accidental abuse of a baby. The baby, although its neck is broken, smiles eerily after the man picks her up. From the objective viewpoint, the dream shows the patient's victimization. From the subjective viewpoint, it shows her own sadism, and her masculine identification as an inadequate parent. From a supervision standpoint, the dream implies, "You may do me damage, but if you then pick me up, I will survive. I will also probably hide my distress."

The second dream supervises the analyst more directly. Again, if we consider a Jungian "reduction" of the dream, it starts with rejection of the baby ("How could I have given birth to such a thing") but this is followed by unremitting physical contact ("I hold him and hold him and hold him"), which brings about a transformation of the baby into "a little boy with wild, curly hair." The supervisory message is that no elaborate intervention is needed. Only "hold me and hold me and hold me."

The dreams thus show the patient's basic personality—the unwanted, irritable baby who is abused and damaged—as well as a possible therapeutic solution, finding a way to the consistent, close holding that she needs.

Symbolically, in the session, Ogden does just that, but it takes time. First, the cycle of vulnerability and defense is lived out by the patient and analyst. Right after telling the first dream, the patient moves quickly from the dream to speak in detail about a project from work. This is like the defensive smiling that the baby does at the end of the dream. The analyst notes this defensiveness and brings her back to the dream. Privately, he works through his own parallel experience of irretrievable loss of his close friend to breast cancer, which helps him become empathic with the patient's own sense of damage and loss.

When he hears the second dream, he notices that, in the words of the dream, the patient picks *it* up and then she holds *him*. This shift, from the inanimate pronoun to the human one, he comments to her, indicates the love that she felt for the child in the dream. He feels uneasy about his precipitous use of the word "love," but this caginess is probably symptomatic of the uneasy countertransference. The patient feels touched and held nevertheless. Her thoughts turn to the analyst seeing her naked and thinking her breasts are too small. This brings to his mind the breast cancer, and his feelings of having not responded adequately when he and his friend discussed her illness. The combination, for the analyst, of experiencing the great love for his friend and the agony of losing her brings a new emotional liveliness into the analytic relationship. It frees him to connect with the patient in an emotional, intimate way, which, the more it can be sustained, the more it will be experienced by the patient as "holding her and holding her and holding her." It also brings out more and more profound associations to the dream from the patient, including the sense that her small breasts make her like a boy, unable to nurse a child.

The following is another example of dreams as supervision. It also shows the value of considering a series of dreams, which develop a theme over time. In this situation, I was working with a patient who was very afraid of treatment. She grew up in a family that was physically and verbally abusive. I thought she really should be in psychoanalysis, but I had not broached the subject with her, because her fear and her level of resistance were so high, and she firmly refused to consider using the couch. But after three years of psychotherapy, once a week, sitting up, she had the following dream:

> I'm in our living room. It's as it always is. The dog is standing in front of me. I'm very upset about the dog. I say to the dog, "Please go on the couch. If you just get on the couch, you'll be OK."

After hearing her dream, I silently look over to the couch in my office. She sees it and says, "Very subtle!"

I say, "To paraphrase Freud, sometimes a couch is just a couch." I also say that in the dream, she might be suggesting to herself to use the couch. She says she might be able to do it after 15 years of therapy.

A year later, she revisits the same theme in another dream: "I was sitting in the chair. You were there (where you are now). Someone came in the door behind me. It was a 30-ish year old woman. She had a gun aimed at you. I had the idea, 'She's definitely not going to shoot him.' I said to her, 'Pull the trigger.'" At this moment, the patient pauses from her narrative of the dream, reaches into her bag, takes out a roll of candy, and says, "Would you like a Life-Saver?" I decline, but am struck by the unconscious offer of a life-saver after she has given the order to shoot me, an irony she does not notice. Then she continues telling the dream:

> "She and I got on the couch. You are immobile, as if you are on 'pause.' I wish I could remember the conversation I had with the young woman. She is definitely caretaking. Then she sits in the chair. I leave."

After hearing her dream, I wonder if it implies that we should change the basic format of the treatment. Perhaps I should become more silent, as if my pause button has been pushed as she says, while still remaining present, listening attentively. She should get on the couch and have an internal dialogue between the different aspects of herself—the murderous aspect and the caretaking aspect—which are depicted in the dream. I tell her this.

Her reaction is still fearful. "You think I would get on the couch with *you* here? No way!" (With this statement, she enacts part of the dream while we are interpreting the dream: She shoots me down, but doesn't really kill me.)

The dream portrays her psychic conflict. She is sure she has her murderousness under control, but then she gives the order to shoot. She fears her family's actual murderousness, and wonders whether one can survive in intimate relations without killer showdowns. She fears that one of us will kill the other. A few weeks later, she has the following dream:

> I come into your office. You are sitting in your usual chair, but there is a tray-table in front of you with a plate of fine china and an elegant napkin. On the chair in which I usually sit, there is a pile of books. I am forced to go to the couch. Somehow my chest opens, and my heart is on your plate. You say, "I am going to eat your heart." I am bleeding, and I wake up.

The dream portrays the dread of being on the couch and what I would do to her. She tells me that a friend of hers had wanted to use the couch with her analyst, but the couch was covered by books. Her friend took this as an indirect message from her analyst not to use the couch. By contrast, in her dream, the books force her onto the couch. Of course, it also raises the question: Is the suggestion she use the couch an academic "bookish" question? Certainly her high level of anxiety and distrust are primary, and must be dealt with before using the couch can be possible.

Some dreams are almost blatant supervision. They describe in bald terms how the patient sees what the analyst is doing. When the meaning of the dream may seem so obvious to a disinterested third party, it is not uncommon for the analyst not to understand the message of the dream, if the analyst's counterresistance is high. For example, an analyst in supervision with me harbored the notion that she knew better than most people how to deal with problems and had a tendency to give her patient advice. The patient had the following dream:

> I had a dream about you last night. It was just weird. You were kind of intervening between me and Joe, my boss. You were doing therapy with him and kind of explaining him to me. You were very strict and not that nice. But I believed in what you were doing. You were trying to emphasize that there were serious problems—and you were kind of saying "I'm working it out with him and it doesn't have anything to do with you."

I wondered whether the dream might be outlining two problems in the treatment, as perceived by the patient: (1) That the therapist is working on other people's problems instead of the patient's, and (2) That the dream is portraying the therapist working on the patient's problems too unilaterally. She is not collaborating with the patient and is literally telling the patient that it has nothing to do with him. This is an extreme of noncollaboration.

In another instance, a psychoanalyst in supervision with me had been working with a patient for more than 10 years. The patient had made a great deal of progress and, in my view, was nearing the time for termination. The analyst saw it differently, but acknowledged that she had a very strong attachment to the patient and might not want him to terminate for her own reasons. The patient had the following dream:

> I kept having a dream last night. I was trying to graduate from high school. I couldn't graduate because I hadn't taken an American History course and I was supposed to take the final exam or do the final paper. One of the people who went to B's wedding, she was a friend of mine there (high school), and she was in the dream and she had already taken the exam and she had failed it.
>
> Now I think it's a dream about therapy—wanting to graduate from therapy and not knowing what in the world I could do to do that. Which means you're the evil horrible history teacher who wouldn't let me graduate.

> In the dream, I kept putting it off until the last possible time you could take the test. And then I didn't show up. And I just kept hoping that the teacher would let me graduate anyway because it was only one course and I had been there long enough—I was there for ten years.

In this case, not only was the dream's meaning blatant, but the patient himself was spelling out its relation to the problem of termination. In supervision, this opened up a discussion of the therapist's countertransference, especially her difficulty with separation.

A psychoanalyst, in an address to a conference about his clinical work, told of a patient who dreamt that he was sitting across from his analyst at a restaurant and could not understand what he was saying. There may be many meanings about the patient condensed into this dream, including that food and communication are related. But if one views the dream as supervision, one would have to suspect that the patient cannot understand what the analyst is saying. Interestingly, many people in the audience, hearing the analyst's presentation, could not themselves understand what he was saying, so it was not very difficult to surmise the meaning of the dream and to empathize with the patient. The analyst, however, did not explore this meaning with the patient, nor did he seem to be aware of its implications about himself.

Every analyst misses references to himself. As noted above, even Greenson, who revived the focus on transference and countertransference aspects of dreams told in analysis, sometimes missed the references to the therapeutic interaction, such as when he didn't notice the reference to his name when a patient dreams of "green raincoats." In this respect, it is worth having a more detailed look at one of his extended vignettes (1967): A female patient begins a session with two dreams: "(1) I am being photographed in the nude, lying on my back in different positions; legs closed, legs apart; (2) I see a man with a curved yardstick in his hand; it had writing on it which was supposed to be erotic. A red, spiny backed little monster was biting this man with sharp tiny teeth. The man was ringing a bell for help, but no one heard it but me and I didn't seem to care" (p. 143).

Greenson interprets as follows: "Being photographed in the nude refers to problems of exposure as penisless. The man with the yardstick whom she ignores apparently represents her analyst. The red monster he is struggling with could represent a projection of or a revenge for her feelings about the male genital." This is all very much along the interpretive lines, so prominent at the time, of finding penis envy in women.

He later says to the patient: "You feel remote and empty because you seem to be afraid to look at that hateful monster inside you." The patient answers: "That monster was red, actually dark red-brown, like old menstrual blood. It was a medieval fiend, like one sees in the paintings of Hieronymus Bosch. I am like that; if I were a painting, that's what I would be, full of all kinds of demons of sex, bowel movement, homosexuality, and hate. I suppose I don't want to face my hate for myself, for Bill, for my baby, and for you. I haven't really changed and I had thought I had made such progress."

Greenson intervenes with the tried and true: "We recently uncovered a new monster: your anger at men's penises and your disgust with your vagina. And you are running away from it by trying to escape into emptiness."

The patient replies: "You sound so sure of yourself, as though you have it all solved. [She is on to the formulaic nature of his interpretations. But then:] Maybe I am running. I read a book about a man giving his wife cognac to get her drunk so she would be a better sexual partner and she pretended to be drunk so she could let out her real feelings. [They are both conning each other.] Maybe I'm like that. I'd really show you men what I could do sexually. I sometimes get the feeling that underneath this meek slave-girl exterior I present, I have a streak of grandiosity. I'd show you poor 'fuckers' how to really use a penis if I had one. Yes, when Bill was trying his damnedest to satisfy me the other night, I looked at him and it flashed through my mind, who's the 'slavey' now. And that yardstick, I recall asking you once, what yardstick do you use to measure neurosis with? [The dream provides the answer: a yardstick with erotic writing on it! This is a marvelous example of a patient's associations setting up a context that makes the manifest content understandable.] I hate to feel stupid and sometimes you and this analysis make me so. I could be as sharp as you, if I dared. But then I become afraid I would lose you or I'd become repulsive to you and you would desert me. I suppose I have to develop more trust in you. I can't expect Bill to take all this—but you ought to be able to. . . ."

Greenson sees her as having a hateful internal penis and a masculine identification which she projects onto her husband and onto him. But perhaps the dream is her attempt to supervise Greenson, to comment on his line of interpretation, as if she is saying: "Stop measuring me sexually! You make my neurosis so sexualized—is there something else? My aggression and my fear of being as sharp as you: You call that my masculine identification—what if it is a healthful striving or my striving for a feminine identification that is not measured by the yardstick of masculine standards?"

Everybody interprets according to the culture of their times and what their personal belief system is. Dreams are *elastic*; they allow such interpretations to take hold. Nevertheless, dreams are also *persistent*; however much the analyst and patient may shape the dream according to the culture, the dream-life keeps pushing the patient's personal insight beyond that of the analyst's viewpoint and often beyond that of the culture. It is one of the most difficult tasks for the analyst and patient to see this expanded horizon portrayed by the dream rather than to constrain the dream within the procrustean bed of what they already know and what they expect to find. Dora's dreams functioned similarly as signposts to her freeing herself from an oppressive family situation despite Freud's sexualizing interpretations. No matter how much we interpret dreams within the confines of our contemporary culture, our dreams retain an essence that goes beyond those cultural constraints.

CHAPTER 18

THE CLINICAL USE OF COUNTER-TRANSFERENCE DREAMS

THE SUBJECT OF countertransference dreams always evokes great interest among clinicians. The preceding two chapters dealt with the ways in which a patient's dreams can be used by the analyst as a kind of supervision, to help the analyst understand his countertransference and thereby be better able to help the patient with his transference. I have presented chapter 16 as a verbal address about five times. The chapter never mentions the analyst's dreams about the patient, yet every time I presented the paper as a public talk, one of the first questions from the audience was always, "What do you think about the analyst's dreams about the patient, and what do you think about the analyst telling his patient such a dream?" Despite the obvious interest in this subject, it is one of the areas of dream interpretation that has been least studied and least written about.

In the film *Analyze This*, Billy Crystal played a psychoanalyst who was frightened by the coercive transference of his patient, a Mafia don. He told one of his dreams to his patient, played by Robert de Niro, who was not pleased. But the analyst's dream turned out to have an important clue to the patient's psychodynamics and the treatment, such as it was, worked out well. But that was Hollywood. Do such things happen in real analyses?

Many analysts whom I know cringe at the idea of telling their own dream to a patient. The very fact that it seems so taboo has discouraged open discussion of the procedure. Many analysts wonder, why do it?

Granted that one's own dreams are extremely informative, is it useful to the patient to tell them to him? Could the information be used otherwise, and would it be more or less effective? Yet how many analysts have actually tried telling a dream to a patient?

I am still quite cautious about telling a patient my own dream, but I have been inspired to conduct some limited research on it in the library and in my practice. As far as I can discover, Jung (1962) was the first psychoanalyst who regularly told patients his dreams about them. He reported doing so with no apparent self-consciousness that this was in any way a radical procedure. Instead, it accorded with his trust of the validity of his own unconscious impressions. According to Marie-Louise von Franz (1998a, p. 28), who knew Jung personally, when Jung had a dream about someone, whether a patient or someone else, he tended to tell it to the person, without commentary or interpretation. The person was then free to decide if and how the dream was relevant.

In one case, Jung (1962) had a dream the night before the first consultation with a patient:

> A young girl, unknown to me, came to me as a patient. She outlined her case to me, and while she was talking, I thought, 'I don't understand her at all. I don't understand what it is all about.' But suddenly it occurred to me that she must have an unusual father complex. That was the dream [p. 138].

When Jung met the girl the next day, she was the daughter of a wealthy Jewish banker. She was suffering from a severe anxiety neurosis, and had already been through one analysis, which was terminated by the analyst because the transference had been so intense that he feared it would destroy his marriage. (This is Jung's description; today, we should probably say that the countertransference was at least as intense.)

The girl was what Jung called "a Westernized Jewess," very enlightened and not terribly connected to her religion. During the consultation, he realized that she was the girl in his dream the previous night. Not being able to detect a father complex in her, he asked her about her grandfather. She appeared moved and upset. Her grandfather had been a Chassid and a Zaddik. It was said that he was a saint and possessed second sight. She dismissed this as "all nonsense." Jung told her that she has her neurosis "because the fear of God has got into you."

The next night, he had another dream. "A reception was taking place in my house, and behold, this girl was there too. She came up to me and asked, 'Haven't you got an umbrella? It is raining so hard.' I actually found an umbrella, fumbled around with it to open it, and was on the point of giving it to her. But what happened instead? I handed it to her on my knees, as if she were a goddess."

Jung told this dream to the patient, and in a week, he tells us, her neurosis had vanished. He concluded the account: "In this case I had applied no 'method,' but had sensed the presence of the numen. My explaining this to her had accomplished the cure. Method did not matter here; what mattered was the 'fear of God.'"

There is perhaps an implied method here. In Biblical times, and still today in some cultures, some dreams are seen as messages from God. To tell someone a dream is to tell them the message from God. Jung's patient was manifestly alienated from her religion, but felt a deep unspoken bond with her grandfather's piety and religiosity. Jung spoke to her within that framework; like a prophet, he tells her the solution to her neurosis through his dream, and she hears it that way and is released from her one-sided secularism and able to return to her dissociated religious roots. The entire account has a Biblical tone to it, brief, terse, and with no ambiguity. Even the language of Jung's dream sounds Biblical—for example, "and behold, this girl was there too."

In another instance, Jung (1962) felt that his work with a woman was stuck. He dreamt: "I was walking down a highway through a valley in late-afternoon sunlight. To my right was a steep hill. At its top stood a castle, and on the highest tower there was a woman sitting on a kind of balustrade. In order to see her properly, I had to bend my head far back. I awoke with a crick in the back of my neck. Even in the dream I had recognized the woman as my patient."

Jung interpreted the dream as a compensation: If he was looking up at her in the dream, it was because he was looking down at her in waking life. He told her the dream and his interpretation, and the treatment again began to move forward.

As with all analysts' dreams, this dream could also have been interpreted primarily within the psychodynamics of the dreamer. We know from Jung's autobiography that he held two contradictory attitudes towards his mother. Most of the time, she chattered on superficially, but he felt that from time to time, especially if she thought that no one was listening, she would say profound and brilliant things. This dream and Jung's interpretation show this double-sided attitude towards his mother and perhaps women in general.

However revealing of Jung's psychology, his telling the dream to the patient may nevertheless have freed up the treatment. More important than whether the dream showed that Jung was looking up or down at the patient is whether the dream opened up a discussion of that psychological issue between them.

Among interpersonal psychoanalysts, Edward Tauber (1952) wrote the first paper about the psychoanalyst who tells patients his dreams about them and collaborates with the patient to understand it. It was very daring in its time, and still seems so to many analysts nearly fifty years later. Tauber tries to interpret the dream with the patient. The paper makes a good case for judicious use of this technique. At the same time, the clinical examples are precise enough to reveal some of the potential pitfalls of such a procedure.

Tauber dreamt: "The patient and analyst are sitting at a small table in a sidewalk café, perhaps in Paris. The patient is saying very little, but has a very troubled expression on his face. He appears worried. The analyst says to him, 'Why not try to tell me what is the matter?'" (p. 332).

Tauber tells this dream and one other dream to his patient. According to Tauber's paper, the patient responds that

> both dreams had a hoax-like quality: although they manifestly indicated the analyst's concern for him, at the same time he suspected that the analyst was perfectly happy with the friendly, unstressed quality of the relationship; and although the analyst was trying to indicate in a sense that he believed they should go deeper into these issues, he had some private reasons for avoiding the challenge.
>
> The analyst found this latter comment thought provoking, and he could not answer it with either a flat denial or an affirmation. The analyst seriously asked himself whether he was guilty of wanting to avoid difficulties. The analyst's association to this was to remember information from outside sources about the patient that was not too favorable. He did not feel free under the circumstances to communicate this information to the patient. The analyst then made some comments about the dream in which he indicated that in one sense he believed it implied that he was having some difficulty obtaining the maximum degree of participation from the patient, and that possibly the dream was an indirect method of conveying to the patient the analyst's desire for deeper collaboration.

This is a critical point in the analysis. If the analysis of the dream is to prove fruitful, the analyst must be able to proceed with the analysis as far as he can go. In this case, Tauber has moved forward with his unconscious, while he feels inhibited about revealing that which is conscious to him. That is always a risky situation. It can almost be a rule of thumb for the analyst: *If you are aware of something consciously that you cannot tell the patient, then do not attempt to leap over the barrier by telling your patient something as full of unconscious communication as a dream.* To tell the patient a dream under such a circumstance is double binding, as if to say: "I cannot tell you what I am aware of about you, but this makes me uncomfortable and awkward with you. I will try to tell you more by telling you a dream, and maybe you will decipher what I know from the dream, but then I will not admit it to you."

In Tauber's example, the patient picks up that this is the case. By identifying the "hoaxlike" quality in the dreams, the patient is noticing the situation as it exists. The analyst cannot then, in good faith, comment to the patient that he is having some difficulty obtaining the maximum degree of participation from the patient. The patient even speculates, correctly, that Tauber has some private reasons for avoiding the challenge.

MY OWN EXPERIENCES OF TELLING A DREAM TO A PATIENT

In my twenty-five years of doing psychoanalysis and psychotherapy, I have on very few occasions told patients about dreams that I had about them. They were always after I had analyzed the dream on my own, and so I felt reasonably comfortable about what the dream meant. I usually told a dream to people who had been in treatment for several years and whom I felt I knew quite well. And in each case, I felt a kind of exasperation about getting through to the patient. That may be one reason that one dreams of a patient—to break a clinical deadlock and to find a new way to think about the clinical interaction.

The first time I told a patient my dream about him, the patient had been in analysis for about four years, and I think we were both finding it rough going. My interpretations, as often as not, led to a closing down of inquiry. I could feel his anxiety in the room, and my comments often led to his becoming mute and looking as if he had become numb. I wondered whether I was helping him at all. A few years later, he told me that he had felt seriously suicidal when we first worked together and that the analysis had saved his life. But at this point, it was still unclear to me whether I was having much impact on him.

The patient went to great extremes to avoid situations in which he might be blamed, and was reticent about his own blaming of others and fantasies of retaliation. He had difficulty working with his dreams; he said, "I'm terrified of being blamed for things out of my control and my unconscious is out of my control." He was also dealing in the sessions with mourning the sudden death of his mother, and reviewing some of the things he loved about her and some that he did not. On the negative side, she had an unusual ability to control and humiliate him. He had particularly painful memories in relation to losing bladder control.

I was finding myself that it was nearly impossible to make interpretations that did not in themselves feel shaming to him. It was during such a feeling of stalemate that I had the following dream: "I am in a dormitory room, and we are having a session. It is dead. My back hurts. I get down on the linoleum floor, and the patient starts laughing like a baby, very loosely."

In the next day's session, the patient started to complain about his fellow workers, felt very depressed, and complained of having "an air of unreality" about him. He felt that he was a romantic with high ideals, and his current girlfriend would berate him for this. In this atmosphere of depressed, pessimistic, and scornful heaviness, I thought of my dream. It felt to me that the dream was a wish that I could somehow make him laugh; I thought of the line from the nursery rhyme, "The little dog laughed to see such sport."

I decided to tell him my dream. He asked me: "Was I laughing at you for being on the floor?" The analysis, I suddenly remembered, began with our telling each other many jokes; he had bragged to his friend that he and I did that, and she had said, "I never got to tell jokes with *my* analyst." I said to him, "I thought you were laughing *with* me at feeling free to let go." The patient paused, then said, "The linoleum makes me think that the room is not as well-furnished as this one. It seems like a semi role reversal. You could say I was laughing at your discomfort. *I* wouldn't, but maybe that's how you would perceive me. There is a ridiculous aspect to it. Like being on the couch; not ridiculous in itself."

In the next session, we went further into my dream. I said that I thought it expressed a wish for him to let go. He asked me why I thought the floor had been linoleum, and I told him that I associate linoleum to the floor of my kindergarten class. When I was a child we used to take naps on blankets on the linoleum floor. Although it was supposed to be a very serious time for rest, we would slide around on the floor, and it was great fun.

The patient perked up, and said, "That's funny. When I was a kid, my kindergarten teacher, Miss C, was wonderful. I remember telling her when my mother had my youngest brother. I had a piece of news no one else had. She took kids to the playground. She just crossed her legs and watched them. She never got nervous, she let us have our freedom."

I became aware, as he said this, of an important aspect of our interaction. My lack of anxiety and letting him have his freedom had a good effect on him up to a point; but if I did too little, he became frightened of being ignored. This was one of the central affective issues in his psychology—the balance between overcontrol and indifference.

In the next session, we did not speak about my dream overtly. He started talking about feeling tense. He then mentioned an opera production that seemed to him to be too plain. He then said that in a world series baseball game, when one team pulls out all the stops, that's when it's good. I wondered if this was a reference to my telling him my dream, which seemed at the time like pulling out all the stops. Pulling out the stops had a double significance: Its traditional metaphoric meaning of relinquishing any inhibitions, and a concrete meaning of relinquishing bladder control, which can be relieving but also embarrassing.

I wondered, "Does this mean that I should proceed further and not be too timid about his resistance? Does this mean that it would be a relief for him not to worry about his control of all things that came out of him?" He went on, talking about offending people inadvertently—like going up to someone's house, asking the father if his son can come out to play baseball, and having the father tell you his son has polio. "So much of what I say could offend people," he said. This was part of the tension that beset our sessions—when he feared that his next association would offend me, he would become silent.

My telling the patient the dream in this case clarified my wish to "break the ice" with him, and it made some small inroad toward that goal. The interaction of my associations to kindergarten with his own history made me aware of some things we had in common that had not been consciously formulated before.

It was also an enactment in the truest sense. My telling him the dream was an enactment of the content of the dream. In the dream, I did something novel to break the ice, and then, having tried it out in the dream, I did something novel in the actual treatment (telling the patient my dream about him).

Several months after I told the patient my dream, I realized that it had also referred to the theme of social class, which we were having trouble discussing. My patient was extremely sensitive to social class differences in the outside world and in the transference. His grandparents were all working class. His father managed to achieve quite a lot in his career, but held onto a basic distrust of management and a pride in working-class values. My patient paid attention to the class divide between us. While my background was more privileged than his, I felt he exaggerated this difference between us. The patient told me the following two dreams:

"I bumped into Francine, a woman I work with, on the street. She was going home. I asked her, 'Do you live near here?' She said 'Yeah.' I said, 'I thought you lived on X Street (near the old address of their office).' She said, 'No, I moved. I live in this neighborhood.' It was 72nd and Broadway, this neighborhood (the neighborhood of my office), although it looked like a neighborhood in London."

The patient then associated: "I was reading a restaurant review about a great new restaurant in that neighborhood in London. It used to be a lower-class neighborhood, but it has been gentrified lately."

Then he continued: "I had another dream before that. I was stabbed with a screwdriver by a clerk at the office. Although he appears normal, he's really nuts, psychotic. He stabs me in the ribs. A 911 call is made. I realized I'm not really stabbed. This is going to be tough to explain. The authorities come. I'm at the hospital. It's the hospital police, not the regular police. I'm relieved. I won't have to explain myself."

We talked about the two dreams. I noticed his concerns about violence and rape. The patient was often at pains to disown any violent feelings and had been personally offended when girlfriends feared violence in him or from men in general. I also noted his reactions to my neighborhood, which had been gentrified. He was both proud of my office and envious of it. He said he had many feelings about the class system, which is much more blatant in England, as he pointed out, although quite present in the United States, too.

Nearly ten months later, I was having a session with the same patient. We had been discussing his difficulties at work. He was not perceived as a "team player." During his years with the same company, and during his analysis with me, he had been advanced from being a clerk to being in a high level of management, but there were still two or three levels of management higher than his. He recently was passed over for promotion. He claimed to be glad, since he felt that the highest levels of management are corrupted, although he also seemed depressed and envious.

I noted that his reluctance to be a team player may have rational aspects. I admired him for not wanting to do things that compromised his intellectual and ethical principles. In fact, I believed that he had advanced as far as he has, despite his personality difficulties, because he was so competent. But I wondered if sometimes he sabotaged himself by being sour and resentful when there were no principles involved, but merely out of some irrational resentment. He found this compelling and came back to the next session with observations of how this might be going on. As we continued to discuss it, I remembered his dream with the screwdriver stabbing, and felt like I had an "Aha" experience. I asked him if he remembered the dream, and he did. I said, "There is a principle that all of the people in a dream are aspects of the dreamer. When we spoke about it, I wonder if we didn't look enough at the person of the clerk who stabs you. I think he is the aspect of you that is still identified with being a clerk at your job, even though you have progressed so far. That aspect of you is sticking yourself with a screwdriver, that is, screwing yourself. Nobody else can see it, but you know it." This self-sabotaging aspect, the clerk in the dream, is, as he described in the dream, crazy. He was holding onto resentments that no longer applied. He was relieved in the dream when he was seen by the hospital police, so he wouldn't have to talk about it. This was his resistance talking. He was relieved that he had not had to explain this aspect of himself to me.

The issues of class and social mobility are obvious in both of his dreams. In the first, Francine has moved to a neighborhood, my neighborhood, which has been gentrified during the last 20 years. And in the second, his clerk-self injures his executive-self in a way that no one else can see and which he is relieved not to talk about. Now, ten months later, he and I had become able to talk about it more openly. He pointed out the blue-collar background of his family and its current effects on him. He would not hire anyone to help him with domestic tasks, because his grandmother worked as a domestic and resented the way her employers treated her. Whenever he heard about generous family foundations, he wondered about how they got their money and presumed it was ill-gotten. He had an ingrained bias and hostility towards anyone with a sense of entitlement or upper-class pretensions or background. We were able to examine the degree to which this stance is realistic and the ways in which he "screws himself" with it. I realize now that my own dream that I told him was also an attempt to deal with the class issues. By putting myself down on the floor, I was attempting to shift the tense balance of his raising me up in the transference, and I was modeling for him a lack of fear of shame. My association to my kindergarten *class* was also related to the questions of social class and hierarchy. The word "class" was overdetermined, and I was trying to return to a time and place in life when class issues were relatively insignificant.

In this case, my telling of the dream served multiple functions. It broke the ice in the transference. It led to the patient having dreams that, in conjunction with my dream, led to a freer exploration of the issue of social class. The combined analysis of my dream and the patient's dream illustrate a kind of mutual analysis of dreams and a breakthrough in both the patient's and my own resistance. It goes along with my view that effective dream analysis often involves a kind of back and forth analysis and re-analysis of dreams. Usually, such re-analysis concerns only the patient's dreams (see chapter 16). But the same principle applies when an analyst tells a patient a dream. The patient may respond with his own dream. The analysis of both the patient's and analyst's dreams may clarify the entire transference/countertransference matrix.

Was there any problem to my telling the patient my dream? In this example, I don't think so. But I have one reservation. The exploration of countertransference has increasingly been recognized as a powerful tool in helping the psychoanalytic process. We have come a long way since the Neanderthal 1980s, when I heard Joyce McDougall present her self-analysis of her countertransference with a woman patient, only to be told by the discussant that she should get back into analysis. Nevertheless, I believe that in the current literature on countertransference disclosure, successful outcomes may be over-represented. In nearly all the examples that I know of from our literature, the process seems benign and is almost always productive (Watson, 1994). This may represent a reporting bias. Psychoanalysts are much less likely to report, "I explored my countertransference with the patient, the patient felt traumatized, and quit treatment." The analyst may not even be aware of what has happened, since patients who have felt traumatized by their analyst often leave treatment suddenly without ever explaining to their analyst what happened. There are at least two common pitfalls: (1) boundary violations implicit in countertransference revelations; and (2) unwillingness of the analyst to consider thoroughly the patient's reinterpretation of the analyst's revelation.

Another problem with our study of the analyst who tells his patient a dream is that we have no written reports from the patient's point of view of what it is like to be told a dream by one's analyst. When I was in analysis, I read Tauber's paper and asked my analyst to tell me a dream in which I appeared, if he ever had one. He never did. Edgar Levenson was in analysis with Edward Tauber and told one of his students, Susan Kolod (1999), about the experience. He said that he found it to be burdensome, intrusive and completely unhelpful. From Levenson's perspective, Tauber would "dump" the dream on him with the implication that Tauber's dream revealed something important about Levenson which Levenson should be eager to try to figure out. I think there is an essential principle here: If you tell a patient one of your dreams, you must be prepared to respect the patient's wish *not* to analyze it.

If you are going to tell a patient one of your dreams, you must also accept the fact that you will be telling your patient much more than you realize. Remember the principle that everyone in the dream represents an aspect of the dreamer. If we take that principle seriously, then the analyst's dream about a patient is also about the analyst. It may follow that the analyst's dream about a patient is really about the crossover between the patient's personality and the analyst's. If that is so, then when the analyst tells a patient such a dream, he may be saying, in effect, "Here is a way that you and I are similar," or "Here is what I would be like if my personality were like yours." Telling a patient a dream implies a very high degree of self-revelation, whether or not the analyst intends it. And so, if you tell your dream, you must be willing to collaborate openly and sincerely with the patient in interpreting your dream.

COUNTERTRANSFERENCE DREAMS WITHOUT THE PATIENT IN THE MANIFEST CONTENT

Traditionally, countertransference dreams have been identified as dreams by the psychoanalyst in which a patient appears in the manifest content (e.g., Whitman, Kramer, and Baldridge, 1969, p. 702). This definition is, by itself, strangely unpsychoanalytic. It presumes that the identity of the figures in the dreams corresponds with their manifest identity, a principle that is not followed in the clinical interpretation of patients' dreams. All dreams of an analyst are potentially countertransference dreams.

An analyst's dream may well be about her or his countertransference about a particular patient, even if that patient does not appear in the manifest content. The connection to the patient may be deduced from the analyst's associations. Rosenbloom (1998) has provided a good example of an analyst's dream in which the patient did not appear in the manifest content, but which the analyst felt, upon awakening, was related to his feelings toward his patient. The patient's mother was dying, and the analyst dreamt of visiting the home of someone who had already died, and was resistant to comply with their wish that he put masking tape on some beautiful works of art that were hanging on the walls, in connection with the Jewish tradition of covering up mirrors during mourning. Rosenbloom did not tell the dream to his patient, but he analyzed it privately, connecting it to guilt about his own sense of inadequate mourning, and to a link between the depressions of his mother and his patient.

THE ANALYST'S VISUAL IMAGE OF THE PATIENT'S DREAM

Besides analyzing his own dreams about a patient, the analyst has another very powerful source of information about his countertransference in work with dreams. If you monitor your own imagery while listening to a patient's dream, you will often find out very precise facts about your countertransference. This is a technique that should be acceptable to psychoanalysts of all schools, and it is often astonishingly productive (Ross and Kapp, 1962). For example, suppose a patient says, "I dreamt I was in the house I grew up in." You will probably then see a mental image of that house. Even if the patient specifies many details, for example, "I went into a white stucco house, with two Corinthian columns in the front, and red shutters around the windows," the analyst may note the specificity of his own image of the house and its surround. If the analyst then examines that image for his own associations to it, he will discover how he has coordinated the patient's dream-house into his own psychodynamics. Usually, locating that house in the analyst's life story will tell him a great deal about the reactions he is having to the patient and how he is connecting the patient's story to his own life experience—both of which may often tell him something about the patient himself. This happens not only with houses, of course, but with anything or anyone else that appears in the dream.

For example, with one of my patients, I noticed that my image of his house also corresponded to the house of a boy who was my friend growing up and who was an excellent athlete. That boy's father was one of the most paranoid people I knew as a child. He was always irritable and menacing. I realized how much this patient evoked feelings in me reminiscent of my feelings toward this boyhood friend, both of admiration and competition, and of my being careful around his touchy and explosive father. The exploration of my own imagery eventually led to my being aware that my patient was also touchy and explosive and helped me address those issues with him.

CHAPTER 19

THE REALLOCATION OF MADNESS

She thought she saw an elephant
when looking in the mirror.
It was a scarecrow in a tent
and no one else could see her.
You really must go sleep, he said,
Your dreams are in arrear.

When I was in training at a psychiatric hospital, I often heard it said that crazier-sounding dreams were typical of psychotic patients. But in the early years of my private practice, through a fluke of the referral process, the bulk of my patients had been diagnosed either as borderline or psychotic, and I started to notice that what I had been taught often did not hold up. On the contrary, at the beginning of treatment with patients who were either borderline or psychotic, I often noticed that while their waking communications could be filled with delusional material, their dreams often were extremely bland and matter of fact. At times, their dreams seemed to give me uncomplicated messages either about their lives or their reactions to treatment which their waking communications did not.

In 1983, I published a paper about this, describing changes in dreams of borderline patients during psychoanalytic treatment. I reported that in many borderline patients, as well as in some ambulatory schizophrenic patients, dreams reported early in treatment tend to be rational and discursive, with relatively little bizarreness. A special form of such a dream was a kind of reportage—that is, the dream portrayed the actual situation of the previous day's session, with little alteration, communicating to the therapist an aspect of the patient's experience of the session that would not be directly verbalized and might be contrary to the manifest affect of the patient during the waking interactions with the analyst. I also noticed that in some patients, as the analysis progressed and their condition improved, their reported dreams tended to become more bizarre and "dreamlike." Contrary to some people's clinical intuition, this development correlated with an improvement in psychic functioning. I would like now to report observations of other clinicians on the same subject and to place the finding in the context of a broader theory of psychopathology and the theory of dreams.

The original purpose of my report was to communicate a clinical finding which was, to my knowledge, essentially new. In the intervening years, however, I have realized that my "discovery" of realistic dreams in borderline and psychotic patients was by no means new. On the contrary, the first thesis of my paper, that borderline patients' dreams tend to be rational and undreamlike, was already known by the great Russian novelist, Fyodor Dostoyevsky, more than a century earlier. In his novel, *Crime and Punishment* (1866), Dostoyevsky wrote:

> In pathological states dreams are often distinguished by an uncommon vividness and sharpness of focus and by an extraordinary conjunction with reality. The scene unfolded may be a monstrous one, and yet the setting and the means of presentation not only probable, but subtly detailed, full of surprises, and at the same time artistically in key with the scene as a whole, so that the dreamer himself, though he were an artist of the caliber of Pushkin or Turgenev, could never have invented them awake. Such dreams, pathological dreams, make a powerful impression on man's disordered, already aroused organism, and are always remembered for a long time [p. 55].

Several psychoanalysts have also happened on the same kind of clinical data, although they have drawn different conclusions. Freud wrote about such nondreamlike dreams several times during his career. He wondered whether they really existed, and changed his mind about this several times. In *The Interpretation of Dreams*, Freud cites Maury (1878): "Il n'y a pas de rêves absolument raisonnables et qui ne contiennent quelque incohérence, quelque anachronisme, quelque absurdité" (p. 55). ("There are no dreams that are absolutely reasonable and that do not contain some incoherence, anachronism, or absurdity.")

At the time, Freud thought Maury was wrong. He thought he himself had had such dreams, but on closer examination decided that impression was false:

> Thus I remember a dream of mine which struck me when I woke up as being so particularly well-constructed, flawless, and clear that, while I was still half-dazed with sleep, I thought of introducing a new category of dreams which were not subject to the mechanisms of condensation and displacement but were to be described as "fantasies during sleep." Closer examination proved that this rarity among dreams showed the same gaps and flaws in its structure as any other; and for that reason I dropped the category of "dream-phantasies" [p. 331].

He later cast doubt on this conclusion; in 1930, he added a footnote to this passage: "Whether rightly I am now uncertain." In between, Freud (1922) wrote:

> There are dreams which are to be distinguished from the usual type by certain special qualities, which are, properly speaking, nothing but night-phantasies, not having undergone additions or alterations of any kind and being in all other ways similar to the familiar day-dreams. It would be awkward, no doubt, to exclude these structures from the domain of "dreams," but still they all come from within, are products of our mental life, whereas the very conception of the purely "telepathic dream" lies in its being a perception of something external, in relation to which the mind remains passive and receptive [p. 208].

Several times in his career, Freud considered the notion of there being two kinds of dreams, realistic and fantastic, but he never settled the question. The mere fact that he raised it was astonishingly prescient of him. All of his writing on this subject was before 1953, when Aserinsky and Kleitman discovered REM sleep, and before dream researchers noted that REM dreams tend to be more "dreamlike," while nonREM dreams tend to have more of the characteristics of waking thought.[1]

---

1. Bettelheim (1985) writes as if rational thoughts during nonREM sleep can simply be categorized as "not dreams," an arbitrary distinction which cannot be sustained. The identification of dreams with REM, also promulgated by Hobson (1988), is made questionable by the data (Foulkes, 1962; Solms, 2000) that approximately 20% of nonREM dreams are indistinguishable from REM dreams.

After Dostoyevsky, there have been several psychoanalysts who have reported similar kinds of dreams in borderline patients. Brunswick (1929) gives an extraordinarily complete account of dreams in her work with a woman whom she diagnoses as "paranoia of the delusional jealousy type" in which "the pathological process is sharply circumscribed." Nearly all of the dreams reported are of the "sane" variety typical of borderline patients. However, the analysis lasted only two and a half months.

In 1952, Paul Federn, a psychoanalyst known for his expertise with psychoses, wrote: "In some diseases, especially in amentia and in manic and melancholic states, normal knowledge seems to have become unconscious and reveals itself in dreams" (p. 151).

In 1972, empirical researcher Rosalind Cartwright observed that many dreams of psychotics were bland. And in 1983, Roy Schafer reported on a patient who, like some of my patients, did his best reality testing in his dreams, until the issue had been worked through psychoanalytically:

> My final example concerns a young man with severe narcissistic, masochistic, and paranoid problems. For a long time he represented his best reality testing only in his dreaming. That is to say, only in his dreaming did he verbally and pictorially represent certain plain truths about himself, his parents, his friends, and his analyst. These were truths he did not dare consciously recognize and explicitly affirm while awake. We learned that by day he would often represent these truths by what were for him their opposites; he would, for example, emphasize only the kindness of others and his own selfishness. That it was a matter of resisting the daytime representation of reality testing became evident through careful analysis of his responding by reversal to instances of the analyst's countertransferential and counterresistant obtuseness, insensitivity, impatience, and ingratiation. This careful analysis of reversal required a good deal of honest, even if reluctant self-observation on the part of the analyst. The interpretation that had to be developed was this: the analysand was dismissing his reality testing as only a dream and substituting waking dreams for reality testing. It developed subsequently that for him clear-sightedness and frankness amounted to loss of control over anal-sadistic and castrating attacks on others; also, a destructive differentiation of his self from a symbiotic and crippling mother; additionally, a sign of

> castratedness in its being based on "feminine" intuition; and finally, a sign of great superiority over others who, he felt, would not be able to stand up under his powerful "truth-telling" [p. 179].[2]

There are enough individual clinicians who have found reportage dreams in borderline patients, and a change to more "dreamlike" dreams as the patients improve in psychotherapy, that it would seem worthwhile to conduct a quantitative study of this phenomenon. It is my current impression that undreamlike dreams can be indicative of serious pathology, but that not all dreams of seriously ill patients at the beginning of treatment are "realistic." In teaching dream courses, students who have no knowledge of this finding often react with much surprise to the "reportage" dreams. They ask, "Is this really a dream?"

The phenomenon of overly rational dreams in borderline patients has ramifications for our general thinking about thought disorder in psychosis and dreaming. It is possible that psychotic pathology involves a shift of "bizarre" thoughts from dreaming to waking, and of more rational thoughts from waking to dreaming. This would also imply changing our view of dreams from the expression of *content* that is latent to the expression of a *whole kind of mental processing* that may be latent. And that which may be latent in psychotic patients may be rational thinking. If we assume that dreams reflect unconscious processes, then the pattern of borderline dream structure may lead us to conclude that it is erroneous to conceptualize unconscious thinking in terms of specific types of content or process as in classical psychoanalytic theory. If we avoid the reified notion of "the unconscious" as an entity (which is limited to any kinds of structural features or types of contents), and adhere to the usage of "unconscious" only as an adjective (describing a quality of experience, without awareness, which may apply to any forms of thinking and emotional states), we may begin to consider in some patients that that which is unconscious may well be the kind of rational thinking and variegated affect that form the bulk of conscious experience in less troubled individuals.

This was akin to Sullivan's view of schizophrenia. He wrote (1962):

> When the schizophrenic has effected his recoil either from everyone (literally, as in some stupors, or relatively as in occasional paranoid manifestations and in hebephrenic develop-

---

2. For other examples, see Guntrip (1968) and Masterson (1981).

> ments), or from any but a few who are highly illusory to him, the thinking is almost entirely a matter of dreams in which his problems are dealt with in activities the peculiarities of which result from the dream-dynamics mentioned in our theoretic section. The striking differences from ordinary dreams arise in part from the magnitude of the conative backgrounds, and in part from the fact that *his sensory channels are not nearly as impervious as in sleep, so that the events which transpire in his proximity take their place in the dream-thinking, in lieu of day-remnants* [pp. 98–99; italics added].

Sullivan argued that the dreams will change on a continuum—the more that any kind of thinking is dissociated, the more it will be forced into dreams. If we think of pathologies with thought disorder as illnesses in which rational thinking is dissociated, then it makes sense that the dissociated rational thinking might find its way into dreams. As Sullivan (1962) observed:

> To the extent that important tendency systems of the personality have to discharge themselves in sleep, to that extent the dream-processes tend to exaggerated personal importance, and to augmented "reality value." That which permits other states of altered consciousness is their condition of dissociation by other tendency systems of the personality—systems apparently invariantly represented in the self [p. 279].

Decades later, Eric Marcus (1992) reiterated this position, pointing out that this is an aspect of psychopathology that medication does not resolve:

> There are many patients who are left with dissociated states in spite of medication, because a specific dissociated area serves defensive functions that have to do with the dynamic psychology of the material dissociated. Medication does not affect dynamic psychology. This is a crucial area for psychoanalytic psychotherapy to attend to in the patients who show these dissociated areas, and almost all very ill patients do. In fact, it is the sicker patients who do not, since they tend to have their psychotic material infiltrate the entire personality structure [p. 191].

The implication here is that psychopathology is, in some cases, a *failure of dissociation*. It follows, then, that the work of psychotherapy is to reinstate adequate dissociation of psychotic material, restoring it to its rightful place in the unconscious and the dream world.

If psychotic patients dissociate rational thoughts from waking life into dreams, it could show up in the pattern of brain activity in the dreams and waking thoughts of psychotics and nonpsychotics. This is an inherently testable hypothesis. Positron Emission Tomography (PET scans) already allows us to identify the areas of the brain that are active during REM sleep (e.g., Maquet et al., 1996). As this methodology is refined, we may be able to scan the brains of waking hallucinating schizophrenics and of dreaming normal subjects, and vice versa, in order to discover the areas of activity that the two have in common and those that are different.

However, there are other possible explanations of seemingly rational dreams in borderline patients. Although it appears that borderline patients actually have special kinds of dreams, there are several possible alternative explanations of the clinical data. One is that the rational dream is, when actually dreamt, more bizarre, but that the patient "cleans it up" for a variety of motivations. I know that this occurred with at least one patient, who read my first paper on the subject (Blechner, 1983) and told me he found it a great relief. He admitted that, before he read my paper, when reporting his dreams to me, he had deliberately tried to remove or alter the parts that seemed "crazy," lest I think him too disturbed. He felt now that, if anything, he would distort them in the opposite direction.

Another possibility is that the phenomenon is due to a different sleep pattern in borderline patients, not to a difference in the essential character of their dreams. Are the sleep-patterns of borderlines different, so that they have more nonREM dream memory? We know that REM dreams tend to be more bizarre and less like waking thought than nonREM dreams. So, we might ask, do borderline and psychotic patients tend to remember more nonREM dreams than REM dreams? And as they improve in psychotherapy, does their basic sleep pattern change (Zimmerman, 1967, 1970), such that they come to remember more REM than nonREM dreams?

Another alternative explanation is that borderline pathology actually leads to a kind of natural REM deprivation, perhaps due to an inordinately high anxiety level or some other factors. In that case, the REM phenomena become displaced into daytime thinking. Ellman (1985; Ellman and Antrobus, 1991), for example, holds that mechanisms of REM occur throughout the day, and that REM deprivation leads to a displacement of phasic activity into nonREM sleep. Such nonREM dreams become more vivid. Ellman speculates that similar displacements occur in schizophrenia. As Levin (1990) writes about this theory: "This position could also explain the often-documented blandness of schizophrenic dreams" (p. 28).

DREAM INCORPORATION OF PSYCHOTIC MATERIAL AS A SIGN OF CLINICAL IMPROVEMENT

In psychotic patients, a favorable sign of successful psychotherapy may be the incorporation of previously delusional material into the patient's dreams. This has been observed by several clinicians besides myself (Blechner, 1983). Arieti (1963) reports on a patient who had delusions that the Russians were invading the city and had interpreted the red sunset over the Hudson as a divine warning that the whole world would become red. Arieti traces this to a letter from her parents announcing that they would come for a visit to New York. The patient had left her southern, conservative family to live in Greenwich Village in a wild way that her parents and she (to some degree) would disapprove of. As the patient improved, she dreamt she was being chased by her parents all over New York City. She saw in this dream scenes similar to those she saw in her acute delusional state, including the scene around the Hudson River. She was afraid and kept hiding. Finally, however, she felt she did not care whether the parents caught her or not. They would not hurt her. She decided she had nothing to hide and went toward the parents to meet them.

Arieti (1963) writes:

> [These dreams], in a certain way, aim at what Sechehaye tries to accomplish with her treatment. But whereas with Sechehaye's method it is quite difficult to set up artificial dreams, with the method that I follow this natural faculty of the individual is spontaneously resorted to after the patient has decreased his pathology and is psychologically prepared for trials, at least in his dream life. The patient no longer tries to deal with his conflicts in an openly psychotic way, but in that psychotic way which is physiologic and available to every human being: the dream-world [p. 27].

Eric Marcus (1992, p. 189) describes a delusional patient who believes that a crown is waiting for him in the White House and tries, in fact, to get into the White House to retrieve it. He is treated with medication and psychotherapy, and the delusion abates. At first the patient gains insight that his delusion is actually a wish. Eventually, the patient is freed of the preoccupying fantasy, and the delusion then appears periodically as a dream.

The phenomenon of the incorporation of psychotic material into dreams as the patient improves continues to be rediscovered. In 1999, Jean-Michel Quinodoz identified what he called "dreams that turn over a page," in which primitive material appears in the dream, which the psychoanalyst may recognize as a sign of psychic integration. The paper was discussed on the Internet (see Williams, 1999, for a summary), and many other clinicians concurred. Lea Goldberg (Williams, 1999), for example, noted in her work with psychotic patients that "losing a delusional thought in waking life could be followed by the content of the thought appearing in a dream but without anxiety" (pp. 849–850).

A schizophrenic man, Ken Steele, who improved dramatically on the antipsychotic medication Risperdal after 32 years of hallucinations, reported a similar incorporation of his psychotic experience into his dreams (Goode, 1999). Goode writes, "And when, as sometimes happens, his voices return in a dream, and he wakes up in the darkness in a cold sweat, the fear only lasts a few minutes. It was, after all, only a dream" (p. 8).

It has been observed that when psychotic patients improve, they sometimes become nostalgic for their lost symptoms (Fromm-Reichmann, 1959). The incorporation of the psychotic material into dreams may thus be experienced as a way-station to sanity, with the psychotic material temporarily taking up residence in night thoughts, where the recovering patient can feel the relief that "it is only a dream."

PART IV

SLEEP, DREAMS, AND THE BRAIN

CHAPTER 20

KNOWING WHAT WE KNOW IN WAKING AND DREAMING

I dream, therefore I exist.

Strindberg

THE STUDY OF dreams brings us to some of the central questions of modern cognitive neuroscience, namely, what do we know, and how do we know that we know it? Can we sometimes know things, without knowing that we know them? And an even bigger problem is how we keep track of reality. How do we know where our experiences and memories come from? How can we tell whether something really happened to us or whether we imagined or dreamt it?

There is a Chinese tale in the Chuang-tzu: "Once Chuang Chou dreamed that he was a butterfly. He fluttered about happily, quite pleased with the state he was in, and knew nothing about Chuang Chou. Presently he awoke and found that he was very much Chuang Chou again. Now, did Chou dream that he was a butterfly or was the butterfly now dreaming that he was Chou?"

Similarly, how do we know the difference between perception and imagery? In other words, when we visualize something while awake, how can we tell whether we are perceiving something in the world or generating our own imagery? The answer is that sometimes we can't. The psychologist Cheves Perky demonstrated in 1910 that when we imagine something visually, it interferes with our ability to see visual details in the real world. This unreliability is of concern to those who study the accuracy of "eyewitness" testimony (e.g., Loftus, 1979; Wells et al., 2000).

Nevertheless, we usually can distinguish mental images from percepts. How? Kosslyn (1994) outlines several cues which may help us distinguish imagery from perception, but notes that this capacity may be diminished during dreaming:

> First, the stimulus-based attention-shifting subsystem operates only during perception; thus, if our attention is suddenly grabbed by an object or event, we are not engaged in imagery. This may not be true during dreams, however: During waking imagery, one always knows the identity of the objects one is imaging; during dreaming, this apparently is not always true. Moreover, the 'rules' of dreaming allow objects to appear in unusual contexts, so it is conceivable that one's mental attention is 'grabbed' during dreaming in a way that is reminiscent of the way it is captured during perception. I have no evidence one way or the other that the same subsystem is used when attention is shifted by stimulus properties during perception and during dreaming, but I tend to doubt it: The connections from the eye to the superior colliculus, which appear critical for the attention-shifting subsystem, are unlikely to be evoked during imagery [pp. 102–103].

Keeping track of whether an image came from the real world, our own waking imagery, or dream imagery is complicated by the fact that memory for dreams is notoriously bad. It is a common experience for those of us who keep dream logs to be almost totally unable to remember some of the dreams we have recorded. To reread the dream log is to be delightfully surprised—that is, is that what I was thinking then?

Donald Symons (1993) has proposed an evolutionary reason for our forgetting of dreams. He argues that if we remembered our dreams better, we might be more likely to confuse memories of actual experiences with memories of dreams. Dream forgetting helps us keep track of reality.

The problem of how we keep track of reality is a special concern of the experimental psychologist, Marcia Johnson. She conducted a study of how we know if something really happened, or that we imagined it, or dreamt it. (See also Rapaport, 1957.) Johnson calls this the study of "reality monitoring."

Johnson conducted a rather unusual and creative experiment (Johnson, Kahan, and Raye, 1984). She invited couples to be subjects in her study. She asked them to tell each other, upon awakening, one of three things: a dream that they had, a "dream" that they made up while awake, or someone else's dream (for which she provided the text). About two weeks later, she performed tests to see how well the people were able to remember these texts: their own dreams, their made-up dreams, and someone else's dreams.

The subjects had to discriminate between memories for their own dreams and memories for dreams that their spouse or partner told them. There were two tests: recollection, in which they had to provide the dreamtext; and recognition, in which they were given a text, and asked to recognize whether it had been an actual dream, a made-up dream, or someone else's dream. The subjects' ability to remember their own dreams was poor (below 20%). However, their performance on recognition tests was quite good, between 72% and 80%. In other words, you may not be able to tell me the dream that you had last month, but if I ask you, "Did you have a dream last month in which a monkey was swinging over your head?," you will probably be able to remember whether or not you did.

In my clinical work I often remember my patients' dreams better than they do (and better than I remember my own dreams). Often a patient does not remember a dream, but when I provide one or two details from the dream, the patient can recall most of it. However, Johnson also notes that "recall depends critically on how readily information is comprehended and organized" (Bransford and Johnson, 1973; Tulving, 1968). It is possible that analyzing a dream and transforming its unusual content into a more linguistically coherent interpretation helps us remember it, whether it is our own dream or one that has been told by someone else. I think, anecdotally, that if a patient tells me a dream at the end of a session and we do not have time to analyze it, I am much less likely to remember the dreamtext in the next session. But it would be useful to get experimental data on this.

There could be a simple experiment:

Write down your dream immediately upon awakening. Then after a certain amount of time (e.g., one week, month, year), try to write it down again. Do this under three conditions: (1) with dreams that you have never told another person; (2) with dreams that you have told to another person, but not discussed further; and (3) with dreams that you have discussed and analyzed with another person. Is the dream remembered any better if you discuss the dream in analysis, if it is given an interpretation, and if the interpretation is felt as "good"? Repeat the experiment with dreams told to a psychoanalyst by a patient, (1) in which the dream is told but not analyzed; (2) the dream is analyzed and the analysis is felt to be "good" by the analyst; and (3) the dream is analyzed but the analysis is not felt to be "good" by the analyst.

Does the relatively poor recall for dreams suggest that repression or dissociation is at work? In repression, it is presumed that psychological forces actively keep us from becoming aware of certain mental experiences. In dissociation, the connection between different thoughts and feelings is suppressed, although the thoughts and feelings themselves may be separately available to memory.

Poor memory for dreams, as shown by lack of recall, is not an all or nothing process. In some cases, it can be released quite readily by recognition, which suggests that dynamic countercathexes might not be the primary source of those failures in recall. If there were powerful psychological forces working against your remembering parts of a dream, one would expect that you would not be able to *recognize* that aspect of your dream either.

Freud discussed the different metapsychologies of repression and dissociation. Repression disguises the content of thoughts; dissociation disguises the connections between thoughts. According to Freud, if there are two related thoughts that are objectionable, the censorship may alter the content of the two thoughts, while leaving their relationship the same; or it may leave the content of the two thoughts the same, but disguise their apparent relationship. The former is repression, the latter dissociation. Freud (1900) writes:

> Two cases may here be distinguished, though in essence they are the same. In the first of these, the censorship is directed only against the *connection* between two thoughts, which are unobjectionable separately. If so, the two thoughts will enter consciousness in succession; the connection between them will remain concealed, but, instead, a superficial link between them will occur to us, of which we should otherwise never have thought. This link is usually attached to some part of the complex of ideas quite other than that on which the suppressed and essential connection in based. The second case is where the two thoughts are in themselves subject to censorship on account of their content. If so, neither of them appears in its true shape but only in a modified one which replaces it; and the two replacing thoughts are chosen in such a way that they have a superficial association that repeats the essential connection which relates the two thoughts that have been replaced. *In both of these*

cases the pressure of the censorship has resulted in a displacement from a normal and serious association to a superficial and apparently absurd one [p. 530].

The first kind of distortion described by Freud is the essence of dissociation. The two ideas are right there, but the person does not see their connection.

DISSOCIATION, PANIC DISORDER, AND DREAMS

Dissociation is a feature of various clinical syndromes. In my experience, it is a fundamental feature of people with panic disorder. In every case of panic disorder that I have treated, the initial interview reveals the same mental situation. The person is having thoughts or experiences that would make any person terribly frightened. But somehow the person with panic disorder has come to dissociate the fearfulness of the situation. The great fear, which anyone would feel, does not disappear. Instead, it is experienced as a thing in itself, unconnected to anything in the person's real life. In such cases, the immediate experience of panic is readily treatable. You can outline to the patient how the situation of X would make anyone frightened. The result is often recognition and relatively rapid alleviation of the panic symptom, which is replaced by great anxiety and confusion about what to do (which is ultimately preferable to suppression of the anxiety pharmacologically, which leaves the danger situation in place).

In such patients, the seriousness of the danger situation can be portrayed in a dream. The strength of the dissociation can be felt by the psychoanalyst, who sees the danger so plainly in the manifest content, while the dreamer himself cannot see it.

For example, a gay man in his thirties, John, presented in psychotherapy with severe panic attacks, day and night (Blechner, 1997a). During the day he would feel as if he were having a heart attack, and he would wake up in the middle of the night in terror. I asked if he was dreaming when he awoke, and he said that at times he was dreaming that he had AIDS. He was involved in a relationship of two-years standing with a man, Leo. A brief inquiry revealed that Leo's prior lover had died of AIDS, yet he never told John, who found it out from someone else three months into the relationship. He mentioned it to Leo, who had a lame excuse for keeping it secret. John rationalized away his immediate suspicion and then forgot about it (except in his dreams).

Leo himself had not been tested for the HIV virus; in fact, he refused to be tested. I commented to John that anyone in a gay relationship in the 1990s should be concerned about AIDS, and that anyone would be especially concerned if their partner had had a longstanding relationship with someone who died of the disease. Their concern would be even greater if the partner had concealed this fact, even more so if their partner had not been tested, and even more so if the partner refused to be tested. John seemed startled by these thoughts, but the panic attacks ceased.

In another case, a young man in his early twenties consulted me for panic attacks. He was very handsome and he knew it. He was living "high," going to fashionable bars and picking up different girls most nights. He rarely used a condom, risking both pregnancy and sexually-transmitted disease. I asked him if he did other self-destructive things, and he answered by telling me a dream[1] that he had had at least four times:

> I am in a bar, a house or somewhere. I am sitting at a table with one or two people and I have one or two beers. All of a sudden, I put my face down on the table, and I couldn't move. I couldn't move. I am screaming to the others, wait, I'm coming, but I have no control over anything.

I noted that one meaning of the dream is that he was ruining his body, and the other people don't notice. He had taken drugs and was using steroids. He had an odd double consciousness of denial and panic at the same time. The dream condensed the loss of control of sexual climax (Wait, I'm coming!) with the general loss of control of his life.

In both of these clinical vignettes, the patients' dreams brought together ideas that suggested obvious terror to me, but the patients had consciously dissociated the connection between the ideas and the affect.

1. This is a sequence that is common in psychoanalysis. As the analyst inquires into a certain area, the patient may respond by telling a dream. In the moment, the patient is not aware of why the dream answers the analyst's question, although it usually does. We could say there is an unconscious metaknowledge of the connection between the dream and the question, or merely that the patient has learned to trust "free association" enough to report the dream when it arises in his awareness seemingly unbidden.

METACOGNITION: MONITORING OUR OWN MINDS

The study of dreams raises important questions about metacognition, which is a kind of record-keeping of the mind. If we know something, do we know we know it? Are there times that we think we know something when we actually don't? And does the reverse happen: We think we don't know something, but we actually do?

There are examples of people who feel during a dream that they have a certain intellectual ability, yet they cannot reproduce it on awakening. Does this show that their intellectual power in the dream was an illusory impression, or does it show that they cannot sustain the intellectual performance in waking or transfer the ability from dreaming to waking? For example, a composer dreamt that if, in the song "Over the Rainbow," she changed one of the pitches, then she would have the power to influence Harold, a man who attracted her, to become her lover. When she told the dream, I asked her if she could say which pitch she changed, and she could not. The dream could be seen merely as a metaphor of her wish to use her compositional power to make a man love her. But one wonders, had she awakened right after the dream, would she have actually been able to identify the pitch—whether or not it would have had the power indicated by the dream?

The area of foreign languages is another good example of metaknowledge in dreams. People may feel that they are fluent in a foreign language, but when placed in situation in a foreign country, they may perceive the limits of their ability to negotiate the language. I am not considering here the deliberate misrepresentation of one's knowledge, but rather the ability, in good faith, to be aware of what one knows.

Vaschide (1911) remarks that it has often been observed that in dreams people speak foreign languages more fluently and correctly than in waking life. But do people actually speak those languages better in their dreams, or do they only have the impression that they are speaking better? Is there any way to test this? One piece of evidence would be if they could wake and say something that they heard in the dream which they do not understand while awake. Then, we could check if a native speaker of that foreign language confirms that the dream quotation was correctly formed in the foreign language.

Something analogous to this has been done in hypnosis. Erika Fromm worked in hypnoanalysis with a young man who was born in Japan but claimed not to know any Japanese. She did an age regression with him to age four, and he started to speak correct Japanese. Fortunately, she was tape recording the session and so was able to confirm that his Japanese, spoken while in trance, was correct (Fromm and Nash, 1997).

There is also the question of precisely what "knowing" means. Do we know something if our behavior shows evidence of having processed certain information even if we consciously do not have awareness of that knowledge? For example, there is evidence that different areas of the brain process visual information for conscious "knowledge" and for object representations that control motor behavior. A patient known as D.F. had damage to the ventral visual areas of his brain that resulted in severe agnosia, yet he could manipulate objects appropriately even if he could not consciously "see" them (Milner and Goodale, 1995). In another example, a patient with ventral damage was shown a picture of a clarinet. He said it was "perhaps a pencil," while his fingers clearly mimicked playing a clarinet. In these cases, our physical actions show evidence of "knowing" something, although we do not consciously know we know it.[2]

Daniel Schacter distinguishes between explicit and implicit knowledge, which correspond, respectively, to conscious and unconscious knowledge. There have been several attempts to determine whether patients who show implicit knowledge "really" know what they do. One of the earliest studies of implicit knowledge in the dreams of neurologically normal people was conducted by Pötzl (1917). He found that tachistoscopic images that were not consciously perceived would show up in the drawings people made of their dreams. The study raised a profound philosophical question: If a dream shows a kind of knowledge, but the dreamer when awake has no idea of the source of the knowledge, then how are we to think of that knowledge?

METAMEMORY

A similar division of mental processes and our awareness of them occurs with memory; we may remember something without knowing we remember it. Schacter (1991) has described a phenomenon known as "metamory" or "memory monitoring," which is knowledge concerning the characteristics of one's own memory performance. For example, you may not be able to remember the capital of Romania, but you may be able to predict accurately whether you would recognize that it is Bucharest if I told you.

---

2. Related data have also come from split-brain patients, in which the different brain hemispheres seem to "know" different things (Gazzaniga, 1989).

All people vary in their ability to estimate the accuracy of their own memory, but there are neuropathological syndromes in which people estimate their memory functioning especially inaccurately. Patients with the memory disorder known as Korsakoff syndrome as well as Alzheimer patients (McGlynn and Schacter, 1989), both of which involve frontal lobe damage (Kaszniak, 1986), tend to evaluate their memory incorrectly, whereas patients with other memory disorders, such as those with damage only to the temporal lobes but without frontal lobe damage, tend to be accurate (Parkin and Leng, 1993). This leads Schacter to propose that the frontal lobes are involved in memory monitoring.[3]

A patient told his analyst a dream, in which there was the phrase "Bodo Igesz" (he pronounced the last word "ee-gesh"). He could not figure it out but had a feeling that it was something he had heard before. He thought it sounded Hungarian and he liked Hungary. The therapist told the patient that it sounded like a transformation of "Bogus Ego." The patient was impressed with this and went on to associate to this idea and to question its application to himself.

The therapist told me of the dream, and I noted that there was a person with exactly that name who was a director at the Metropolitan Opera. I had seen the name in programs of the opera, and I suspected the patient had, too. Since the patient worked in a music-related field, the significance of this name may have been quite different for him. If the analyst had dreamt of Bodo Igesz, it would likely have meant bogus ego. And clearly, the analyst thought that the patient did have a bogus ego, and used the dream interpretation as a vehicle to communicate this bad news. The patient could work with it, and one assumes that no terrible clinical harm was done, and that inevitably some insight into the patient's own dynamics may have occurred. But it points out how the dream thought can be constructed rather than deciphered. Of course, one could argue that Bodo Igesz was an overdetermined dream construction—that it was a condensation of "bogus ego" and the name of the person who worked at the Met. One could never prove that this is *not* so, but it would be more convincing if the concept of "Bogus Ego" had emerged from the patient's associations, rather than the analyst's.

This incident also highlights the fact that we can have a feeling that something that comes to mind is a memory, without being able to recall what it is a memory of. The dreamer had a feeling that he had heard

---

3. This goes along with Mesulam's (1981) proposal that there are systems integrating various cortical and subcortical regions in both hemispheres in the coordination of one function.

the name Bodo Igesz before, but could not remember where. This is another variation of metamemory—a "feeling of memory."

I had a vivid experience of metamemory in connection with one of my dreams: In it, I was looking for a library whose address is "Le cercle d'Auteuil." When I awoke, I had the distinct feeling that there was in fact such an address.

When I had the dream, I had not been in Paris for two years, but over my lifetime, I have been there many times. I thought that I might have once seen a reference to "Le cercle d'Auteuil" and then forgotten it mostly. I continued to ask about it. I wrote to a French friend who now lives in America, but who spent the first three decades of his life in Paris. He told me that Auteuil was a suburb of Paris; there used to be a series of trams around Paris, and that one of them might well have been called "Le cercle d'Auteuil."

Then I got out my guides to Paris. It listed a "rue d'Auteuil," a "boulevard d'Auteuil," and a "porte d'Auteuil." There is a restaurant named "Beaujolais d'Auteuil" and another named "Relais d'Auteuil." Still no "cercle!" It seemed that either there really is a "cercle d'Auteuil" which I have not been able to find, or my mind, having witnessed the other versions of d'Auteuil, might have created it.

Now we have to ask: Does it matter whether there is, indeed, a "cercle d'Auteuil" or not, as far as understanding my dream is concerned? The classical psychoanalytic view of dreams would probably answer no. Freud, I believe, would have argued that "Le cercle d'Auteuil," if it did exist, represented indifferent material which was being brought into service to express some important piece of latent content.

But if "Le cercle d'Auteuil" really exists, that might lead to understanding something about the dream. The time when I saw it might be an important clue to the dream's meaning. And where does the "feeling" of knowing come from? We can see that knowing that one knows something is not an all-or-none phenomenon. One can have a feeling that one knows something, without knowing just what it is that one knows. This may just be a form of knowing with a low level of confidence. But it may tell us something more about the phenomenology of knowing and remembering.

In clinical work with dreams, we repeatedly encounter situations in which memory is better than metamemory; we know more than we think we know. This is experienced most dramatically with traumatic experiences, although dreams can illustrate memory for other kinds of material as well, as Pötzl (1917) and others have shown. This has led to the question of the degree to which we can use dreams as reliable evidence of memories of which the dreamer is not conscious. We often see this in discussions by groups of clinicians, who see evidence in a dream of a traumatic experience. Sometimes the dreamer consciously remembers these experiences; sometimes not.

In dreams, a trauma may be represented, which others hearing the dream will notice, but the dreamer herself does not identify. The difference is that in dreams, it is more common that when the dream interpreter points out the trace of trauma, the dreamer can recognize it and may sometimes recall a relevant memory. But in telling the dream, the dreamer does not notice how the dream rerepresents the trauma.

This occurs often in dream analysis groups. For example, a participant in a dream group reported the following dream:

> I was in a resort, and the queen of Ghana is connected to it. There is great joy going on, a celebration, because she has arranged for an explosion which is going to be greatly liberating. Everyone is jumping up and down. But then, we hear suddenly that we had better run for cover. The bomb may be going off in the resort by mistake. We are all running. Someone says, Get down! The police are coming and maybe they are going to start shooting. I climb into a fireplace with a curtain and turn off the lights. I'm waiting there. Someone climbs in. I don't want to let her in, but she does anyway.

There was a great deal of discussion of the meaning of the dream, and I will not go into all the details here. But there was a sense among the group members that the dreamer's climbing into the fireplace seemed related to the Holocaust, and that the dreamer was either a Holocaust survivor or descended from one. The dreamer was, in fact, the child of Holocaust survivors. He knew this, but, in reporting the dream, he had no idea that anything in the dream referred to the Holocaust. Once the connection was made by the group, he claimed that the dream made much more sense to him, referring to his general sense of danger in the world, and the relation of various real dangers to him with those of the Holocaust to his relatives.

PROCEDURAL KNOWLEDGE IN WAKING AND DREAMING

The rules of reality testing, which we struggled as children to learn, require us to dismiss as unreal that which we have learned *cannot* be, as well as some things that *ought not* be. This is one message of the story of "The Emperor's New Clothes": If it cannot be that the emperor is parading naked through the streets, then it is not so. We learn to dismiss as a passing illusion many things that our sensorium registers, but which do not follow our rules of how the world should work.[4] Children, not having yet learned this, can often see what we adults cannot—except in our dreams, for there we find the survival of our early capacities for perception and thinking unfettered by reality testing.

The examination of mutual contradictions between what one knows can happen and what one perceives happening is part of what psychoanalysts call reality testing. It is something that develops over time; children may violate it without anxiety until a parent corrects them repeatedly. A young boy told his mother: "I just heard our dog speak." Mother said, "No, dear, that cannot be. You must have imagined it." The boy takes in his mother's lesson that dogs do not speak. But his perception had been that he heard the dog speak. He learns from this experience, not only that dogs do not speak, but that immediate sense impressions are not to be trusted if they violate knowledge of how the world works. Over time the boy learns to fine tune this belief. Dogs and other animals may speak in stories and on television, but not in "real" life.

This knowledge is part of "common sense," which Marvin Minsky (Dreifus, 1998) has defined as "knowing maybe 30 or 50 million things about the world and having them represented so that when something happens, you can make analogies with others. . . . you can push something with a stick but not pull it. You can pull something with a string, but you can't push it."

In dreams the requirements of reality testing are lessened, though not entirely and not to the same degree in all dreams. When we are awake and recall our dreams, we tend to notice when the rules of reality testing were violated, but we do not notice when they were retained. While many strange and bizarre things may happen in our dreams, we do not usually notice how many normal facts of common sense and procedural knowledge, like those mentioned by Minsky, are retained in the action of our dreams. Helmholtz, one of the great scientists of the nineteenth century, was impressed by this fact (Helmholtz, 1863, p. 223):

4. When I was doing my doctoral dissertation (Blechner, 1977), I discovered a special case of this in music perception. I found that professional musicians tended not to hear small differences in pitch that were not deemed harmonically relevant, whereas nonprofessionals heard those differences more reliably. Our perceptions are shaped by what we have learned is important.

> The voluntary impulse for a specific movement is a psychic act which subsequently is also perceived as a change in sensation. Now is it not possible that the first act causes the second by purely psychic means? It is not impossible. Something like this happens when we dream. While dreaming, we believe we are executing a movement and we then continue dreaming that what actually happens is a natural consequence of that movement, as would have occurred also during a waking state. We dream that we are stepping onto a boat pushing off from the shore, gliding out on the water and seeing how the surrounding objects change their positions, etc. *Here the expectation of the dreamer, that he is going to see the consequences of his activities, seems to produce the dreamed perception in a purely psychic way. Who can say how long and drawn out such a dream could become? If everything in a dream happened extremely regularly, according to the natural order, it would be no different than being awake except for the possibility of waking up, and the interruption of this dreamed sequence of images* [p. 223].

This is an important observation. Helmholtz is noting that in dreams much of our procedural knowledge still holds true (although we must add, not all of it). Usually, we do not notice the extent of this—the fact, for example, that the laws of gravity apply in most of our dreams, although we notice when those laws are violated. This may lead us to wonder: What is the brain mechanism by which procedural knowledge can be overridden? In clinical neurology, there are several syndromes in which prior knowledge fails to constrain our expectations and adjustments of action sequences that are necessary for goal-directed behavior. There are cortical versions of this problem, in which knowledge of categorical structure of object or action representations may be lost (as in the agnosias). There are also subcortical lesions (usually of the basal ganglia) in which over-learned/automatic action sequences (or habits) may be compromised (Bilder, personal communication[5]; Mesulam, 1985; McCarthy and Warrington, 1990).

---

5. Bilder has also offered an interesting theory of the neuropsychological significance of such dreams: "I think a more general issue arises in attempting to understand how these constraints are liberalized in dream states. Specifically, what are the mechanisms underlying the generation of expectations, assessment of 'mismatch' between those expectations and incoming sensory information, and then making adjustments to one's expectations and action programs to reduce mismatch (which is associated with arousal and the sense of anxiety/discomfort).

Shortly after his mother died, one of my patients dreamt that his mother came into his bedroom and asked him if he wanted the light on. She started looking through one of his drawers. She left the room, and suddenly he saw the drawer moving along the floor toward the bed. He thought, "Maybe mom is under the bed." He looked, and she wasn't there. He picked up the drawer and walked toward the living room. As he walked past the kitchen, the burners were on with no pots. He asked his mother something, and she responded something.

Usually during the analysis of a dream, we especially notice the events that do not conform to common sense. This dream has a combination of natural events that conform to common sense and some strange ones that do not. The drawer moving along the floor by itself does not. In this case, the dreamer, *in the dream*, finds it strange and looks for evidence that his mother is secretly controlling the drawer's movement, but she is not. The dream captures the sense of his mother's presence and her absence, and the sense that she could have an uncanny influence on his life, even after her death.

But the dream also has events that do conform to common sense. The first part in which mother enters the room could have happened in the natural world. The same is true of her looking through his drawers (overdetermined, with a sexual connotation), which she might have done in real life, although probably not while he was present. The dream actually has a progression from expectable things, to slightly strange, to seemingly impossible, then back through strange, and back to normal. The dreamer was most struck by the uncanny part, the drawer moving

---

I have suggested (Bilder, in preparation) that there are several major mechanisms that do this. One is a primarily 'cortico-cortical' system, where autoregulatory control is provided by a fundamental duality in the evolution of cortex. This system provides fine-grained control and is capable of making subtle adjustments to both expectations and behavioral programs to reduce mismatch. The other system is 'cortico-limbic' and is engaged when there are larger mismatch events, and more radical alteration of expectations and actions is needed to reduce mismatch. In dreaming, it is interesting to consider which aspects of these systems may be 'off line.' It seems likely that the usual cortico-cortical systems (especially the usual fronto-posterior resonant networks) are not active as these would be during conscious states. If true, you would expect to see posterior cortical networks (i.e., the sensory representation systems, including representations of some actions) functioning according to more 'local' network facilitations, and less under the constraints of the usual frontal and striatal expectation biases. This would yield more radical 'jumps' from one state to another, failure of these to be controlled by prior knowledge/expectations, and more 'synthetic' activation states where usually incongruous sensory experiences could co-occur."

by itself. In this instance, he has a meta-awareness, during the dream, of the break from reality and tries to solve the mystery.

We have not paid enough attention to this: How is it that our procedural knowledge of the world is incorporated into the structure of a dream, and what determines when it is not (when violations of our procedural knowledge find their way into our dream)? Is there an orderliness to the determination of which rules of reality are retained or violated, or when? We do not know that. We notice some regularities. For example, flying in dreams is common, especially in children's dreams. And what determines whether the departures from reality strike us as odd *in the dream*?

We shall consider these questions further in the next two chapters.

CHAPTER 21

WHAT DREAMS CAN TELL US ABOUT THE BRAIN

> The factual is already theory. The blue of the heavens reveals to us the chromatic law of optics. Only do not look behind the phenomena, they themselves are the doctrine.
>
> Goethe, *Wilhelm Meister*

THE EMINENT DREAM researcher Allan Rechtschaffen once wryly observed that we seem to have learned a great deal about the biology of dreaming without really knowing what dreaming is the biology of (Rechtschaffen, 1964).[1] This is a question worth taking seriously; studies of the biology of the brain, however important, need to be coordinated with studies of experiential psychology if they are to remain relevant to understanding human functioning. Rechtschaffen's comment leads us to ponder: How can clinicians who study dreams in the consulting room help those who study the biology of dreaming in the laboratory? Clinicians are in a privileged position. They hear and analyze dreams several times every day. They need to examine those dreams carefully, not only to discover meaning, but to note both the kinds of patterns that occur and the kinds that never occur in the manifest dream.

1. Even the role of REM sleep is still far from certain. An opthalmologist, David Maurice (1998), has proposed that the main function of REM sleep is the maintenance of the eye. The rapid eye movements keep the fluids in the eye moving which keeps the cornea oxygenated. Without REM, the cornea might not receive adequate oxygen, and new blood capillaries might grow which would impede vision.

Freud's *The Interpretation of Dreams* was not just about dreams. It was an attempt to develop a model of how the mind works. Freud used dream phenomena as evidence for the functions and structure of the mind. He looked at the forgetting of dreams and came up with the idea of repression. He looked at the imagery of dreams and came up with the idea of regression. Now, after more than a century, armed with more clinical experience and greater knowledge of the brain, we need to extend Freud's studies, with closer examination of the phenomenology of dreams in relation to brain function.

Freud's goal of deriving a model of mind from dream phenomenology has drawn less and less attention from modern psychoanalysts for several reasons. First, the ever-increasing specialization that has occurred in all areas of research has led nonspecialists to be intimidated, and so clinicians have tended to limit their focus to clinical matters. The enormous developments within cognitive neuroscience have increasingly taken over the study of the mind/brain, and it is difficult for clinical psychoanalysts to keep pace with the developments in neuroscience. Clinical findings are excellent generators of hypotheses, but they are hard to control scientifically. Psychoanalysts have been intimidated by their lack of quantitative data.

Neurobiologists today are hunting for the brain bases of dreaming by studying first-hand data of brain function with ever-evolving new technology. In the old days, we had only EEG records. Today, we have many other, more sophisticated tools, such as CAT scans, Positron Emission Tomography (PET), Functional Magnetic Resonance Imaging (fMRI), and magnetoencephalography (MEG) which can more accurately track the activity of different parts of the brain during dreaming. And we have neuropsychologists, like Mark Solms (1997), studying how dreaming changes when the human brain is damaged by external injuries, such as a gunshot or head trauma, or by internal injuries, such as a brain-damaging stroke.

All of these studies examine how changes in the brain lead to changes in dreaming. I am proposing here that we also think in the opposite direction: by studying the kinds of "disordered" thinking that can occur in dreams, we may get clues about how the mind/brain is organized. By studying the possibilities for disorganization, we will learn the principles of brain organization. I will suggest routes from phenomenology to biology, instead of the other way around.

In 1907, Jung proposed that dreaming was the sleeping equivalent of schizophrenia. He wrote that if the dreamer walked about and acted like a person awake, we would have the clinical picture of dementia praecox.

This hypothesis inspired great hope—hope that if we understood dreams, we would understand schizophrenia and then be able to cure it. But it has not worked out that way so far. It was thought that if we deprived people of dreaming and of REM dreaming in particular, they would become psychotic. But that also didn't work out. People deprived of REM were found to have more anxiety, difficulties learning and concentrating, and reduced ability to cope with stress, but they did not become psychotic (Greenberg et al., 1992). The most reliable finding is that people deprived of REM spend more time in REM dreaming when left alone—the REM rebound effect. We know that there is a need for REM, but we do not know precisely what we need REM for.

REM AND DISSOCIATION

There is a surprising angle on REM sleep suggested by the work of the neurologist V. S. Ramachandran (Ramachandran et al., 1996). He was studying a stroke patient whom he called Mrs. BM, who had the syndrome known as anosognosia. Her left arm was paralyzed, but as sometimes happens to patients who have strokes on the right side of the brain, Mrs. BM denied that there was anything wrong with her arm. The Italian neurologist Eduardo Bisiach and his colleagues (1992; see also Vallar et al., 1990) found that if you inject ice cold water into the patient's left ear canal, you set the patient's eyes moving rapidly back and forth. While experiencing this nystagmus, the patient stopped denying her disability.

Ramachandran connects this temporary remission of anosognosia by inducing nystagmus with the phenomena of REM dreams. He accepts the view that dreaming is more common in REM sleep, and that during REM dreams disturbing facts about the self that are usually dissociated may come into more awareness. He also raises the possibility that patients with anosognosia might acknowledge their paralysis in their REM dreams.

While nobody knows exactly how the rapid eye movement leads to a release of dissociation, there may be even more evidence of this. In recent years a novel treatment of post-traumatic stress disorder has appeared known as EMDR, eye-movement desensitization and reprocessing. Patients who have had a past trauma are asked to track a clinician's left-right finger movement, so that their eyes shift rapidly back and forth, and to report their thinking, which is reported to lead to reduced dissociation and eventual resolution of the trauma. Could the

Bisiach cold-water injections in the ear, REM sleep, and EMDR all share a common mechanism by which eye movements, or correlated brain processes, relieve dissociation?

This suggests another intriguing possibility—that REM dreams may be more effective at relieving dissociation than nonREM dreams. We know from Foulkes (1962) that approximately 10–15% of nonREM dreams are indistinguishable from REM dreams. But even if a nonREM dream has the vividness and bizarreness of a REM dream, is it less effective in bringing together dissociated material? This question would be worth studying.

WHICH PSYCHOPATHOLOGY DOES DREAMING RESEMBLE?

Jung's analogy of dreaming and schizophrenia has been challenged by several thinkers. Sullivan (1953) found the analogy of dreams with schizophrenia to be inaccurate and suggested that night terrors, with their contentless terror, were much closer to the experience of schizophrenia, especially the stage of catatonic terror.

Hobson (1993) has argued that dreams are not like schizophrenia, but rather more like delirium. He writes, "There is no separation of thoughts and feelings in dreams, as occurs in schizophrenia" (p. 42). This is not accurate. I have heard quite a few dreams, for example, in which there is a pleasant situation, but the dreamer nevertheless feels dread. But there are certainly some dreams that resemble delirium more than schizophrenia.

Dreams can also mimic other psychopathological states. For example, some dreams mimic obsessive-compulsive disorder quite closely. The dreamer will state that he got to a certain point in the dream "and then the dream went on and on for hours." Sometimes the dreamer will even awaken, and when back to sleep return to the obsessional preoccupation. For example, Sullivan (1953) described the carryover in his own experience of an obsessional preoccupation from a nightmare into waking life. He had a frightening dream about a spider, and when he awoke from the dream, he continued to see the spider-spot on the sheet. Sullivan considered this a mini-schizophrenic event; Sullivan always saw obsessionalism and schizophrenia as closely related.

A psychiatrist in psychoanalytic treatment had the following dream:

> I am having lunch. I get to my office and realize that I had forgotten about two appointments, my patient on Wednesday at

> 2:20 and the next one. I am not sure who. I wonder, How could I do this? Then I am at a reception (I am not sure where. It is something between my office and a hotel lobby.) The patient whom I see on Mondays at 6:50, Mr. A, is there. Someone arrives who is related to him. Mr. A takes me aside and asks, "Could we have our session somewhere else, so that Mr. B (the man who has arrived who knows Mr. A) will not know that I am in therapy with you?" I say, "OK." I go down a hallway. There are open rooms alongside it, as in a clinic, although they seem to be decorated as residential rooms. I get to one, and my son is in it. This looks like a good one, so I ask him to leave. He says cheerfully that he will. I look at the key for the room, and it has one number on it. I write it down, as a note to give to my patient, about where to meet me. But then I look at the door, and it has a different number on it. I think that I should write a note to Mr. A that explains the difference in numbers. I get stuck on this, it seems, for hours of dreaming. It is like an obsessional thought: how will I explain this to him, and will he be able to find the room? I think the obsession in the dream is the constant checking back and forth between the two numbers, as if I cannot believe that the two numbers are different, and as if any amount of checking back and forth will remedy the situation.

The dream feels to the dreamer like the uncontrollable checking of a person with obsessive-compulsive disorder. He says, "I do not tend to do such checking while awake. What happened in my brain, that it got stuck at this spot?"

The dreamer, skillful at diagnosing obsessional disorders, finds himself the victim of an obsessional disorder in the dream. He went on associating to the need for good boundaries in working as a psychiatrist and some recent clinical situations that were troublesome from that perspective. But the dream also functioned as a kind of compensation. His conscious wish for clear boundaries was balanced in the dream by a wasteful over-concern with boundaries. The dream illustrates the transformation of paranoid anxiety into obsessionalism—the patient's fear that the person who has entered the room will know he is in therapy (which is a fear experienced by the dreamer also) becomes transformed in the dream into the dreamer's endless preoccupation with the difference in room number.

Dreams may mimic many forms of psychopathology and neuropathology. The fact is that some dreams are like schizophrenia, some are like delirium, and some are like something else, pathological or not. Clinicians know that some dreams are like panic attacks, obsessional ruminations, hysterical conversion symptoms, or manic episodes. And some are just like everyday experiences, more or less emotional. As I pointed out in chapter 19 ("The Reallocation of Madness"), some dreams are rather similar to waking thoughts. People who hear them ask, "Was this really a dream?"

Why is there such variety in dreams, and why are so many pathologies, psychiatric and neurological, mimicked or reproduced in dreams? This is a fundamental problem whose solution has barely been worked out. I offer a broad proposal: *During sleep, the various sectors or modules of the mind can be individually modified or their connections reorganized. The connections of the mental apparatus may be shifted around, and not always shifted in the same way*. We do not know whether all kinds of reorganization are possible, or if not, what constraints there are and what controls which kind of reorganization occurs.

To explore this issue, we must study dreams closely for their varieties of experience and their implications for brain organization. Our task is to suggest some of these neurological modifications *based on the phenomenology of dreaming*. Our observations will tell us which kinds of experiential reorganization are possible. And in doing so, we might get a better idea of how the brain is organized during sleep and waking.

Freud's model of regression in dreaming implied a discrete, unidirectional flow of information in waking—from sensory contact with the world through the perceptual system and into the memory system. He felt that in dreaming, this sequence was reversed. Input from the sensory system was blocked, and the perceptual system received input from images stored in memory.

Freud's proposal was brilliant in its time, but it needs to be revised today in light of new information about the mind/brain. We know that the transformation of raw sensory data into percepts is more complex than Freud thought. It occurs in many stages, and information of differing complexity is processed in different parts of the brain. The full development of such a theory is still being worked out (see for example, McClelland and Rumelhart, 1986; Zeki, 1993; Churchland, 1995). The thinking today, among many scientists, is that mental functioning is best described by a model of parallel distributed processing (PDP). This means that information does not flow only in one direction, but instead there may be multiple pathways for information that can shift independently. For example, with vision, light may start by entering the eye and stimulating the retina. The information may then be transmitted to the lateral geniculate nucleus, and then on to the visual cortex. But this is only one route for visual information. The information may be divided at many points and processed simultaneously in many different ways. In addition, there are many recurrent feedback loops along the way that feed the partially processed information back into the system. Similarly, the connections of the perceptual information with memory can involve many kinds of feedforward and feedback mechanisms.

Freud's proposal that, in dreaming, the flow of information processing is reversed probably needs to be reassessed.[2] How can you simply reverse a process with multiple lines of information flow and with recurrent feedback loops? But we can modify Freud's idea and propose that in dreaming, the flow of information, if not simply reversed, is *changed*. But how is it changed? That is a great research project still to be done, although we already have some fascinating early results. Using PET scans, Braun et al. (1998) have demonstrated attenuated activity in primary visual cortex and increased activity in the extrastriate cortex and in limbic and paralimbic regions during REM. This implies that during REM dreams, the visual association cortices and paralimbic regions *may* operate as a closed system, with internal generation of affectively toned imagery. Using such new technology, research in this area is progressing rapidly, although many questions remain to be explored.

THE SPECIAL COGNITION OF DREAMS

Here is where psychoanalysts and others who work with dreams phenomenologically can be of help. They can identify and catalogue the kinds of cognitions that are common in dream life and relatively absent from waking life. These observations can then be formulated into proposals of the kinds of processing of information and emotion that differentiate dreams from waking mental life. Such proposals may help guide neurophysiologists about where to look, about which mental functions may be functionally and neurologically separable from one another, and how, in sleep, these mental functions are reorganized.

We can then update Freud's regression model. I would like to propose a model—that in dreams, different levels of perceptual processing can provide *input* to the final "percept" of the dream. They can all do so separately, and without the usual coordination of waking consciousness. If this is so, then *the specifics of bizarre dream experiences may*

---

2. However, when Freud proposes multiple mnemonic systems, he seems to be anticipating the PDP model.

be a source of data about the different levels of perceptual processing. By careful examination of the experiences in dreams, we may gain insight into the workings of our mind/brains.

I know that this is a far-reaching hypothesis and will require a great deal of research to test it. But we already have some relevant data. Let us start with one example of a seemingly bizarre dream formation. A dreamer says, "I knew she was my mother, although she didn't look like her." Any clinician who hears dreams regularly can tell you that such statements are not at all uncommon.

It surprises me that this is not usually surprising to people. Many people, when reporting a bizarre experience in a dream, will prepare the listener by saying, "It was the strangest thing . . ." or "I don't really understand how this could happen, and yet . . ." But when people see someone in a dream whose identity doesn't match their appearance, they usually don't need a qualifying preface to describe the experience—at least my patients don't. They take it for granted that I will know what they mean. It is a commonplace bizarreness of dream life. In our waking lives, we would not normally say, "It didn't look like my mother, but I knew it was she." Such statements could quickly get one psychiatrically hospitalized. Yet somehow we feel comfortable reporting such experiences when they occur in a dream. Open any text with multiple dream examples, and you are likely to find an example of this experience quickly. I have been collecting them for a while. Here are a few examples:

"I'm sitting in a dream beside a man I don't recognize, but I know in the dream is my father" (Boas, 1994, p. 155). Or: "At that moment, I spied Popeye lying on the ground, only he looked like my patient" (Myers, 1987, p. 43). Or: "I was the opposite of what I actually look like. I was tall and lanky like Katharine Hepburn, but not particularly attractive" (Fosshage and Loew, 1987, p. 10).

In all of these examples, the dreamer recognizes a character's identity, even though the person's appearance does not match the identity. There is a disjunction between appearance and identity. I call such occurrences "disjunctive cognitions." Two aspects of cognition do not match each other; the dreamer is aware of the disjunction, yet that does not prevent it from remaining. In waking life, most sane people would assume that they mis-saw or misidentified the person, and correct for it; but not necessarily in dreams.

What might be happening in terms of brain processing with such dreams? Let us first consider what we know about facial recognition. One theory of facial recognition is that the visual information passes from the retina through the optic nerve to the lateral geniculate nucleus and thence to the cortex, for discrimination of the features by the feature discrimination area. There is thought to be an additional location in the temporal lobe specifically dedicated to facial recognition, called the facial recognition area. The feature discrimination area may be providing one input to the dream, while the facial recognition area may be providing a different input.

The neurological account of the disjunctive cognition does not invalidate the psychological account. Both are valid, and it is possible that considerations of meaning coordinate the brain reorganization, or vice versa. A dream interpreter interested in meaning may well inquire as to how the dreamer knew that it was his mother, and also what were the physical details of the dream figure that did not look like mother. In doing so, it may be possible to see the dream image as a condensation of the physical attributes of one person and the emotional attributes of the mother, or some other combination, and thereby come to some better understanding of how the dreamer feels about his mother.

An excellent example of this may be found in the book *Dream Interpretation* by Fosshage and Loew (1987). In their fascinating clinical study, the dreams of Martha, a patient in psychoanalysis, are shown to six psychoanalysts, each from a different school of thought, and they are asked to offer their ideas on interpretation. Martha's second dream includes the disjunctive cognition: "My mother was in there going through my purse. She didn't look like my mother" (p. 11). The six psychoanalysts examining this material said:

1. Freudian: "The mother in the dream, who is also the psychotherapist, looked different because she was investigating the sexual contents of her mind. Her real mother was 'guarded and evasive.' The mother in the dream was more genital and incited Martha to be sexually active" (p. 41).
2. Jungian: "Here we deal with the intrusion of the mother, who is not her real mother and cannot be gotten rid of by efforts of will. In presenting a figure who is not the actual person it purports to be, the dream points to an entity 'like mother' from the outset, that is, to subject level significance. It refers to the 'mother in her,' to whatever qualities, values, or attitudes the mother engendered in her. The mother's standards or feelings in her are the intruders in her 'room,' her personal inner space or individuality" (p. 71).
3. Culturalist: "Furthermore, the dream mother 'didn't look like my mother.' Might she have been hiding from herself a revulsion

more intense than anything she was ready to acknowledge?" (p. 105).

4. Object relational: [Author's note] He does not discuss this aspect of the dream. This is startling. The Freudian and Jungian say that the mother does not look like her mother because she represents, not the real mother, but the internal object. Does the object-relational analyst say nothing about it because he does not think it important? Or does he think it such an ordinary occurrence, because for him everyone in the dream represents an internal object, that it does not deserve mention?
5. Phenomenological: "In the first instance, Martha's mother does not look like her mother. When her mother behaves in the way of raping Martha's intimate sphere, she appears bodily different. The phenomenon of bodihood is but the carrying out of human existence in the sphere of the body. As such, it refers immediately and directly to the totality of the existential relationship. That the bodily appearance of the mother is strange and unfamiliar indicates that Martha does not recognize this behavioral modus as belonging immediately to her existential relation to her mother, in which she herself exists as a helpless, defenseless daughter. This is surprising when we think of Martha's first association in which she reports exactly analogous behavior of herself and her mother. It would seem that Martha has not wakingly recognized what her tolerance of this behavior of her mother means for her, nor how much of her independence and personal integrity she loses by her submission and helplessness to this relational mode" (pp. 168–169).
6. Gestalt: "We could consider her mother to be an introject, the part of herself that is hurt, tearful, rarely angry, that she might like to spit up" (p. 206).

Thus, most of the clinicians agree that the person who does not look like who she is represents not the person herself but the internal object, the internalized mother. The focus among these analysts is not the division of the brain function, but the division between actual people in the outer world and of internalized "people" that we all carry in us (whether you call them internal objects, introjections, personifications, or some other technical term).

But here we face an intriguing possibility. The fact that we can divide our percepts between internal and external objects must have a mechanism in the brain. *What is the brain basis for internal object representations?*

Is the neural anatomy that allows internal object relations related to the separate brain areas involved in feature perception and identity perception? For any psychoanalyst interested in a neurally-grounded psychoanalytic science, this seems to be an essential question, even though we may not yet have definitive answers, given current neurological knowledge.

Psychoanalysts, I think, should be excited by this. It suggests a manifestation in dreams of fundamental conceptions of psychoanalysis—namely, transference and object representations—and holds out the possibility of identifying the neurobiological mechanisms of these phenomena. Most psychoanalysts assume that we all keep mental representations of other people in mind, and that our relations with other people are colored if not actually shaped by these mental representations. Unconsciously, we may see our mother in any number of women—or men, for that matter. So when the dreamer says, "I knew it was my mother although it didn't look like her," he may be acknowledging a common knowledge that transference exists.

But in a sense, the process of interpretation may lead us not to pay enough attention to the simple experience in such a dream. We may ask, is it not odd to feel so certain about the identity of the person in the face of contradictory physical evidence? What does this division tell us? It suggests that the processes of seeing the physical attributes of a person are not identical, perhaps not even isomorphic, with the recognition of the identity of that person. But is there any other evidence that those processes are separate in our minds?

Ordinary introspection of our waking thoughts might not support such an idea. Most people equate seeing the person with recognizing the person's identity. We have the quaint experience in the Bible of the blind Isaac being approached by Jacob, disguised with animal fur on his hands. Isaac says, "The voice is the voice of Jacob, but the hands are the hands of Esau." But we know this to be the effect of a trick on a blind man. Surely those of us with our sensorium intact make no such confusions.

But before we reject out of hand the notion that seeing someone and recognizing his identity are separable, we should look to the field of neuropsychology. There, we find that some people who have suffered strokes or other brain damage have a syndrome known as prosopagnosia (from the Latin *prosopon* for face, and *agnosia*, lack of knowledge, hence the lack of knowledge of faces). A man with prosopagnosia may look at his wife of 50 years, see all of her features clearly, and yet not recognize who she is. Collateral information, like the sound of her voice, may help him identify her, but if he just looks at her face, he may not recognize her. In such people, the process of seeing is intact, but the process of facial recognition is not (Bodamer, 1947). A woman with prosopagnosia might ask her husband to speak, because she cannot tell who he is from looking at his face. She can see her husband's face clearly; she just cannot recognize who it is.

This sort of experience is hard to grasp for normal people. People with prosopagnosia can find it exasperating to explain their condition to other people. For example, a woman wrote (Restak, 1994):

> I warn people now. If we have a wonderful exchange and are going to be friends for life, I say, Look, if we meet again outside . . . and I wouldn't recognize you, just give me the code word. The code word is something we talked about and then I would recall what we talked of.
>
> People complain I don't greet them. So I warn them beforehand. It is very embarrassing. I live in an active community . . . and I ask now after four years in the community, "Who is this?" Now people cannot understand it. I ask friends of mine who do not know I have this problem, "Who is this?" They are amazed. "Of course, she is so and so"[3] [pp. 90–91].

Scientists are identifying the parts of the brain that are responsible for different aspects of face recognition (see Mesulam, 1998). Gorno-Tempini et al. (1997) found that in humans, identifying unfamiliar faces activates one area of the brain, the unimodal visual association areas in the fusiform region, while the recognition of familiar faces also activates another area of the brain, the lateral midtemporal cortex. This division of function can be found in subhuman primates, too. Perrett et al. (1982) have found that in the macaque monkey, there is a specific region of the cortex responsive to faces. From such findings, we have come to recognize that the process of facial recognition is indeed very complex and may be achieved by a part of the brain that is different from the brain areas involved in general visual analysis. (See Farah, 1995, for a thorough discussion of whether facial recognition is merely an aspect of very complex visual analysis or is indeed special, and compare with Tranel et al., 1988.)

We thus have a case of several kinds of data, from human neuropathology, from experimental brain research with animals, and from

3. For other vivid accounts of this syndrome, see Humphreys and Riddoch (1987) and Lhermitte et al. (1972).

dreams all showing that the processes of feature perception and identity recognition can be separated. In normal waking consciousness, the two work in tandem. That may be one of the reasons it is hard in psychoanalysis for people to become aware of their internal "objects." But perhaps the person-recognizing module of the brain can see mother even when the physical features show "not mother." In dreams, psychosis, neuropathological syndromes, and very intense transference states, this division shows up more clearly than in normal waking consciousness.

The dream experience of disjunctive cognition of features and identity is not exactly the same as the experience of the prosopagnosic. The prosopagnosic sees the face but does not know who it is. For him, facial recognition is not working, or, if it is working, it is not available to consciousness. The dreamer sees the person but knows it is someone else. For him, facial identification is working, but is dissociated from feature recognition. We theorize that during dreaming the facial recognition and feature recognition modules are *providing input* rather than analyzing the information provided by external stimulus sources.

Perhaps a closer analogue to the experience of prosopagnosia is the dream experience of seeing someone but not recognizing him or her, such as: "There was a man standing nearby. I couldn't tell who he was." In such circumstances, there is an inability to recognize the person. But the similarity of this dream experience to prosopagnosia would depend on whether the features are clear but the identity is not; if the entire visual experience is poorly defined, then the situation is more like trying to see in the dark than like prosopagnosia.

In any case, we are not looking for identical experience between the dream and the neuropathological syndrome but rather a convergence of data; the important aspect that unites prosopagnosia and both of these dream experiences is the disjunction of perception of visual features and identity recognition.

OTHER DISJUNCTIVE COGNITIONS

Some of the disjunctive cognitions in dreams are more subtle. A dreamer may have a sense of direction that conflicts with her knowledge of direction. Consider the following dream of one of my patients: "I am running across a flat open plain. I am heading west. On my left (south) was a railroad train, which was running at the same speed as I (or so it seemed—it might have been a distance away and really going faster).

Behind it was a mountain range with a sunset or sunrise. I woke up really disoriented." She knows she is heading west, even though the sun is rising or setting in the south. She is very aware of perspective (the relative speed of the train), but the direction makes no apparent sense.

Loss of directional sense is a common consequence of parietal lobe damage, although the kind of loss is different, depending on whether the damage is to the right or left parietal lobe. Right parietal damage is more often associated with loss of directional sensitivity that is independent of the body space (such as the sense of true compass directions), while left parietal damage is associated with more severe loss of sensitivity for directions that must be mapped with respect to one's own body orientation in space (e.g., right-left orientation). The latter is a key component of the so-called Gerstmann syndrome (Gerstmann, 1927), where it is associated with disorders of writing and arithmetic ability. (Interestingly, the same patient had another dream in which there was a preposterous mathematical calculation.) It is possible that my patient's dream shows the possibility that the two parietal lobes are capable of independent operation during dreaming, although other conclusions are also possible.

It is important for us to note not only which kinds of disjunctions occur in dreams, but also which kinds do not. That is a very difficult task. One is on much shakier ground when asserting that something does not occur than that it does. Who knows if it does occur, but you have just not observed it? For an individual clinician even more caution is needed, since data come from a relatively small sample of dreamers. So any hypotheses here are offered with even more caution than those until now and await the confirmation or rejection of other clinicians and those researchers who study large dream samples that are collected from non-clinical populations (such as the large dream log from the University of California, Santa Cruz that is available on the Internet).

With that caveat, there may be value to discovering which dimensions of cognition cannot be disjunctive (if there are any) in dreaming. Can, for example, the color qualia of a percept differ from the recognized color? I have never heard someone tell a dream in which "it looked green but I knew it was blue." The specifics of what can happen in dreaming could then be compared with those of experiments on waking perception of multi-dimensional stimuli, especially the phenomenon of "illusory conjunctions" in normal subjects (Treisman and Gelade, 1980) and related phenomena in patients with the parietal-lobe damage of Balint's syndrome (Robertson et al., 1997).

I would also like to inquire further into the specifics of the cognitive disjunction between feature recognition and identity recognition that are possible in a dream. The most common form of this dream experience, at least according to my clinical experience, is for the dreamer to sense the disjunction between appearance and identity but for identity to be stated in positive terms. In the previous example, from Fosshage and Loew, the dreamer says: "My mother was in there going through my purse. She didn't look like my mother." The dreamer senses that she didn't look like mother, but she knew anyway that it was her mother.

It is less common—at least in my clinical experience—for people to say, "It looked like my mother, although I knew it was *not* my mother." In fact, I have not been able to find a single example of this in my records of patients' dreams or my own. I am waiting to hear from other clinicians or researchers if this ever occurs. If this tendency is true for the general population of dreamers, it is an important fact. How exactly we should understand this *asymmetry* is open to debate. One explanation could be that identity recognition, at least in dreams, is a positive process, not a negative one. If we imagine clashing inputs from feature recognition and identity recognition, and if identity recognition is the stronger input, it then must always result in a positive identity. "Not my mother" is an idea, not a percept.

This phenomenon of dream life has a correlate in our theory of transference and object representations. We tend more commonly to transfer primary representations of identity onto new people, but less commonly to deny the identity of those we perceive. In other words, transference more commonly wreaks proactive transformations, rather than erasing perceived identities.

Does a dreamer ever dream, "I was walking. It didn't look like me, but it was me." I have not heard precisely that dream. The closest I have heard is a dream in which a woman dreamer appeared in a dream both as herself and as a man. Of course, if you adopt Jung's subjective viewpoint, people dream all the time about people who do not look like them, but really are an aspect of them. But the subjective viewpoint is based on dream interpretation, not on the untransformed experience of the manifest dream.

In the following chapter, we will look further at the kinds of disjunctions that do or do not occur.

CHAPTER 22

ENDONEUROPSYCHIC PERCEPTION

We shall not cease from our exploration
And the end of all our exploring
Will be to arrive where we started
And know the place for the first time.

T. S. Eliot

THE STUDY OF disjunctive cognitions in relation to neuropathological syndromes may be related to what Freud called "endopsychic perception." Freud meant by this term that psychopathological symptoms like hallucinations and delusions also have a positive value for researchers, in that they may suggest how the human mind is organized and structured. For example, delusions of being watched may be considered a projected "endopsychic perception" of the superego. Freud (1933) wrote:

> [Psychotics] have turned away from external reality, but for that very reason they know more about internal, psychical reality and can reveal a number of things to us that would otherwise be inaccessible to us.
>
> We describe one group of these patients as suffering from *delusions of being observed.* They complain to us that perpetually, and down to their most intimate actions, they are being molested by the observation of unknown powers—presumably persons—and that in hallucinations they hear these persons reporting the outcome of their observation: 'now he's going to say this, now he's dressing to go out' and so on. Observation of this sort is not yet the same thing as persecution, but it is not far from it; it presupposes that people distrust them, and expect to catch

> them carrying out forbidden actions for which they would be punished. How would it be if these insane people were right, if in each of us there is present in his ego an agency like this which observes and threatens to punish, and *which in them has merely become sharply divided from their ego and mistakenly displaced into external reality*? [p. 59; italics added].

In this fascinating discussion, Freud is suggesting that the delusions of madmen reflect an insight into the organization of the mind. The delusion of being judged is an "endopsychic perception" of the morally judging aspect of the personality; the internal psychic agency, the punitive superego, is perceived as being outside the self. But the delusion itself may be evidence of the existence of the internal agency.

We may wish to expand "endopsychic perception" into an area we will call "endoneuropsychic perception." By that we mean that certain psychological phenomena may represent an insight into the organization of the brain. We are extending Freud's principle from metapsychology to neuropsychology, a focus that Freud himself originally adopted in the "Project" and which he would probably not have abandoned had he lived a century later.

This may lead us to wonder if other strange dream experiences might be suggestive of kinds of brain organization that we cannot intuit from waking introspection.[1] We recur to the sweeping general hypothesis of the preceding chapter: *Wherever disjunctive cognitions occur, the two aspects of cognition are handled in different brain areas whose mutual influence is suppressed or shifted during sleep.*

While one of the most common disjunctive cognitions involves a mismatch of a person's identity and his appearance, there are many other kinds. Consider the following dream reported by Panksepp (1998): "Somehow I knew that it is the Union and Confederate armies of the Civil War, although everything visual in the dream corresponds to our contemporary times" (p. 126). While there is no individual facial recognition involved here, the disjunction is still between appearance and identity. (In addition, there is a combination of two different eras in time, a subject which we will consider further below.) Or: "I am asleep in my bed at home. I know I'm in bed, in my room—but I have no tangible sensations in regard to my surroundings. It is pitch black and like a vacuum" (LaRue, 1970, p. 7, quoted in Domhoff, 1993, p. 299). Or:

---

1. Most of the exhaustive studies of large dream samples have focused on content (e.g., Hall and Van de Castle, 1966). We need to reexamine large dream samples for this sort of structural analysis.

"The dream doesn't really take place in my parents' apartment. There is a bookcase there in what used to be my bedroom" (Blechner, 1995a).

In these examples, there is a disjunction of person, place, or object recognition from simple perception. We can recognize any one of these identities in our dreams *despite* our perception.

Another fine example of disjunctive cognition occurs in the dream of Freud's patient, the so-called "Lovely Dream," which we have already examined from another perspective. At one point the dreamtext reads: "He walked with such difficulty and so laboriously that he seemed glued to the spot."

It is a common experience in dreams that one attempts to move and yet nothing happens. This may be another example of endoneuropsychic perception, an oneiric registration of the fact that during sleep, voluntary muscular movement is for the most part inhibited. Hobson (1988) observed this, but used it as evidence that such dream events are not meaningful. *I wish to stress that the connection of the dream experience with the reorganization of the brain during sleep does not invalidate the psychological meaning of the dream. The dream may reflect brain organization, and the dreamwork may still use those correlated brain phenomena as tools to express meaning.*[2]

It is like Milton's sonnet on his blindness. The blindness was not caused in order to write his sonnet. But once he had become blind, he used his experience to create one of the most beautiful sonnets in English. Similarly, the dreamwork may use the endoneuropsychic perception of paralysis in the service of creating the dream narrative.

This follows the same principles that Freud used when analyzing dreams with a "somatic stimulus," that is, unusual somatic disturbances caused by illness or by disruptions from the environment. For example, needing to urinate, we may dream of waterfalls. Hearing an alarm clock, yet being unwilling to awaken, we may incorporate a ringing sound, as in a fire alarm, into the narrative of the dream. The dream incorporates these external stimuli, and the dream narrative uses them for personal expression.

But another somatic stimulus source is the operation of the brain itself. That is, the brain is observing its own psycho-neural activity and portraying it metaphorically and directly in dream formations. We do not recognize these sources of dreams because our conscious knowledge of brain activity is sorely inadequate. Yet by careful examination of the

---

2. Another intriguing possibility is that the dream content *causes* the changes in brain activation.

experiences in dreams, we may gain insight into the workings of our mind/brains.

Later in the "Lovely Dream," the movement inhibition is relieved: "At the top of the rise he was able to walk much more easily." Again, we may wonder if this change in dream content correlates with changes in the brain, such as a reduction in the level of inhibition of the motor neurons. At this point in time, it is probably beyond the capacity of neuroscience to answer these questions. But with the rapid progress being made in brain imaging during sleep, it may not be long before data on this subject can be collected. We already have studies in which the directions of dream movement and the directions of eye movements were found to be correlated (e.g., Herman et al., 1984). We can imagine a study in which the activity levels in a dreamer's brain are charted against the content of his dream, to see how they match up.

The study of dream phenomenology may identify other disjunctive cognitions which may then be considered in connection with the data of neuropathological syndromes and of animal research. We may also look to certain neuropathological syndromes for suggestions about the kinds of disjunctive cognitions that might occur in dreams. The total data picture will be informative no matter how it turns out, if we carefully study which disjunctions occur in dreams, in brain damage, in both, or only in one. I shall not go into the full details here of these connections, but only suggest some of the possibilities. In some cases, I will examine mental processes that are observed in waking individuals with brain dysfunction and then consider whether there are analogues in dream phenomena. In other cases, I will proceed in the opposite direction, first looking at certain dream phenomena and then considering whether there are analogues in brain dysfunction.

In chapter 20, we explored the difference between knowing and knowing that you know. The question, which also could be called "knowledge versus meta-knowledge," is especially fascinating in certain neuropathological syndromes. In several of these syndromes, people seem to have lost conscious perceptual or cognitive abilities, but objective tests show that they retain the ability to perceive, think, or remember, although the information from those processes is not readily accessible to consciousness. Their ability or knowledge has become "implicit." They don't know they have the knowledge, but we can show that they do.

Our knowledge of these phenomena increased dramatically during the twentieth century. In 1911, Claparède (1911) gave an especially vivid account of information retention without memory. He described a 47-year-old woman with Korsakoff's syndrome, a form of memory loss:

> I was able to show, by means of learning experiments done by the saving method, that not all ability of mnemonic registration was lost in this person. What is worthy of our attention here was her inability to evoke recent memories voluntarily, while they did arise automatically, by chance, as recognitions.
>
> When one told her a little story, read to her various items of a newspaper, three minutes later she remembered nothing, not even the fact that someone had read to her; but with certain questions one could elicit in a reflex fashion some of the details of those items. But when she found these details in her consciousness, she did not recognize them as memories but believed them to be something "that went through her mind" by chance, an idea she had "without knowing why," a product of her imagination of the moment, or even the result of reflection.
>
> I carried out the following curious experiment on her: to see whether she would better retain an intense impression involving affectivity, I stuck her hand with a pin hidden between my fingers. The light pain was as quickly forgotten as indifferent perceptions; a few minutes later she no longer remembered it. But when I again reached out for her hand, she pulled it back in a reflex fashion, not knowing why. When I asked for the reason, she said in a flurry, "Doesn't one have the right to withdraw her hand?" and when I insisted, she said, "Is there perhaps a pin hidden in your hand?" To the question, "What makes you suspect me of wanting to stick you?" she would repeat her old statement, "That was an idea that went through my mind," or she would explain, "Sometimes pins are hidden in people's hands." But never would she recognize the idea of sticking as a "memory" [pp. 68–70].

We, as outside observers, would deduce that the patient had some mental record of the pin prick, but she, from her subjective viewpoint, had no conscious memory of it. Her brain had access to the knowledge, but her conscious mind did not. This is a feature found in several "disconnection" syndromes (Geschwind, 1965). We can show experimentally that the information is there, but the person does not know that she knows what she knows. And if she is unaware of having that knowledge, is it correct to say that *she* knows it?

Researchers who try to describe these phenomena using ordinary language run into trouble of the kind that we discussed in chapter 4 ("Who Creates, Has, Remembers, Tells, and Interprets the Dream?"). Tranel and Damasio (1985) call this "knowledge without awareness" or "covert recognition." Alternatively, we could say that "her brain has the information, but she doesn't know it." Weiskrantz (1997) calls it "memory without experienced remembering." This is a suggestive phrase. How is "memory" different from "remembering?" The implication of Weiskrantz' phrase is that memory requires no awareness; remembering does.

Another agnosia is "visual agnosia," in which the eyes are normal, but vision is not, because of damage to various areas in the brain responsible for processing visual information. The patient loses an aspect of visual perception, while visual sensation remains normal. Critchley (1966) provides a clear example: "A sixty year old man woke from a sleep unable to find his clothes, though they lay ready for him close by. As soon as his wife put the garments into his hands, he recognized them, dressed himself correctly and went out. In the streets, he found he could see things, but not tell what they were" (p. 289).

And then there is blindsight, a condition in which people claim not to be able to see anything in part or all of their visual field, but in which they show the ability to use certain visual information in the environment without realizing that they can do so. For example, if a man with blindsight is asked to say what is the shape of an object in front of him, he will not be able to say what it is. But if given two choices, he will tend to pick the right choice. If asked to reach for an object, he will reach in the right direction, even though he claims not to be able to see it. And if tested with different shaped objects, his hand will assume the correct shape before trying to grasp the object (Weiskrantz, 1986).

We might say that people with blindsight have perception without conscious sensation, or that they have vision without seeing. They register visual information in their environment, and can learn to use it, without ever feeling like they are seeing. Weiskrantz (1986), in discussing blindsight, distinguishes between "seeing" and "feeling that there is a stimulus there." His blindsighted patient may not see a visual stimulus, but nevertheless feel that something has happened:

> With increasing stimulus salience, e.g., luminous contrast or velocity of movement, he may start to acknowledge a "feeling" that something is happening and is usually able to locate where the feeling comes from in space. The feeling may have spatial

> properties, in the sense that he may feel that there is something coming out from the screen. It may also have a "wave-like" impression, or be like "moving my hand in front of my eyes when the room is totally dark." He nevertheless denies that such feelings are "seeing"[3] [p. 168].

This is a kind of experience that is familiar to us in dreams. Dreamers often describe the awareness of an event or of a presence, without being able to specify much in the way of further details or to identify the modality of perception within the dream. People say, "Someone else was there," but cannot describe the person visually. It is just a feeling. Many representations of dreams in film have this quality of shadowy "presences" that are not clearly defined.

The discussion of blindsight shows us the limitations of our current language to describe information-processing functions separately from our experience of them. The complexities lead to astonishing verbal productions. Consider the following from Natsoulas (1982, p. 88), when he compares the degree of awareness in blindsighted patients to that of a sleepwalker:

> For, in order for the sleepwalker to manoeuvre in this way, he must have some perceptual awareness of the environment. But, of course, such a person remains a sleepwalker; he does not know what he is doing, or that he intends to do anything, or that he is having perceptions in his environment while sleepwalking. The acts of consciousness which are his perceptual awarenesses during the episode are not conscious acts of consciousness [p. 88].

Not conscious acts of consciousness? Shall we then have to posit unconscious acts of consciousness? We see here the perpetually recursive nature of consciousness with its various meta-levels: awareness, awareness of awareness, awareness of awareness of awareness, etc.

PAIN WITHOUT SUFFERING

Some neurological syndromes do not involve knowledge but experience. There is the example of people with trigeminal neuralgia, who suffer

3. A deficit analogous to blindsight has also been found in regard to the sense of touch (Paillard et al., 1983).

severe facial pain. Some intractable cases were treated with psychosurgery; they were given prefrontal lobotomies by the surgeon Pedro Almeida Lima, who had helped Egas Moniz develop the procedure (Damasio, 1994; see also Freeman and Watts, 1950). After the surgery, one of the patients looked relaxed and happy. When asked about the pain, he replied cheerfully, "Oh, the pains are the same, but I feel fine now, thank you." According to Damasio:

> Clearly, what the operation seemed to have done, then, was abolish the emotional reaction that is part of what we call pain. It had ended the man's suffering. His facial expression, his voice, and his deportment were those one associates with pleasant states, not pain. But the operation seemed to have done little to the image of local alteration in the body region supplied by the trigeminal nerve, and that is why the patient stated that the pains were the same. While the brain could no longer engender suffering, it was still making "images of pain," that is, processing normally the somatosensory mapping of a pain landscape [p. 266].

This is an astonishing event. One feels the sensations of pain without the emotional concomitants of unpleasure—we could call it *pain without suffering*. Such clinical findings suggest that the faculty of registering sensations and of feeling them in an emotional sense are in some way separable in the brain. And a person can lose the capacity for one without losing the capacity for the other.

Of course, this can happen without psychosurgery. It is well documented that soldiers in wartime can be severely injured, yet they may help their fellow soldiers in an extraordinary way and not feel the pain of their own injuries while doing so.

Ramachandran and Blakeslee (1998) describe a neurological syndrome known as "pain asymbolia." Such patients claim to feel pain, but that it doesn't hurt. Sometimes they also start giggling when pricked with a pin. There is often damage to the insular cortex, a structure that, according to Ramachandran, "receives sensory input, including pain from the skin and internal organs, and sends its output to the limbic system (such as the cingulate gyrus) so that one begins to feel the strong aversive reaction—the agony—of pain" (p. 208). Ramachandran argues that the dissociation between the perceived threat and the discordant lack of emotional sense of danger is responsible for the relieved laughter.

We may consider, does the separation of pain and suffering ever occur in dreams? In what way?

Freud (1900) noted that dreams can produce a denial of pain. He gives as an example a time when he had a painful boil on the base of his scrotum, which made walking extremely difficult. He dreamt that he was riding on horseback (something that he never did in actuality) and saw the dream as a denial of the physical pain that he was feeling while awake (pp. 229–230). So here the dream created a situation that in waking life would have been painful, but in sleep the dreamer has no pain.

There are a number of other ways that pain appears in dreams. Of primary interest to us is pain that is experienced (or not experienced) by the dreamer. Although I do not have statistical data on this, it seems to me much more common to dream that someone else has pain in the dream than for the dreamer to feel the pain in the dream.

There are quite a few examples in which the dreamer has one of the characters in the dream in a situation causing physical pain, but the dreamer does not feel the pain herself. For example, Freud (1900) described a woman who had to wear a painful apparatus at night following an operation and in her dream made "herself analgesic while ascribing her pains to someone else" (p. 233). Also, in Freud's "Irma dream," Freud heard Irma complain terribly about her pains, but Freud did not feel them himself in his dream.

In cases where the dreamer does feel pain in the dream, it is often due to an external stimulus causing the pain. This occurred in the famous dream of Maury (1878). He dreamt that during the Reign of Terror, he watched several scenes of murder. Then he was brought to trial himself, questioned, condemned, and led to execution by the guillotine. The blade fell, he felt his head separated from his body, and woke up in extreme anxiety, only to realize that the top of the bed had fallen on his cervical vertebrae just as the guillotine blade did in the dream.

In my experience, it seems to be relatively rare for a dreamer to experience physical pain first hand in a dream. Cases in which the dreamer feels pain and there is no external sensory stimulus causing pain during the dream seem to me to be rarer still, if they ever happen at all. I have been able to find only two dreams that might fit this category in my entire file of patients' dreams (which contains several thousand dreams), and it is questionable whether they in fact fit the category. In one, a woman dreamt that men broke into her home: "They tied me up in bed, and they made my husband leave. I knew the script, I knew just what was going to happen. There were two men. One cut my shoulder with a razor. I knew that was going to happen too, but it hurt. I was reading the script, to find out who did it and why. I never found out." In this dream, the dreamer distances herself from the pain by knowing what will happen. Nevertheless, the cut to her shoulder is painful.

The second example for which I have no record of a physical stimulus causing the physical pain in the dream came from a divorced man who dreamt: "I had been at a family event. I was riding in my car, taking my daughter home to her mother. I see a figure on the side of the road, a witch all in black. She grabs onto my knuckle with her teeth. I'm gritting my teeth. It was my ex-wife, of course. I realize she wasn't holding on that tight. I pulled back my arm and punched her." He then associated to the dream: "It was horrible but manageable. She hurt me but I was able to defend myself. The hurt wasn't that bad. It was like she had no teeth." Unfortunately, I did not ask the dreamer if there was anything causing actual pain to his finger when he had the dream. Emotionally, of course, the dreamer experienced a great deal of pain during the divorce.

There are a few examples from the dream log of the University of California, Santa Cruz, that bear on this issue, although in these cases, too, we cannot ask the dreamer for more detail. In one (No. 205, 10/12/87), a man cuts himself with a blade, but, to his surprise, he feels no pain. The dream starts with his being on trial for something like embezzlement.

> During the course of this trial, they had called for a physical examination of me, like an operation, even—they wanted to make cuts in my body to examine something—not going all the way inside to the organs, and so forth, but kinda superficial cuts where you cut the skin in long straight lines down the arms and down the torso. Maybe something to do with bacteria or something, I don't know. I was real concerned about that, but I was not real concerned about the trial in general. . . . But this physical examination thing concerned me quite a lot. There's kind of a conflict here. I have the impression that I have already had this examination, and it didn't really work the way they thought it was going to. But I think that isn't logical because that wouldn't have happened and there wouldn't have been any point in me being concerned about it further, but I was—I was concerned about having it done correctly, and fascinated with the procedure itself. And so there weren't actually any cuts on my body, it's as though they had tried to and it wouldn't do it. So

> I was interested in that, and I just decided I'd do it myself. I got something to cut with . . . and I got something like a razor blade and started to make these cuts myself. It surely would be awkward if you did that—lying down, and trying to even make the sort of cut I'm talking about with one arm, without looking at it, but it's as though I wasn't doing it that way, it's as though I was doing it from outside my body. And I was a little bit ragged and awkward at it at first, but eventually I got the hang of it and—this is how it seemed awkward to me, as though I was doing it from right over my body, and—just like you would a doll, you know—straight down, and I discovered that it was awkward to do—the right-hand side of my body (lying on the ground), which seems to be the left-hand side from the position I'm actually cutting in. So, what I needed to do is to move around, so I moved down to where I was really facing the side of my body to do that. This is all very slow and awkward, but there wasn't any blood or anything. Well, I did that, and I don't know anything more about it—*it obviously didn't hurt particularly, I know I kept expecting it to—I kept expecting it to feel at least, you know, like it does when you cut yourself* (italics added), so I was a little bit surprised that it didn't bleed, but I wasn't worried about there being any real damage or anything because I knew I would heal up. And quite sure that I knew I'd heal up without scars, too. Just didn't seem that big a deal. But now I felt like I had done it, for them. That they would be happy now. It was like I have accomplished whatever it was they wanted me to do for them.

In another dream (No. 349, 11/24/91), a woman is at a librarians' meeting.

> I chat for a bit, and actually my back has begun to hurt and is getting worse—lots worse. I complain of it and somebody sympathizes, asks what happened, I say I got it from sitting on my little squashy couch. One of the librarians I know, sitting in the back row, says Daniel here should give me a talk on how to take care of your back. I say I've heard it, thank you, plenty of it, I couldn't stand any more. I'm squatting right now to relieve it, and get up saying I'm gonna go do my back exercises.

Since the dream mentions her back exercises, it is likely that she experienced regular trouble with her back, so we suspect that the back pain in the dream had a somatic source.

We need more research that explicitly addresses the issue of pain in dreams. From the limited data that I have been able to find, however, it appears that in dreams we rarely experience physical pain without an actual somatic stimulus. This is striking considering how common it is to feel unpleasant and painful *emotions* in dreams, such as anxiety, dread, and terror.

In describing various kinds of disjunctive cognitions, the reader may have noted that we have difficulty describing in language the kinds of separation of function that are observed in many kinds of brain dysfunction; the results often sound like oxymorons or other odd linguistic constructions. Here is a list of those I have discussed:

1. Knowledge without awareness
2. Vision without seeing
3. Sense of touch without feeling
4. Retention without memory, or having information but not knowing it
5. Pain without suffering

Such neurological syndromes make us aware of functional divisions in the brain/mind which we would probably not intuit from mere introspection: vision/seeing; pain sensation/pain experience; actual illness/sense of being healthy; seeing familiar faces/recognizing them; and having information/remembering. But if we paid more attention to the phenomenology of our dreams, we might also become aware of these divisions and of others that have not yet been identified.

VISUAL DISORDERS IN DREAMS AND BRAIN DYSFUNCTION: 1. MONOCHROMATIC DREAMS AND ACHROMATOPSIA

Some people with normal waking color vision report that their dreams lack color. In fact, according to Hall (1953; see also Van de Castle, 1994), only about one-third of dreams have color in them.[4] A few people dream entirely in color, and a somewhat larger percentage never experience color in dreams, while the majority of people see color in some dreams. These statistics have been questioned (Tauber and Green, 1962), and

4. The precise numbers are: 29% of dreams are in partial or full color, 31% for women, 24% for men (Van de Castle, 1994, p. 298).

Kahn et al. (1962) found that if people are asked about color in their dreams, the incidence is found to be much higher, closer to 70–80% of dreams. However, even when special inquiry by researchers elicits some color percepts in dreams, it is not clear that there is color as much as in the waking visual field. We do not know to what degree even those dreams that *have color in them* are *in color.* I once heard a dream in which most of the characters were in black and white and two of the characters were in color.

Hall (1953) could find no significance in who dreams in color, nor could he find any content differences in chromatic vs. achromatic dreams. He concluded: "Our search has been fruitless. . . . We have come to the conclusion that color in dreams yields no information about the personality of the dreamer. It is merely an embellishment on the dream and does not signify anything in itself" (p. 46).

However, there may be other significance to the strange fact that some people who are not colorblind seem to dream without color. What does this suggest about the human mind/brain? Before attempting an answer, let us consider the varieties of human colorblindness.

There are various degrees of colorblindness. In colloquial speech, people who say they are colorblind usually mean that they cannot distinguish certain colors from one another, such as red from green. But there are forms of colorblindness known as achromatopsia in which people live in a totally black-and-white world (Sacks, 1997). This condition may be due to a genetic defect which leads to an eye syndrome known as rod monochromancy. The defect may also be in the brain. This is known as central achromatopsia and is caused by a highly circumscribed cortical lesion, bilaterally on area V4 on the fusiform gyrus (Zeki, 1990, 1993).

It is odd that many dreams seem to be achromatic, since most of our waking vision seems to be in color. Where does this come from? One possible answer, supported by the research of Kahn et al. (1962), is that two-thirds of our dreams are not really without color, but that if the color in them is not notable, we do not report it.

There is also the fact that our color perception is much more acute in the center of our visual field. In the margins of our vision, there is very little color perception, although our conscious minds do not usually note this.

And, perhaps most significant, all of us see less color at low levels of illumination. At night, when awake, we can often distinguish the shapes of objects but not their colors. The rods in our cornea can register shapes in such low light conditions, but the cones cannot register color. Such vision is called *scotopic.*[5] Is our dreaming at night in some way an analog of this vision at low levels of illumination? Do perceptual modules perhaps set themselves for creating percepts of low illumination in some dreams?

2. PERIPHERAL VISION WITHOUT CENTRAL VISION

A dream experience of loss of vision in the center of the visual field has been reported. As noted above, Ullman (1973) tells of a dream that was about "a certain kind of blindness" affecting himself and other people:

> Peripheral vision was intact enough to create, at times, the doubt that the blindness existed. There was a certain distressful wavering between doubt and certainty. I became aware in the dream that the blindness could be compensated for by a very simple expedient. It involved shifting the angle at which a series of steps were arranged so that they could be mounted vertically rather than at the usual incline, thus enabling the person ascending them to guide himself by what he could feel with his hands rather than by what he could see with his eyes. In this way, so it seemed in the dream, the illusion of normality was maintained [pp. 289–290].

The dream occurred after three significant events: four days after Ullman heard a lecture about how ordinary Germans overlooked the brutal killing of a Jewish child during the Holocaust; three days after John F. Kennedy was shot; and one day after Lee Harvey Oswald was murdered. Ullman interprets the dream in terms of his thoughts about Freud blinding himself to the importance of social conflict, as well as Ullman's own blindness to unpleasant truths:

> Subjectively, I am saying something about myself and what I have to do to maintain my own emotional distance and blindness from certain unpleasant truths [about violence in our own culture]. Objectively, I am saying something about the world and the way it lends itself to personal manipulation. A paradoxical

5. Astronomers use this fact to their advantage; when trying to detect very faint stars through a telescope, they "look off" the central fovea, so that the image falls on a region of the retina rich in light-sensitive rods (Gregory, 1973).

> social truth seems to come out of the dream, namely, the very process one relies on to cover up the blindness presumably also enables one to climb up the ladder of success [p. 291].

But looking at the dream from our current concern, we would have to wonder how Ullman's dream might suggest something about the organization of vision in the brain. Indeed, we find that the loss of focal vision with the retention of peripheral vision is quite common with certain lesions of the primary occipital cortex. It can also occur at the sensory level, through retinal damage (macular degeneration).

I discussed Ullman's dream with Robert Bilder, a neuropsychologist at the Center for Advanced Brain Imaging in Orangeburg, NY, who identified a different aspect of the dream that is significant for the understanding of brain function. Bilder told me that, from his point of view, "the most interesting aspect of the dream is the substitution of somatosensory representations for visual representations to guide goal directed action, and that this use of a separate sensory input stream was able to maintain the 'illusion of normality.' This is intriguing because normally, loss of key sensory inputs is associated with distress ['mismatch'] and a real sense of abnormality [consider vulnerability to hallucinations/delusions when sensory inputs are compromised, as is hypothesized in dementia and part of the experience of healthy people undergoing sensory deprivation]" [personal communication, March 5, 2000].

AMNESIAS

There are many types of amnesia, and it is remarkable how many of them can be mimicked in dreams. Consider the following dream:

> I was in a foreign country. I rented a car, drove out of town, and got lost. I didn't know which town I was in, nor which town I came from. I asked some tourists if they had a map, but the maps had no city names on them, only the outline of the land masses. I ask at a hotel and they also cannot tell me the name. Then I realize that if I look at the car-rental agreement, it should say the name of the town to which I must return.

The dream had many personal meanings, including the dreamer's feeling "lost" in his life, uncertain which road to take, metaphorically.

However, the dreamer was also very concerned about middle-aged memory loss. He had been reading articles about memory loss and was unsure if his memory problems were normal for someone in middle age, were caused by excessive drinking, or were due to some other factor. His first association to the dream was: "Last night, I had a large strong drink before dinner and got drunk. Is my dream foretelling my memory loss, or indicating the loss that is already there?" He was thus wondering, in the terms we have been using, if his dream was an endoneuropsychic perception of organic memory loss. At the least, the *fear* of alcohol-induced memory loss was made real in the dream.

REDUPLICATIVE PARAMNESIAS

There is a subset of amnesic syndromes known as reduplicative paramnesias, in which a person is convinced that a familiar place or person has been duplicated (Pick, 1903). There are two main subsets: reduplication of place and reduplication of person.

In reduplication of place, a patient may say: "This is the second hospital I've been in. It looks just like the hospital I was in yesterday." But he will not make the deduction that since they look the same, they are the same place. This clinical phenomenon raises an intriguing problem. It is virtually automatic for normal people to deduce, "If I was there yesterday, and it looked the same, I must be in the same place." What is the function of the mind responsible for this deduction? Since it is an ability that can be lost with certain kinds of brain damage, can we discover the neuroanatomical basis of this ability? We know that an analogous phenomenon can occur in dreams, as cited earlier: "The dream doesn't really take place in my parents' apartment. There is a bookcase there in what used to be my bedroom" (Blechner, 1995a).

There is the related phenomenon of "reduplication of person." A man may say, "I have two wives, the woman who visited me in the hospital today and the woman who called last night." Such a statement shows a deficit related to reduplication of place, but also involves human identity—in this case, the knowledge that a woman experienced in different time frames and different contexts is a single person. There is also the related phenomenon of Capgras syndrome (Capgras and Reboul-Lachaux, 1923), in which a patient will see someone familiar, like a parent or spouse, and feel convinced that the person is an impostor.

Robinson and Freeman (1954) defined self-continuity as recognition of a stable self that can change over time, and they proposed that their lobotomized patients lost this sense of self-continuity. Patients with reduplication of person may be considered to have lost the sense of what might be called *other-continuity*; other people no longer have a stable identity that can change over time. Thus, one patient claimed that he had two families—the one that he had before his hospitalization, and the other upon his release a year later. The children in his new family looked like his old ones, but were taller. The patient may be aware of the bizarreness of this percept and maintain it nevertheless. Consider the following segment of a clinical interview with a patient who believed that his first wife set up a woman who looked like her to take her place (Stuss, 1991).

> **Examiner:** So all of a sudden you came out of the hospital and you went back in the same house with a whole different family.
> **Subject:** Well, that is about the size of it, yes.
>
> **E:** How can you account for that?
> **S:** I don't know. I tried to understand it myself, and it was virtually impossible to understand it.
>
> . . .
>
> **E:** I think you are pulling my leg.
> **S:** I am not. I am trying to be truthful.
>
> **E:** You are not trying to pull the wool over my eyes.
> **S:** No, I am not trying to. . . .
>
> **E:** If somebody would tell you that story, what would you say to them?
> **S:** I would find it extremely hard to believe, and I probably should be defending myself more so. I have not to date, I have not tried in any way, shape, or manner or tried to divorce the first wife [pp. 72–73].

There are a number of theories of reduplication of person. One theory is that it is due primarily to psychodynamic factors. Another is that there are multiple neural pathways for facial recognition which divides the cognitive information from the more affectively laden information. It may be that affective information is critical to the identification of people who are close to us. By this theory, the Capgras patient sees the features of his mother without having the "feel" of mother. Thus, he assumes that she is an impostor (Ellis and Young, 1990; Young et al., 1993; Ellis et al., 1997).

Does reduplication of person and place have an analogue in dream experiences? I believe it may. Dreamers sometimes report that the same person may appear in a dream twice, in two impersonations. Certainly this can happen with the self, for example: "I was in the fight and I was also watching it from above." Of course, if one assumes that every character in the dream is an aspect of the dreamer, then there are as many impersonations of the dreamer as there are characters. This was the basis of Jung's interpretation using the subjective approach. But from a research standpoint, we can consider multiple impersonations only in the manifest, not in the latent content of the dream.

At the same time, we asked earlier whether dreams ever occur of the type, "It looked like my mother, but I knew it was not her." I noted that I had not heard such dreams. Yet if there were such dreams, they would be a direct analog of Capgras' syndrome, in which a person looks like a loved one but is experienced as an impostor.

TRANSPOSITION OF TIME IN DREAMS

In their dreams, people often mix objects and feelings from different eras in time. The notion of time travel, a popular theme in science fiction, could well have originated in dreams. In our dreams we often revisit places and experiences that are emotionally important to us. Our dreams can transform our time sense, mixing old and new aspects of things. It is common, for example, for people who have left a job to dream of their old workplace, sometimes years later. The workplace may be clearly recognizable, but certain features of it are changed. The dream may come at a time when the new work situation is questionable, and the dreamer may unconsciously be revisiting the reasons for leaving the old job. The dream may reflect an unconscious solution, something along the lines of: "My old job, changed in this way, would be best."

The changes may also reflect changes in the dreamer. One of my patients dreamt that she returned to the hospital where she used to work: "It was totally changed. The staff was very young." The dreamer was about to have a significant birthday which made her feel old. The staff in the dream was very young relative to how old she now felt. But then, in the dream, her old boss told her to do something objectionable, and she was able to say "No!" in a way she was never able to when she was actually there, but which she was now able to do much more easily as her personality had developed. The dream portrayed both the good and bad aspects of her increased age and maturity.

Another woman dreamt: "In the dream, I am my current age [65] and my mother is 32. She is ignoring me." Although she knew that this combination of ages was impossible in the waking world, it felt compelling to her. She explained: "My mother was 32 on Kristallnacht in Austria. I was only three years old. I cannot remember anything from that time. But my relatives tell me it was horrible. My uncle came to our apartment with his face all bloodied. My mother left the house to search for my father. He had been sent to a concentration camp, but she was able to bring him back. I have no memory of the time, but I think that whatever happened then has stayed with me forever. In some sense, my mother, as I react to her and to her stand-ins in my life, is always that 32-year-old woman, no matter what my actual age."

The transposition of time in a dream, like the disjunction between feature perception and identity recognition, is an aspect of bizarreness that usually does not surprise people. It suggests another important connection between dreaming and organic psychosis. In both, the past can be experienced as if it is the present. If you ask an amnesic patient who confabulates, "What did you do last night?" he may tell you that he was at Mary's restaurant with five other people. You know that he was in the hospital last night. If you tell his wife of his response, she may tell you, "Yes, he was at that restaurant with those five people, but that was five years ago." The patient may have no realization that his memory, although correct, has been transposed in time.

Dreamers frequently report something similar: "I was at my parents' house. It looked like it did 20 years ago, but I was there as an adult."

Such dreams may represent an endoneuropsychic perception of our memory system. They may be revealing to us something that memory researchers have increasingly accepted, that memory is not a passive storehouse of the records of our past experiences, a biological file cabinet in which the pages stay constant over the years. Instead our memories are constantly revised and re-revised as our lives progress, and can be melded with current experience.

The transpositions in time in a dream may also show various fixations or obsessions with the past, or a process of comparison of the present with the past. A man in his thirties dreamt, "I was with my high school sweetheart. We were all adult, although I haven't seen her in years." The man was unhappy in his marriage, and this dream revealed his nostalgia for his old girlfriend. In the dream she went on to show him a large tattoo on her thigh, which she did not possess when he dated her, but which he saw as a sign of modern, experimental, free-thinking women. His current wife would never get a tattoo, but he felt that his former girlfriend would.

We already discussed how there may be an asymmetry concerning dreams that have a disjunction between feature perception and identity recognition. It seems to be much more common to dream "It didn't look like my mother, but I knew it was her" than "It looked like my mother, but I knew it was not her." There may be a similar asymmetry with time transposition (David Olds, personal communication). According to my records, it is not unusual to dream, "We were back in the house I grew up in, but I was my current age." It is much less common to dream, "I was in my current house, but I was a child." I have no record of the latter sort of dream, but we would need a much larger sample, collected from many dream researchers, to state categorically that such a dream does not occur or occurs only very rarely. If such a dream does not occur, it would be significant for our theory. It might indicate a division in the brain of our sense of the time of our self representation separate from our sense of time about other aspects of our experience, and an asymmetry in how these can be combined.

When hearing a dream in which there is an apparent transposition in time, we must be careful to specify where and how the insight into the transposition of time occurs. Does the insight into the transposition of time occur in the dream itself or does it come after the fact, as the dream is told during waking life? In other words, the disparity in time may be a product of secondary revision. Sometimes, but not always, the dreamer has no awareness during the dream of the disparity in time. It is an important experiential distinction. If the dreamer while asleep has no insight into the transposition of time, that would suggest a closer analogue of the brain state during the dream with the brain state in the neuropathological syndrome.

VARIETIES OF AWARENESS DURING SLEEP AND DREAMING

There are many varieties of awareness of sleeping and dreaming. I have heard reported all sorts of gradations and interpenetrations of sleep and dreaming. These include:

1. The most common state of dreaming is a kind of agnosia. We don't realize that we are dreaming. As the dream is going on, we think it is really happening. Thus, in "normal" dreaming, our reality monitoring is faulty.

2. There is also a phenomenon known as "lucid dreaming," in which the dreamer is aware that she is dreaming. Some lucid dreamers also claim to be able to direct the outcome of the dream during the dream. We might also call it "metadreaming," in line with other metacognitions—an accurate awareness that one is dreaming. Metadreaming would then, of course, also include inaccurate awareness of dreaming—either an assumption that one is dreaming when one is awake, or an assumption when one is dreaming that one is not. (The latter is the most common metacognition of dreaming.)
3. A person in a dream is tired and takes a nap. "In the dream I got tired. So I lay down and took a nap."
4. A person in a dream has a dream. "In the dream, I fell asleep and then I dreamt . . ." Also, in the ancient Chinese book, *The Chuang-tzu*: "Still all of them, when they dream know not that they dream, and at times they dream that they are engaged in dreaming: only at the moment that they waken do they know they have but dreamed" [Parsifal-Charles, 1986, p. 65].
5. A person tells the dream within the dream after having the dream (see Blechner, 1995a): "And then in the dream, I told you the dream."
6. People have the experience during a dream of waking up from their sleep. In fact, they are still dreaming.

There are still other gradations of "reality awareness" of the sleep state and the dreaming experience. One can be aware in a dream of being asleep without being aware that one is dreaming, and the fact of being asleep becomes part of the manifest content. This was reported to me by a man who had a dream a few nights before a seminar in Manhattan which he had organized himself and at which he was to be the keynote speaker. "In the dream, the seminar is in Albany, and I forgot to tell them that it's in Albany. *In the dream, I realized that I was asleep but not that I was dreaming*. I thought, I have to wake up to tell them."

This is awareness that one is asleep, but not that one is dreaming. The situation seemed completely real to the dreamer. Being aware that he was asleep, he felt the need to wake up in order to act on the concern of the dream (he was not aware that his concern about notifying the others was part of a dream until he *did* wake up). This example is particularly strange, in that the dreamer seems to lack, in his dream, the procedural knowledge that if he is thinking while asleep, he must be dreaming.

How should we conceive of these dreams and of what they might say about consciousness? They may be evidence of the recursive nature of consciousness, and that this recursiveness also occurs in the sleep state. These phenomena raise many questions about consciousness: Do the processes of self-awareness of one's state operate differently during sleep and dreaming? What does it mean to "know" that one is asleep or to know that one is dreaming? How does the sleeping mind create the illusion of going to sleep, or of waking up while asleep? Or the illusion of remembering a dream and telling it, as part of the dream? How many recursions are possible in the self-awareness of waking and sleeping?

There are many other gradations of experience and involvement in our dreams. Sometimes we feel in our dreams as if we are passively watching a movie. Sometimes we feel that we are in the middle of the action of the dream. And other times, we feel that we are watching ourselves take part in the dream. What causes these different degrees of involvement, our stance in relation to the dream, from different visual, spatial, and experiential perspectives?

One theory is that the experience of the dream is correlated with (or, in a stronger version, determined by) feedback, during the creation of the dream, from different parts of the brain. It is possible that during dreaming the areas of the brain connected with perceptual input or with muscular output are variously activated during dreaming. For instance, if there is motion in the dream, then there may be feedback from the brain centers connected to the skeletal musculature. If the dream is verbal, then there may be feedback from speech centers. John Antrobus (1991), one of the proponents of this view, writes: "Imaged physical participation in the dream may depend on feedback from larger skeletal musculature. Conceptual-verbal dreams may be dependent on feedback from subcortical speech centers. The passive watching of images may well identify a default condition when proprioceptive feedback is strongly inhibited" (p. 104).

PERCEPTUAL "FILLING IN" AND DREAMS

There are a number of examples in which people with defective perceptual systems "fill in" the gaps in their perceptual fields. For example, in 1760, Charles Bonnet described the occurrence of vivid visual hallucinations in his grandfather, who was psychologically normal but visually impaired. Charles Bonnet's syndrome, in which people with deteriorated vision start to have hallucinations, has recently been found to be much more common than once thought. It occurs among more than 10% of elderly people with visual disturbances such as macular degeneration. Many people with it try to hide the fact that they are hallucinating for fear of being thought psychotic. In fact, most patients with Bonnet's syndrome show no signs of psychosis besides their hallucinations, and they benefit from being told that such hallucinations are normal.

An important question is: to what degree are Charles Bonnet hallucinations similar to dreams in the same patient? One woman said (Teunisse et al., 1996), "In my dreams I experience things which affect me, which are related to my life. These hallucinations, however, have nothing to do with me" (p. 796). But some patients thought their visions could have psychological significance. One elderly childless man was intrigued by recurrent hallucinations of a little girl and boy and wondered whether these hallucinations reflected his unfulfilled wish to be a father. One widow hallucinated her recently deceased husband three times a week.[6] So in these latter two examples, the visions fulfill a wish, much as some dreams do.

Teunisse et al. tabulated the characteristics of Bonnet hallucinations. For example, 63% of patients reported that the hallucinations were always in color, which is almost double the rate reported by Hall for dreams. However, it would be useful to collect the dreams of patients with Bonnet's syndrome and to compare them systematically with the hallucinations. Such a study might clarify the relationship between waking visual nonpsychotic hallucination and dream hallucination.

In another example of perceptual filling-in, the neurologist V. S. Ramachandran tells of a patient named Josh in his early thirties with a scotoma (blind spot). A steel rod had pierced the back of Josh's skull, damaging part of the primary visual cortex. As a result, he had a scotoma about the size of a palm in his left visual field.

In a series of ingenious experiments, Ramachandran studied the ways that Josh "filled in" his visual field. In one instance, he presented him with two rows of numbers: 1, 2, 3 at the top of the scotoma and

---

6. This is not unique to Bonnet's syndrome. In actuality, one of the most common *waking* hallucinations is for a person who has lost a close relative to "see" the relative (Rees, 1975; see also Marris, 1958; Yamamoto et al., 1969). Such "hallucinations" are experienced by approximately 50% of widows and widowers and are a normal part of grieving. They are usually experienced without anxiety and are not considered pathognomic for schizophrenia (Blechner, 1997a). Dead relatives also commonly reappear alive in dreams.

7, 8, 9 at the bottom. Would Josh's brain fill in the visual field with the missing numbers? At first, Josh reported that he saw a continuous vertical column of numbers. But when Ramachandran (Ramachandran and Blakeslee, 1998) asked him to read off the numbers, Josh said, "Um, one, two, three, um, seven, eight, nine. Hey, that's very strange. I can see numbers, but I don't know what they are. . . . They don't look blurred. They kind of look strange. I can't tell what they are—like hieroglyphics or something" (p. 101).

In Ramachandran's view this was

> a curious form of temporary dyslexia in Josh. Those middle numbers did not exist, were not flashed before his eyes, yet his brain was making up the textural attributes of the number string and completing it. This is another striking demonstration of division of labor in the visual pathways. The system in his brain that deals with surfaces and edges is saying, "There is numberlike stuff in this region—that's what you should see in the middle," but since there are no actual numbers, his object pathway remains silent and the net result is illegible "hieroglyphics" [p. 102].

These findings are very suggestive for our study of dreams. We often hear from dreamers something like "I saw a message written there, but I couldn't make out what it said." It also happens auditorily, "I heard him say something to me, but I couldn't make it out." We know there is a message, we know it is using language, but we don't know the content. This may be an example of dreams getting input from the section of our brains involved in perceiving "languageness" without further input from the section that decodes actual words.

And if that is so, which related phenomena of dreams might tell us about other ways that aspects of our stimulus world are divided in perceptual processing? For example, in the large sample of dreams from non-clinical populations collected at the University of California, Santa Cruz, there is the following dream (Dream No. 5, 1985): "On the way out, P.T. takes the guy aside and says something very stern and final-sounding in French. I knew it was French but I don't understand it and that was the reason he was using it, so that I wouldn't be embarrassed or have to hear something I wouldn't want to."

The dreamer may have been able to dream of some words that only sounded like French without being able to specify what they were. Could this suggest that there is separate processing of the sound of a language from the constituent words? Many of us are able to recognize the sound of a certain language without being able to speak it.

There are many dream formations in which certain aspects of the stimulus are specified and others are unclear. It is common, for example, for a dreamer to say, "There was a man there, but I didn't know who it was." The dreamer is sure of the gender of the person, a man, but not more of the identity. Could this suggest that the perception of gender is wired in separately from other aspects of identity?

Let us go back for a moment to the child's dream of the seal/boat: "They were crossing the channel, and for some reason needed another boat. They were frightened, but then a seal swam up to them. They thought it was just a seal, but then they looked and under the water it was a whole boat, it was huge, so they climbed onto the seal/boat, and it brought them to the shore of mainland." The child puts together a seal and a boat; both are objects that can navigate through water. That is an aspect that they share, but one is animate and the other inanimate. We know that children don't place as much store by the animate/inanimate distinction as adults. Children like to imagine that the inanimate world can come to life. Teacups dance and books speak. Read any child's book and you will find many examples of this. Children say, "Goodnight, moon." As the child develops, he or she learns to suppress this tendency, although as adults, when we say things to our children like "Here comes Mr. Wind!" we may be rediscovering our capacity for blurring the animate/inanimate distinction. Does this capacity also survive in our dreams?

Ramachandran uses his observations of Josh to suggest which aspects of the stimulus world can be constructed by the brain and how the brain may divide up the different aspects of the world during perceptual processing. But this is precisely along the lines that we have been exploring in relation to dream condensation and symbols. Would it not be wonderful to see whether and how perceptual "filling-in" aligns with our experiences in dreams?

Ramachandran makes the distinction between conceptual filling in and perceptual filling in. This distinction is actually one of conscious versus unconscious control. We all can *imagine* what is behind our heads, but we can consciously and deliberately change our minds about what that is. Perceptual filling in is done by neurons that are not in our conscious control. The patient with a scotoma can consciously perceive the visual field filling in, without feeling that he can control it. It often takes place over time; when Josh was shown a pattern of flashing black dots on a red background, he claimed to see the outline of his scotoma.

Ramachandran asked him, "But Josh, what do you see inside the scotoma?" Josh replied, "Well, it's very strange, doctor. For the first few seconds, I saw only the red color bleeding into this part of the screen, but the twinkling black dots did not fill in. Then after a few seconds, the dots filled in, but they weren't twinkling. And last, the actual twinkle—the motion sensation—filled in as well" (p. 102).

Ramachandran says that the "filling in seems to occur at different speeds for different perceptual attributes like color, motion (twinkle) and texture. Motion takes longer to fill in than color, and so on. Indeed, such differential filling in provides additional evidence that such specialized areas do exist in the human brain. For if perception were just one process happening in a single location in the brain, it should happen all at once, not in stages" (p. 102).

And what are those specialized areas? We may wonder if dreams might give us information about this. Are different aspects of identity processed separately, and which are they? Is gender processed separately from identity, as we noted above? If we start to listen to our patients' dreams from this perspective, we will be able to generate important hypotheses that can be tested.

I am raising these questions without definitive answers—we cannot have definitive answers without data, and once relevant data are collected, we shall have to consider the significance of those data. My intention here is to draw our attention to the potential sources of data, and the potential connections (or distinctions) that there may be between what occurs in dreams and in neuropathological syndromes, so that we may better understand the relationship between psychology and brain processes.

The connection between dreams, psychopathology, and neuropathology is the dream frontier that has been least explored. At this frontier, both clinicians in the consulting room and brain scientists in the laboratory can proceed boldly and find that each field of inquiry can contribute to the other. Throughout this book, I have tried to attend to both the meaning and the science of dreams, always stressing that we can turn to dreams both for their clarification of the dreamer's psychological concerns and for clues about how the brain operates. If we attend to the neuropsychology of dreams and to the meaning of dreams with equal vigor, we may one day achieve what Freud originally hoped to develop—a unified science of brain and mind.

REFERENCES

Alpert, J. (1995) Dreams, trauma, and clinical observation. *Psychoanalytic Psychology*, 12:325–328.

Altman, L. L. (1975) *The Dream in Psychoanalysis*. New York: International Universities Press.

Antrobus, J. (1990) The neurocognition of sleep mentation. In: *Sleep and Cognition*, ed. R. Bootzin, J. Kihlstrom & D. Schacter. Washington, DC: American Psychological Association.

Antrobus, J. (1991) Dreaming: Cognitive processes during cortical activation and high afferent thresholds. *Psychological Review*, 98:96–121.

Arieti, S. (1963) The psychotherapy of schizophrenia in theory and practice. Psychiatric Research Report No. 17, American Psychiatric Association.

Arkin, A., Hastey, J. & Reiser, M. (1966) Post-hypnotically stimulated sleep-talking. *Journal of Nervous and Mental Disease*, 142:293–309.

Aristotle (1955) On sleep. In: *Aristotle: Parva Naturalia*, ed. W. Ross. Oxford, UK: Clarendon Press.

Arnold-Foster, M. (1921) *Studies in Dreams*. London: Allen & Unwin.

Artemidorus (1990) *The Interpretation of Dreams: Oneirocritica*, trans. R. White. Torrance, CA: Original Books.

Aserinsky, E. & Kleitman, N. (1953) Regularly occurring periods of eye motility and concurrent phenomena during sleep. *Science*, 118:273–274.

Baars, B., Cohen, J., Bower, G. & Berry, J. (1992) Some caveats on testing the Freudian slip hypothesis. In: *Experimental Slips and Human Error*, ed. B. Baars. New York: Plenum.

Bartlett, F. (1932) *Remembering: A Study in Experimental and Social Psychology*. Cambridge, UK: Cambridge University Press.

Bass, A. (1995) Dream analysis as a relational event: Commentary on Blechner's "The Patient's Dreams and the Countertransference." *Psychoanalytic Dialogues*, 5:27–44.

Benedetti, G. (1989) Träume von Psychotherapeuten psychotischer Patienten. *Daseinsanalyse*, 6:248–259.

Benjamin, J. (1988) *The Bonds of Love*. New York: Pantheon.

Benson, D. & Geschwind, N. (1985) Aphasia and related disorders: A clinical approach. In: *Principles of Behavioral Neurology*, ed. M. Mesulam. Philadephia: Davis, pp. 193–238.

Bettelheim, B. (1985) Afterword. In: *The Third Reich of Dreams*, by K. Beradt. Wellingborough, Northhamptonshire: Aquarian Press.

Bilder, R. & LeFever, F., eds. (1998) *Neuroscience of the Mind on the Centennial of Freud's* "Project for a Scientific Psychology." New York: New York Academy of Sciences, *Annals Vol. 843.*

Binswanger, L. (1928) *Wandlungen der Auffassung und Deutung des Traumes von den Griechen bis zum Gegenwart.* Berlin: Springer.

Bisiach, E., Rusconi, M. & Vallar, G. (1992) Remission of somatophrenic delusion through vestibular stimulation. *Neuropsychologia*, 29:1029–1031.

Blechner, M. J. (1977) Musical skill and the categorical perception of harmonic mode. *Haskins Laboratories Status Report on Speech Research*, 52:139–174.

Blechner, M. J. (1983) Changes in the dreams of borderline patients. *Contemporary Psychoanalysis*, 19:485–498.

Blechner, M. J. (1992) Working in the countertransference. *Psychoanalytic Dialogues*, 2:161–179.

Blechner, M. J. (1994) Projective identification, countertransference, and the "maybe-me." *Contemporary Psychoanalysis*, 30:619–630.

Blechner, M. J. (1995a) The patient's dreams and the countertransference. *Psychoanalytic Dialogues*, 5:1–25.

Blechner, M. J. (1995b) Schizophrenia. In: *Handbook of Interpersonal Psychoanalysis*, ed. M. Lionells, J. Fiscalini, C. Mann & D. B. Stern. Hillsdale, NJ: The Analytic Press, pp. 375–396.

Blechner, M. J. (1996) Comments on the theory and therapy of borderline personality disorder. *Contemporary Psychoanalysis*, 32:68–73.

Blechner, M. J., ed. (1997a) *Hope and Mortality*. Hillsdale, NJ: The Analytic Press.

Blechner, M. J. (1997b) Psychoanalytic psychotherapy with schizophrenics: Then and now. *Contemporary Psychoanalysis*, 33:251–262.

Blechner, M. J. (1998) The analysis and creation of dream meaning: Interpersonal, intrapsychic, and neurobiological perspectives. *Contemporary Psychoanalysis*, 34:181–194.

Blechner, M. J. (2000a) On dreams that turn over a page. Letter, *International Journal of Psychoanalysis*, 81:174.

Blechner, M. J. (2000b) Confabulation in dreaming, psychosis, and brain damage. *Neuro-Psychoanalysis*, 2:23–28.

Blechner, M. J., Day, R. S. & Cutting, J. E. (1976) Processing two dimensions of nonspeech stimuli: The auditory-phonetic distinction reconsidered. *Journal of Experimental Psychology: Human Perception and Performance*, 2:257–266.

Boas, F. (1994) *The Way of the Dream: Conversations on Jungian Dream Interpretation with Marie-Louise von Franz*. Boston: Shambhala.

Bodamer, J. (1947) Die Prosopagnosie. *Archiv Psychiatrische Nervenkrankheiten*, 179:6–54.

Boisen, A. (1960) *Out of the Depths*. New York: Harper.

Bollas, C. (1987) *The Shadow of the Object: Psychoanalysis of the Unthought Known*. London: Free Association Books.

Bonime, W. (1962) *The Clinical Use of Dreams*. New York: Basic Books.
Bonime, W. (1986) Collaborative dream interpretation. *Contemporary Psychoanalysis*, 14:15–26.
Bonnet, C. (1760) *Essai analytique sur les facultés d'âme*. Copenhagen: Philbert.
Bransford, J. & Johnson, M. (1973) Consideration of some problems of comprehension. In: *Visual Information Processing*, ed. W. Chase. New York: Academic Press, pp. 383–438.
Braun, A., Balkin, T., Wesensten, N., Gwadry, F., Carson, R., Varga, M., Baldwin, P., Belenky, G. & Herscovitch, P. (1998) Dissociated pattern of activity in visual cortices and their projections during human rapid eye movement sleep. *Science*, 279:91–95.
Brenneis, C. B. (1994) Can early childhood trauma be reconstructed from dreams? *Psychoanalytic Psychology*, 11:429–447.
Brenner, C. (1955) *An Elementary Textbook of Psychoanalysis*. New York: International Universities Press.
Bringuier, J.-C. (1989) *Conversations with Jean Piaget*. Chicago: University of Chicago Press.
Brunswick, R. M. (1929) The analysis of a case of paranoia. *Journal of Nervous & Mental Disease*, 70:1–22, 155–179.
Bullard, D. M., ed. (1959) *Psychoanalysis and Psychotherapy: Selected Papers of Frieda Fromm-Reichmann*. Chicago: University of Chicago Press.
Burke, W. F. (1992) Countertransference disclosure and the asymmetry/mutuality dilemma. *Psychoanalytic Dialogues*, 2:241–271.
Caligor, L. (1981) Parallel and reciprocal processes in psychoanalytic supervision. *Contemporary Psychoanalysis*, 17:1–27.
Caligor, L. & Caligor, J. (1978) The dream in psychoanalytic therapy. In: *Psychoanalytic Psychotherapy*, ed. G. Goldman & D. Milman. Reading, MA: Addison-Wesley.
Caligor, L. & May, R. (1968) *Dreams and Symbols*. New York: Basic Books.
Capgras, J. & Reboul-Lachaux, J. (1923) L'illusion des "sosies" dans un délire systematisé chronique. *Bulletin de la Société Clinique Médicine Mentale*, 2:6–16.
Carroll, L. (1976) *Complete Works*. New York: Vintage.
Cartwright, R. D. & Ratzel, R. (1972) Effects of dream loss on waking behaviors. *Archives of General Psychiatry*, 27:277–280.
Casement, P. (1991) *Learning from the Patient*. New York: Guilford Press.
Churchland, P. (1995) *The Engine of Reason, the Seat of the Soul*. Cambridge, MA: MIT Press.
Claparède, E. (1911) Récognition et moïté. Trans. as "Recognition and 'Meness,'" in *Organization and Pathology of Thought*, ed. D. Rapaport. New York: Columbia University Press, 1951, pp. 58–75.
Crick, F. & Mitchison, G. (1983) The function of dream sleep. *Nature*, 304:111–114.
Crick, F. & Mitchison, G. (1986) REM sleep and neural nets. *Journal of Mind and Behavior*, 7:229–249.

Critchley, M. (1966) *The Parietal Lobes*. London: Hafner.

Curtis, H. & Sachs, D. (1976) Dialogue on the changing use of dreams in psychoanalytic practice. *International Journal of Psycho-Analysis*, 57:343–354.

Damasio, A. (1985) Disorders of complex visual processing: Agnosias, achromatopsia, Balint's syndrome, and related difficulties of orientation and construction. In: *Principles of Behavioral Neurology*, ed. M. Mesulam. Philadelphia: F. A. Davis, pp. 259–288.

Damasio, A. (1994) *Descartes' Error*. New York: Putnam.

Darwin, C. (1859) *On the Origin of Species by Means of Natural Selection or the Preservation of Favoured Races in the Struggle for Life*. London: Murray.

Davie, T. M. (1935) Comments upon a case of "periventricular epilepsy." *The British Medical Journal*, (3893)293–297.

Delaney, G. (1991) *Breakthrough Dreaming*. New York: Bantam.

Dement, W. & Kleitman, N. (1957a) Cyclic variations in EEG during sleep and their relation to eye movements, body mobility and dreaming. *Electroencephalography & Clinical Neurophysiology*, 9:673–690.

Dement, W. & Kleitman, N. (1957b) The relation of eye movements during sleep to dream activity: An objective method for the study of dreaming. *Journal of Experimental Psychology*, 53:89–97.

Dennett, D. (1991) *Consciousness Explained*. Boston: Little, Brown.

Domhoff, G. (1991) An introduction to "The two provinces of dreams" (Commentary on Hall's paper). *Dreaming*, 1:95–98.

Domhoff, G. (1993) The repetition of dreams and dream elements: A possible clue to a function of dreams. In: *The Functions of Dreaming*, ed. A. Moffitt, M. Kramer & R. Hoffmann. Albany, NY: State University of New York Press, pp. 293–320.

Domhoff, G. (1996) *Finding Meaning in Dreams: A Quantitative Approach*. New York: Plenum.

Dostoyevsky, F. (1866) *Crime and Punishment*, trans. S. Monas. New York: New American Library, 1968.

Dreifus, C. (1998) A conversation with Dr. Marvin Minsky: Why isn't artificial intelligence more like the real thing? *The New York Times*, July 28, F3.

Durang, C. (1999) Interview by Tim Sanford, unpublished. Available from Playwrights Horizon, New York, NY.

Edelman, G. (1973) Antibody structure and molecular immunology. *Science*, 180:830–840.

Edelman, G. (1987) *Neural Darwinism*. New York: Basic Books.

Eeden, F. van (1913) A study of dreams. *Proceedings of the Society for Psychical Research*, 26:431–461.

Ekstein, R. & Wallerstein, R. (1958) *The Teaching and Learning of Psychotherapy*. New York: International Universities Press.

Ellis, H. & Young, A. (1990) Accounting for delusional misidentification. *British Journal of Psychiatry*, 157:239–248.

Ellis, H., Young, A., Quayle, A. & De Pauw, K. (1997) Reduced autonomic responses to faces in Capgras delusion. *Proceedings of the Royal Society of London (Biology)*, 264:1085–1092.

Ellman, S. (1985) Toward a psychoanalytic theory of drive: REM sleep, a CNS self-stimulation system. *Clinical Psychology Review*, 5:185–198.

Ellman, S. & Antrobus, J. (1991) *The Mind in Sleep*. 2nd ed. New York: Wiley.

Erikson, E. (1954) The dream specimen of psychoanalysis. *Journal of the American Psychoanalytic Association*, 2:5–56.

Evans, C. & Newman, E. (1964) Dreaming: An analogy from computers. *New Scientist*, 419:577–579.

Fairbairn, W. R. D. (1940) Schizoid factors in the personality. In: *Psychoanalytic Studies of the Personality*. London: Routledge, 1952, pp. 3–27.

Fairbairn, W. R. D. (1944) Endopsychic structure considered in terms of object-relationships. In: *Psychoanalytic Studies of the Personality*. London: Routledge, 1952, pp. 82–136.

Farah, M. (1995) Dissociable systems for visual recognition: A cognitive neuropsychology approach. In: *An Invitation to Cognitive Science, Vol. 2: Visual Cognition*, ed. D. Osherson. Cambridge, MA: MIT Press.

Federn, P. (1952) *Ego Psychology and the Psychoses*. New York: Basic Books.

Ferenczi, S. (1913) To whom does one relate one's dreams? In: *Further Contributions to the Theory and Technique of Psycho-Analysis*. New York: Brunner/Mazel, 1980, p. 349.

Ferenczi, S. (1916) Interchange of affect in dreams. In: *Further Contributions to the Theory and Technique of Psycho-Analysis*. New York: Brunner/Mazel, 1980, p. 345.

Ferenczi, S. (1925) Contradictions to the "active" psycho-analytical technique. In: *Further Contributions to the Theory and Technique of Psycho-Analysis*. New York: Brunner/Mazel, 1980, pp. 217–230.

Ferenczi, S. (1927) Review of Rank's *Technik Der Psychoanalyse: I. Die Analytische Situation. International Journal of Psycho-Analysis*, 8:93–100.

Ferenczi, S. (1932) *The Clinical Diary of Sándor Ferenczi*, ed. J. Dupont (trans. M. Balint & N. E. Jackson). Cambridge, MA: Harvard University Press, 1988.

Fisher, C. (1954) Dreams and perception. *Journal of the American Psychoanalytic Association*, 2:389–445.

Fisher, C. & Paul, I. (1959) The effect of subliminal visual stimulation on images and dreams: A validation study. *Journal of the American Psychoanalytic Association*, 7:35–83.

Fisher, S. & Greenberg, R. (1996) *Freud Scientifically Appraised*. New York: Wiley.

Fiss, H. (1991) Experimental strategies for the study of the function of dreaming. In: *The Mind in Sleep*, ed. S. Ellman & J. Antrobus. New York: Wiley, pp. 308–326.

Fodor, J. (1998) *Concepts: Where Cognitive Science Went Wrong*. Oxford: Oxford University Press.

Fosshage, J. (1983) The psychological functions of dreams: A revised psychoanalytic perspective. *Psychoanalysis and Contemporary Thought*, 6:641–669.
Fosshage, J. & Loew, C., eds. (1987) *Dream Interpretation: A Comparative Study*. New York: PMA Publishing.
Foucault, M. (1986) Dreams, imagination, and existence. *Review of Existential Psychology and Psychiatry*, 19:29–78.
Foulkes, D. (1962) Dream reports from different stages of sleep. *Journal of Abnormal & Social Psychology*, 65:14–25.
Foulkes, D. (1985) *Dreaming: A Cognitive-Psychological Analysis*. Hillsdale, NJ: Lawrence Erlbaum Associates.
Foulkes, D. (1999) *Children's Dreaming and the Development of Consciousness*. Cambridge, MA: Harvard.
Franz, M.-L. von (1998a) *Dreams*. Boston: Shambhala.
Freeman, W. & Watts, J. (1950) *Psychosurgery: In the Treatment of Mental Disorders and Intractable Pain*. Springfield, IL: Thomas.
French, T. & Fromm, Erika O.[1] (1964) *Dream Interpretation: A New Approach*. New York: Basic Books.
Freud, S. (1877) Beobachtungen über Gestaltung und feineren Bau der als Hoden beschriebenen Lappenorgane des Aals. *S.B. Akad. Wiss. Wien* (Math.-Naturwiss. Kl.) I Abt, 75:419.
Freud, S. (1895) Project for a scientific psychology. *Standard Edition*, 1:283–397. London: Hogarth Press, 1966.
Freud, S. (1900) *The Interpretation of Dreams. Standard Edition*, 4 & 5. London: Hogarth Press, 1958.
Freud, S. (1901) *The Psychopathology of Everyday Life. Standard Edition*, 6. London: Hogarth Press, 1960.
Freud, S. (1905) Fragment of an analysis of a case of hysteria. *Standard Edition*, 7:1–122. London: Hogarth Press, 1953.
Freud, S. (1910) Five lectures on psycho-analysis. *Standard Edition*, 11:9–55. London: Hogarth Press, 1957.
Freud, S. (1913) An evidential dream. *Standard Edition*, 12:267–277. London: Hogarth Press, 1958.
Freud, S. (1918) From the history of an infantile neurosis. *Standard Edition*, 17:7–122. London: Hogarth Press, 1955.
Freud, S. (1920) Beyond the pleasure principle. *Standard Edition*, 18:7–66. London: Hogarth Press, 1955.
Freud, S. (1922) Dreams and telepathy. *Standard Edition*, 18:195–220. London: Hogarth Press, 1955.

1. I spell out the first name of Erika O. Fromm to distinguish her from Erich Fromm. The two have been confused in many dream bibliographies. Erika O. Fromm was married to Paul Fromm, who was Erich Fromm's cousin.

Freud, S. (1923a) Remarks upon the theory and practice of dream-interpretation [1922]. *Standard Edition*, 19:109–122. London: Hogarth Press, 1961.

Freud, S. (1923b) The ego and the id. *Standard Edition*, 19:12–66. London: Hogarth Press, 1961.

Freud, S. (1923c) Psycho-analysis. *Standard Edition*, 18:235–254. London: Hogarth Press, 1955.

Freud, S. (1931) Female sexuality. *Standard Edition*, 21:225–246. London: Hogarth Press, 1961.

Freud, S. (1933) Revision of the theory of dreams. In: *New Introductory Lectures on Psycho-Analysis. Standard Edition*, 22:7–30. London: Hogarth Press, 1964.

Freud, S. (1940) An outline of psychoanalysis [1938]. *Standard Edition*, 23:165–171. London: Hogarth Press, 1964.

Fromkin, V., ed. (1973) *Speech Errors as Linguistic Evidence*. The Hague: Mouton.

Fromm, Erich (1951) *The Forgotten Language*. New York: Rinehart.

Fromm, Erika O. (1998) Lost and found half a century later: Letters by Freud and Einstein. *American Psychologist*, 53:1195–1198.

Fromm, Erika O. & Nash, M. (1997) *Psychoanalysis and Hypnosis*. Madison, CT: International Universities Press.

Fromm-Reichmann, F. (1950) *Principles of Intensive Psychotherapy*. Chicago: University of Chicago Press.

Fromm-Reichmann, F. (1959) *Psychoanalysis and Psychotherapy*. Chicago: University of Chicago Press.

Gackenbach, J. & LaBerge, S., eds. (1988) *Conscious Mind, Sleeping Brain: Perspectives on Lucid Dreaming*. New York: Plenum.

Gardiner, M. (1983) The Wolf Man's last years. *Journal of the American Psychoanalytic Association*, 31:867–897.

Garma, A. (1940) *Psychoanalysis of Dreams*. New York: Aronson, 1974. (Originally published in Spanish.)

Gazzaniga, M. (1989) Organization of the human brain. *Science*, 245:947–952.

Gerstmann, J. (1927) Fingeragnosie und isolierte Agraphie: Ein neues Syndrom. *Zeitschrift für Neurologie und Psychiatrie*, 108:152–177.

Geschwind, N. (1965) Disconnexion syndromes in animals and man. *Brain*, 88:237–294, 585–644.

Gibson, J. J. (1966) *The Senses Considered as Perceptual Systems*. Boston: Houghton Mifflin.

Gibson, J. J. (1979) *The Ecological Approach to Visual Perception*. Boston: Houghton Mifflin.

Gill, M. M. (1982) *Analysis of Transference I: Theory and Technique*. New York: International Universities Press.

Gill, M. M. & Hoffman, I. Z. (1982) *Analysis of Transference II: Studies of Nine Audio Recorded Psychoanalytic Sessions*. New York: International Universities Press.

Gitelson, M. (1952) The emotional position of the analyst in the psychoanalytic situation. *International Journal of Psycho-Analysis*, 33:1–10.

Goldenberg, J., Mazursky, D. & Solomon, S. (1999) Creative sparks. *Science*, 285:1495–1496.

Goode, E. (1999) With help, climbing back from schizophrenia's isolation. *The New York Times*, January 30, pp. A1, 8.

Gorno-Tempini, M., Price, C., Josephs, O., Vandenberghe, R., Cappa, C. F., Kapur, N. & Frackowiak, R. (1998) The neural systems sustaining face and proper-name processing. *Brain*, 121:2103–2118.

Greenberg, R., Katz, H., Schwartz, W. & Pearlman, C. (1992) A research-based reconsideration of the psychoanalytic theory of dreaming. *Journal of the American Psychoanalytic Association*, 40:531–550.

Greenson, R. (1967) *The Technique and Practice of Psychoanalysis*. New York: International Universities Press.

Greenson, R. (1970) The exceptional place of the dream in psychoanalytic practice. *Psychoanalytic Quarterly*, 39:519–549.

Gregor, T. (1981) "Far, far away my shadow wandered . . .": The dream symbolism and dream theories of the Mehinaku Indians of Brazil. *American Ethologist*, 8:709–720.

Gregory, R. (1973) *Eye and Brain: The Psychology of Seeing*. New York: McGraw-Hill.

Grinstein, A. (1983) *Freud's Rules of Dream Interpretation*. New York: International Universities Press.

Groddeck, G. (1923) *The Book of the It*. New York: International Universities Press, 1976.

Grotstein, J. (1979) Who is the dreamer who dreams the dream and who is the dreamer who understands it? *Contemporary Psychoanalysis*, 15:110–169.

Grünbaum, A. (1984) Repressed infantile wishes as instigators of all dreams: Critical scrutiny of the compromise model of manifest dream content. In: *The Foundations of Psychoanalysis: A Philosophical Critique*. Berkeley: University of California Press, pp. 216–239.

Guntrip, H. (1968) *Schizoid Phenomena, Object Relations, and the Self*. New York: International Universities Press.

Gutheil, E. (1951) *Handbook of Dream Analysis*. New York: Washington Square Press, 1966.

Hacking, I. (1990) *The Taming of Chance*. Cambridge, UK: Cambridge University Press.

Hall, C. (1953) *The Meaning of Dreams*. New York: Harper.

Hall, C. & Van de Castle, R. (1966) *The Content Analysis of Dreams*. New York: Appleton Century Crofts.

Hamilton, E. & Cairns, H. (1961) *Plato: The Collected Dialogues*. Princeton, NJ: Princeton University Press.

Hartmann, E. (1995) Making connections in a safe place: Is dreaming psychotherapy? *Dreaming*, 5:213–228.

Hartmann, E. (1998) *Dreams and Nightmares*. New York: Plenum.
Haskell, R. (1985) Dreaming, cognition, and physical illness: Part II. *Journal of Medical Humanities and Bioethics*, 6:109–122.
Helmholtz, H. von (1863) Sensations of tone. In: *Helmholtz on Perception: Its Physiology and Development*, ed. R. M. Warren & R. P. Warren. New York: Wiley, 1968.
Herman, J., Erman, M., Boys, R., Peiser, L., Taylor, M. & Roffwarg, H. (1984) Evidence for directional correspondence between eye movements and dream imagery in REM sleep. *Sleep*, 7:52–63.
Hersh, T. (1995) How might we explain the parallels between Freud's Irma dream and his 1923 cancer? *Dreaming*, 5:267–287.
Heynick, F. (1993) *Language and Its Disturbances in Dreams*. New York: Wiley.
Hillman, J. (1979) *The Dream and the Underworld*. New York: Harper & Row.
Hobson, J. A. (1988) *The Dreaming Brain*. New York: Basic Books.
Hobson, J. A. (1993) *The Chemistry of Conscious States*. Boston: Little Brown.
Hobson, J. A. (1999) The new neuropsychology of sleep: Implications for psychoanalysis. *Neuro-Psychoanalysis*, 1:157–183.
Hobson, J. A. & McCarley, R.W. (1977) The brain as a dream state generator: An activation-synthesis hypothesis of the dream process. *The American Journal of Psychiatry*, 134:1335–1348.
Humphreys, J. & Riddoch, M. (1987) *To See or Not to See: A Case Study of Visual Agnosia*. Hillsdale, NJ: Lawrence Erlbaum Associates.
Hunt, H. (1989) *The Multiplicity of Dreams*. New Haven, CT: Yale University Press.
Isakower, O. (1938) A contribution to the patho-psychology of phenomena associated with falling asleep. *International Journal of Psycho-Analysis*, 19:331–345.
Jackendoff, R. (1987) *Consciousness and the Computational Mind*. Cambridge, MA: MIT Press.
Jacobi, J. J. (1973) *The Psychology of C. G. Jung*. New Haven, CT: Yale University Press.
Johnson, M. (1991) Reality monitoring: Evidence from confabulation in organic brain disease patients. In: *Awareness of Deficit After Brain Injury*, ed. G. Prigatano & D. Schacter. New York: Oxford, pp. 176–197.
Johnson, M., Kahan, T. & Raye, C. (1984) Dreams and reality monitoring. *Journal of Experimental Psychology: General*, 113:329–344.
Jones, E. (1957) *The Life and Works of Sigmund Freud*. New York: Basic Books.
Jones, R. M. (1970) *The New Psychology of Dreaming*. New York: Grune & Stratton.
Joseph, B. (1985) Transference: The total situation. *International Journal of Psycho-Analysis*, 66:447–454.
Jung, C. G. (1907) The psychology of dementia praecox. In: *Collected Works, Vol. 3*, trans. R. Hull. New York: Pantheon Books, 1960.
Jung, C. G. (1909) The analysis of dreams. In: *Dreams*, trans. R. Hull. Princeton, NJ: Princeton University Press, 1974, pp. 3–12.

Jung, C. G. (1934) The practical use of dream analysis. In: *Dreams*. Princeton, NJ: Princeton University Press, 1974, pp. 85–110.

Jung, C. G. (1944) *Psychology and Alchemy*. In: *Collected Works, Vol. 12*. Princeton, NJ: Princeton University Press, 1953.

Jung, C. G. (1948) General aspects of dream psychology. In: *Dreams*. trans. R. Hull. Princeton, NJ: Princeton University Press, 1974, pp. 23–66.

Jung, C. G. (1960) *Analytical Psychology: Its Theory and Practice*. New York: Pantheon.

Jung, C. G. (1962) *Memories, Dreams, Reflections*. New York: Vintage.

Jus, A., Jus, K., Villeneuve, A., Pires, A., Lachance, R., Fortier, J. & Villeneuve, R. (1973) Studies on dream recall in chronic schizophrenic patients after prefrontal lobotomy. *Biological Psychiatry*, 6:275–293.

Kaempffert, W. (1924) *A Popular History of American Invention*. New York: Scribners.

Kahn, E., Dement, W., Fisher, C. & Barmack, J. (1962) Incidence of color in immediately recalled dreams. *Science*, 137:1054–1055.

Kanzer, M. (1955) The communicative function of the dream. *International Journal of Psychoanalysis*, 36:260–266.

Kaszniak, A. (1986) The neuropsychology of dementia. In: *Neuropsychological Assessment of Neuropsychiatric Disorders*, ed. J. Grant & K. Adams. New York: Oxford, pp. 172–220.

Keating, E. & Gooley, S. (1988) Disconnection of parietal and occipital access to the saccadic oculomotor system. *Experimental Brain Research*, 70:385–398.

Kekulé, A. (1890) Benzolfest-Rede. *Berichte der Deutschen Chemischen Gesellschaft*, 23:1302–1311. Trans. O. Benfey (1958), Kekulé and the birth of the structural theory of organic chemistry in 1858. *Journal of Chemical Education*, 35:21–23.

Kenny, A., ed. (1994) *The Wittgenstein Reader*. Oxford: Blackwell.

Khan, M. M. R. (1976) The changing use of dreams in psychoanalytic practice: In search of the dreaming experience. *International Journal of Psychoanalysis*, 57:325–330.

Kihlstrom, D. (1986) The cognitive unconscious. *Science*, 237:1445–1452.

Klein, D. (1994) The utility of guidelines and algorithms for practice. *Psychiatric Annals*, 24:362–367.

Klein, M. (1932) *The Psycho-Analysis of Children*, rev. ed. New York: Delacorte Press, 1975.

Klein, M. (1946) Notes on some schizoid mechanisms. In: *Envy and Gratitude and Other Works, 1946–1963*. New York: Delacorte Press, pp. 1–24.

Klein, M. (1952) Mutual influences in the development of the ego and id. In: *Envy and Gratitude and Other Works, 1946–1963*. New York: Delacorte Press, pp. 57–60.

Kolod, S. (1999) We're together in dreams. Paper presented to the Division of Psychoanalysis, American Psychological Association, New York, April 16.

Kosslyn, S. (1994) *Image and Brain*. Cambridge, MA: MIT Press.
Kraepelin, E. (1906) *Über Sprachstörungen im Traum*. Leipzig: Engelman.
Kramer, M. (1993) The selective mood regulatory function of dreaming: An update and revision. In: *The Functions of Dreaming*, ed. A. Moffitt, M. Kramer & R. Hoffmann. Albany: State University of New York Press, pp. 139–195.
Kramer, M. (2000) Does dream interpretation have any limits? An evaluation of interpretations of the dream of "Irma's injection." *Dreaming*, 10:161–178.
LaBerge, S. (1985) *Lucid Dreaming*. Los Angeles, CA: Jeremy Tarcher.
Lakoff, G. (1988) Cognitive semantics. In: *Meaning and Mental Representation*, ed. U. Eco, M. Santambriogio & P. Violi. Bloomington: University of Indiana Press.
Lakoff, G. (1993) How metaphor structures dreams: The theory of conceptual metaphor applied to dream analysis. *Dreaming*, 3:77–98.
Lakoff, G. & Johnson, M. (1980) *Metaphors We Live By*. Chicago: University of Chicago Press.
Lakoff, G. & Johnson, M. (1999) *Philosophy in the Flesh: The Embodied Mind and Its Challenge to Western Thought*. New York: Basic Books.
Langer, S. (1967) *Problems of Art*. New York: Scribner.
Langs, R. J. (1978) *The Listening Process*. New York: Aronson.
Lasky, R. (1989) Some determinants of the male analyst's capacity to identify with female patients. *International Journal of Psycho-Analysis*, 70:405–418.
Lavie, P. & Hobson, J. A. (1986) Origin of dreams: Anticipation of modern theories in the philosophy and physiology of the eighteenth and nineteenth centuries. *Psychological Bulletin*, 100:229–240.
Levenson, E. (1972) *The Fallacy of Understanding*. New York: Basic Books.
Levenson, E. (1983) *The Ambiguity of Change*. New York: Basic Books.
Levenson, E. (1987) The interpersonal (Sullivanian) model. In: *Models of the Mind and Their Relationship to Clinical Work*, ed. A. Rothstein. New York: International Universities Press, pp. 49–67.
Levenson, E. (1991) *The Purloined Self*. New York: Contemporary Psychoanalysis Books.
Levin, R. (1990) Psychoanalytic theories on the function of dreaming: A review of the empirical dream research. In: *Empirical Studies of Psychoanalytic Theories, Vol. 3*, ed. J. Masling. Hillsdale, NJ: The Analytic Press, pp. 1–53.
Lewin, B. (1973) Sleep, the mouth and the dream screen. In: *Selected Writings of Bertram Lewin*, ed. J. Arlow. New York: Psychoanalytic Quarterly.
Lhermitte, J., Chain, F., Escourolle, R., Ducarne, B. & Pillon, B. (1972) Étude anatomoclinique d'un cas de prosopagnosie. *Revue Neurologique*, 126:329–346.
Libet, B. (1992) The neural time-factor in perception, volition and free will.

In: Libet, B. (1993) *Neurophysiology of Consciousness*. Boston: Birkhäuser, pp. 255–272.

Libet, B. (1993) *Neurophysiology of Consciousness*. Boston: Birkhäuser.

Libet, B., Gleason, C., Wright, E. & Pearl, D. (1983) Time of conscious intention to act in relation to onset of cerebral activity (readiness potential): The unconscious initiation of a freely voluntary act. *Brain*, 106:623–642.

Lippmann, P. (1998) On the private and social nature of dreams. *Contemporary Psychoanalysis*, 34:195–221.

Loftus, E. (1979) *Eyewitness Testimony*. Cambridge, MA: Harvard University Press.

Malcolm, J. (1982) *The Impossible Profession*. New York: Random House.

Maquet, P., Péters, J.-M., Aerts, J., Delfiore, G., Degueldre, C., Luxen, A. & Franck, G. (1996) Functional neuroanatomy of human rapid-eye-movement sleep and dreaming. *Nature*, 383:163–166.

Marcus, E. (1992) *Psychosis and Near Psychosis*. New York: Springer Verlag.

Marris, P. (1958) *Widows and Their Families*. London: Routledge & Kegan Paul.

Martin, L. (1986) "Eskimo words for snow": A case study in the genesis and decay of an anthropological example. *American Anthropologist*, 88:418–423.

Masson, J. (1985) *The Complete Letters of Sigmund Freud to Wilhelm Fliess 1887–1904*. Cambridge, MA: Harvard University Press.

Masterson, J. F. (1981) *The Narcissistic and Borderline Disorders*. New York: Brunner/Mazel.

Maurice, D. (1998) The Von Sallmann lecture of 1966: An ophthalmological explanation of REM sleep. *Experimental Eye Research*, 66:139–145.

Maury, L. F. A. (1878) *Le Sommeil et les Rêves*. Paris.

McCarley, R. W. (1992) Human electrophysiology: Basic cellular mechanisms and control of wakefulness and sleep. In: *American Psychiatric Press Textbook of Neuropsychiatry*, 2nd ed., ed. S. Yudofsky & R. Hale. Washington, DC: American Psychiatric Press, pp. 29–55.

McCarthy, R. & Warrington, E. (1990) *Cognitive Neuropsychology*. New York: Academic Press.

McClelland, J. & Rumelhart, D. & the PDP Research Group (1986) *Parallel Distributed Processing: Explorations in the Microstructure of Cognition*. Cambridge: MIT Press.

McGlynn, S. & Schacter, D. (1989) Unawareness of deficits in neuropsychological syndromes. *Journal of Clinical and Experimental Neuropsychology*, 11:143–205.

McKeon, R., ed. (1968) *The Basic Works of Aristotle*. New York: Random House.

Meltzer, D. (1978) Routine and inspired interpretations. In: *Countertransference*, ed. L. Epstein & A. Feiner. New York: Aronson.

Meltzer, D. (1984) *Dream-Life*. Perthshire: Clunie Press.

Menaker, E. (1981) Otto Rank's contribution to psychoanalytic communication. *Contemporary Psychoanalysis*, 17:552–564.

Mesulam, M.-M. (1981) A cortical network for directed attention and unilateral neglect. *Annals of Neurology*, 10:309–325.
Mesulam, M.-M. (1985) *Principles of Behavioral Neurology*. Philadelphia: F. A. Davis.
Mesulam, M.-M. (1998) From sensation to cognition. *Brain*, 121:1013–1052.
Meyer, L. B. (1956) *Emotion and Meaning in Music*. Chicago: University of Chicago Press.
Milner, A. & Goodale, M. (1995) *The Visual Brain in Action*. Oxford: Oxford University Press.
Mitchell, S. (1998) The analyst's knowledge and authority. *Psychoanalytic Quarterly*, 67:1–31.
Motley, M. (1995) Slips of the tongue. *Scientific American*, September, pp. 116–129.
Myers, W. (1987) Work on countertransference facilitated by self-analysis of the analyst's dreams. In: *The Interpretation of Dreams in Clinical Work*, ed. A. Rothstein. Madison, CT: International Universities Press, pp. 37–46.
Nabokov, V. (1981) *Lectures on Russian Literature*. New York: Harcourt Brace Jovanovich.
Natsoulas, T. (1982) Conscious perception and the paradox of "blind-sight." In: *Aspects of Consciousness*, ed. G. Underwood. New York: Academic Press, pp. 79–109.
Neisser, U. (1967) *Cognitive Psychology*. New York: Appleton-Century-Crofts.
Newman, E. & Evans, C. (1965) Human dream processes as analogous to computer programme clearance. *Nature*, 206:534.
Niederland, W. (1965) The role of the ego in the recovery of early memories. *Psychoanalytic Quarterly*, 34:564–571.
Nietzsche, F. (1886) *Beyond Good and Evil*. New York: Vintage, 1989.
Ogden, T. (1982) *Projective Identification and Psychotherapeutic Technique*. New York: Aronson.
Ogden, T. (1989) *The Primitive Edge of Experience*. Northvale, NJ: Aronson.
Ogden, T. (1997a) Reverie and interpretation. *Psychoanalytic Quarterly*, 66:567–595.
Ogden, T. (1997b) Reverie and metaphor. *International Journal of Psychoanalysis*, 78:719–732.
Olds, D. (1994) Connectionism and psychoanalysis. *Journal of the American Psychoanalytic Association*, 42:581–611.
Oppenheim, A. (1956) The interpretation of dreams in the ancient Near East with a translation of an Assyrian dreambook. *Transactions of the American Philosophical Society*, 46(3):179–373.
Padel, J. (1987) Object relational approach. In: *Dream Interpretation: A Comparative Study*, rev. ed. J. Fosshage & C. Loew. New York: PMA Publishing, pp. 125–148.
Paillard, J., Michel, F. & Stelmach, G. (1983) Localization without content: A tactile analogue of "blind sight." *Archives of Neurology*, 40:548–551.

Palombo, S. (1984) Recovery of early memories associated with reported dream imagery. *American Journal of Psychiatry*, 141:1508–1511.
Palombo, S. (1985) Can a computer dream? *Journal of the American Academy of Psychoanalysis*, 13:453–466.
Panksepp, J. (1998) *Affective Neuroscience*. New York: Oxford University Press.
Parkin, A. & Leng, N. (1993) *Neuropsychology of the Amnesic Syndrome*. Hillsdale, NJ: Lawrence Erlbaum Associates.
Parsifal-Charles, N. (1986) *The Dream: 4,000 Years of Theory and Practice*. West Cornwall, CT: Locust Hill Press.
Perky, C. (1910) An experimental study of imagination. *American Journal of Psychology*, 21:422–452.
Perrett, D., Rolls, E. & Caan, W. (1982) Visual neurones responsive to faces in the monkey temporal cortex. *Experimental Brain Research*, 47:329–342.
Pick, A. (1903) On reduplicative paramnesia. *Brain*, 26:260–267.
Pötzl, O. (1917) The relationship between experimentally induced dream images and indirect vision. *Psychological Issues*, 2:41–120, 1960. (First published in: *Zeitschrift für Neurologie und Psychiatrie*, 37:278–349.)
Pribram, K. (1998) A century of progress? In: *Neuroscience of the Mind on the Centennial of Freud's* "Project for a Scientific Psychology," ed. R. Bilder & F. LeFever. New York: New York Academy of Sciences, *Annals Vol. 843*, pp. 11–19.
Pullum, G. (1991) *The Great Eskimo Vocabulary Hoax*. Chicago: University of Chicago Press.
Pulver, S. (1987) The manifest dream in psychoanalysis: A clarification. *Journal of the American Psychoanalytic Association*, 35:90–115.
Quinodoz, J.-M. (1999) "Dreams that turn over a page": Integration dreams with paradoxial regressive content. *International Journal of Psychoanalysis*, 80:225–238.
Ramachandran, V., Levi, L., Stone, L., Rogers-Ramachandran, D., McKinney, R., Stalcup, M., Arcila, G., Zweifler, R., Schatz, A. & Flippin, A. (1996) Illusions of body image: What they reveal about human nature. In: *The Mind-Brain Continuum: Sensory Processes*, ed. R. Llinás & P. Churchland. Cambridge, MA: MIT Press.
Ramachandran, V. & Blakeslee, S. (1998) *Phantoms in the Brain*. New York: William Morrow.
Ramsay, O. & Rocke, A. (1984) Kekulé's dreams: Separating the fiction from the fact. *Chemistry in Britain*, 20:1093–1094.
Rank, O. (1926) Die analytische Situation. In: *Die Technik der Psychoanalyse, Vol. 1*. Vienna: Deuticke.
Rapaport, D., ed. (1951) *Organization and Pathology of Thought*. New York: Columbia University Press.
Rapaport, D. (1957) Cognitive structures. In: *The Collected Papers of David Rapaport*, ed. M. Gill. New York: Basic Books, pp. 631–664.
Rechtschaffen, A. (1964) A discussion of W. Dement's "Experimental Dream

Studies." In: *Science and Psychoanalysis*, ed. J. Masserman. New York: Grune & Stratton, pp. 162–171.
Rechtschaffen, A. & Mednick, S. (1955) The autokinetic word technique. *Journal of Abnormal and Social Psychology*, 51:346.
Rees, W. D. (1975) The bereaved and their hallucinations. In: *Bereavement: Its Psychosocial Aspects*, ed. B. Schoenberg, I. Gerber, A. Wiener, A. Kutscher, D. Peretz & A. Carr. New York: Columbia University Press.
Reik, T. (1948) *Listening with the Third Ear*. New York: Farrar Straus.
Reis, W. (1951) A comparison of the interpretation of dream series with and without free association. In: *Dreams and Personality Dynamics*, ed. M. F. DeMartino. Springfield, IL: Charles C. Thomas, 1959, pp. 211–225.
Reiser, M. (1993) *Memory in Mind and Brain: What Dream Imagery Reveals*. New Haven, CT: Yale University Press.
Reiser, M. (1997) The art and science of dream interpretation: Otto Isakower's teachings revisited. *Journal of the American Psychoanalytic Association*, 45:891–907.
Restak, R. (1991) *The Brain Has a Mind of Its Own*. New York: Harmony Books.
Restak, R. (1994) *The Modular Brain*. New York: Scribner.
Robertson, L., Treisman, A., Friedman-Hill, S. & Grabowecky, M. (1997) The interaction of spatial and object pathways: Evidence from Balint's syndrome. *Journal of Cognitive Neuroscience*, 9:295–317.
Robinson, M. & Freeman, W. (1954) *Psychosurgery and the Self*. New York: Grune & Stratton.
Rorem, N. (1994) *Knowing When to Stop*. New York: Simon & Schuster.
Rosch, E. (1977) Human categorization. In: *Studies in Cross-Cultural Psychology*, ed. N. Warren. London: Academic.
Rosen, V. (1955) The reconstruction of a traumatic childhood event in a case of derealization. *Journal of the American Psychoanalytic Association*, 3:211–221.
Rosenbloom, S. (1998) The complexities and pitfalls of working with the countertransference. *Psychoanalytic Quarterly*, 67:256–275.
Ross, W. & Kapp, F. (1962) A technique for self-analysis of countertransference: Use of the psychoanalyst's visual images in response to patient's dreams. *Journal of the American Psychoanalytic Association*, 10:643–657.
Ryle, G. (1949) *The Concept of Mind*. New York: Barnes & Noble.
Sabini, M. (1981) Dreams as an aid in determining diagnosis, prognosis, and attitude toward treatment. *Psychotherapy & Psychosomatics*, 36:24–36.
Sacks, O. (1973) *Awakenings*. Garden City, NY: Doubleday.
Sacks, O. (1997) *The Island of the Colorblind*. New York: Knopf.
Sandler, J. (1976) Countertransference and role-responsiveness. *International Review of Psycho-Analysis*, 3:43–47.
Schachtel, E. (1959) *Metamorphosis*. New York: Basic Books.
Schacter, D. (1991) Unawareness of deficit and unawareness of knowledge in patients with memory disorders. In: *Awareness of Deficit after Brain*

Injury, ed. G. Prigatano & D. Schacter. New York: Oxford, pp. 127–151.

Schafer, R. (1983) *The Analytic Attitude*. New York: Basic Books.

Schavelzon, J. (1983) *Freud, un Paciente con Cancer*. Buenos Aires: Editorial Paidos.

Schimel, J. (1969) Dreams as transaction: An exercise in interpersonal theory. *Contemporary Psychoanalysis*, 6:31–38.

Schur, M. (1972) *Freud: Living and Dying*. New York: International Universities Press.

Searles, H. (1955) The informational value of the supervisor's emotional experiences. *Psychiatry*, 18:135–146.

Seligman, M. & Yellen, A. (1987) What is a dream? *Behavior Research and Therapy*, 25:1–24.

Share, L. (1992) *If Someone Speaks, It Gets Lighter: Dreams and the Reconstruction of Infant Trauma*. Hillsdale, NJ: The Analytic Press.

Sharpe, E. F. (1937) *Dream Analysis*. New York: Norton.

Silberer, H. (1914) *Probleme der Mystik und ihrer Symbolik*. Vienna.

Smith, C. (1995) Sleep states and memory processes. *Behavior and Brain Research*, 69:137–145.

Smith, D. (1999) Fresh look at a syntax skewer. *The New York Times*, June 9, E1–4.

Solms, M. (1997) *The Neuropsychology of Dreams*. Mahwah, NJ: Lawrence Erlbaum Associates.

Solms, M. (1999) Commentary on "The new neuropsychology of sleep." *Neuro-Psychoanalysis*, 1:183–195.

Spence, D. (1982) *Narrative Truth and Historical Truth*. New York: Norton.

Squier, L. & Domhoff, G. (1998) The presentation of dreaming and dreams in introductory psychology textbooks. *Dreaming*, 8:149–168.

States, B. (1995) Dreaming "accidentally" of Harold Pinter: The interplay of metaphor and metonymy in dreams. *Dreaming*, 5:229–245.

Stekel, W. (1943) *The Interpretation of Dreams*. New York: Washington Square Press, 1967.

Stern, D. (1997) *Unformulated Experience*. Hillsdale, NJ: The Analytic Press.

Stevens, A. (1996) *Private Myths: Dreams and Dreaming*. Cambridge: Harvard University Press.

Stolorow, R. & Atwood, G. (1982) The psychoanalytic phenomenology of the dream. *Annual of Psychoanalysis*, 10:205–220.

Strunz, F. (1993) Preconscious mental activity and scientific problem-solving: A critique of the Kekulé dream controversy. *Dreaming*, 3:281–294.

Stuss, D. (1991) Disturbance of self-awareness after frontal system damage. In: *Awareness of Deficit after Brain Injury*, ed. G. Prigatano & D. Schacter. New York: Oxford University Press, pp. 63–83.

Sullivan, H. S. (1953) *The Interpersonal Theory of Psychiatry*. New York: Norton.

Sullivan, H. S. (1962) *Schizophrenia as a Human Process*. New York: Norton.

Sullivan, H. S. (1972) *Personal Psychopathology*. New York: Norton.

Sullivan, H. S. (1973) *Clinical Studies in Psychiatry*. New York: Norton.
Swinney, D. (1979) Lexical access during sentence comprehension: (Re)consideration of content effects. *Journal of Verbal Learning and Verbal Behavior*, 18:645–668.
Symons, D. (1993) The stuff that dreams aren't made of: Why wake-state and dream-state sensory experiences differ. *Cognition*, 47:181–217.
Tauber, E. (1952) Exploring the therapeutic use of countertransference data. *Psychiatry*, 17:331–336.
Tauber, E. & Green, M. (1962) Color in dreams. *American Journal of Psychotherapy*, 16:221–229.
Teunisse, R., Cruysberg, J., Hoefnagels, W., Verbeek, A. & Zitman, F. (1996) Visual hallucinations in psychologically normal people: Charles Bonnet's syndrome. *The Lancet*, 347:794–797.
Thompson, R. (1930) *The Epic of Gilgamesh*. Oxford, UK: Oxford University Press.
Thorner, H. (1957) Three defences against inner persecution. In: *New Directions in Psychoanalysis*, ed. M. Klein, P. Heimann & R. Money-Kyrle. New York: Basic Books, pp. 282–306.
Tolstoy, L. (1878) *Anna Karenina*, trans. C. Garnett. New York: Dodd Mead, 1966.
Tranel, D. & Damasio, A. (1985) Knowledge without awareness: An autonomic index of facial recognition by prosopagnosics. *Science*, 228:1453–5.
Tranel, D., Damasio, A. & Damasio, H. (1988) Intact recognition of facial expression, gender, and age in patients with impaired recognition of face identity. *Neurology*, 38:690–696.
Treisman, A. & Gelade, G. (1980) A feature-integration theory of attention. *Cognitive Psychology*, 12:97–136.
Tulving, E. (1968) Theoretical issues in free recall. In: *Verbal Behavior and General Behavior Theory,* ed. T. Dixon & D. Horton. Englewood Cliffs, NJ: Prentice-Hall, pp. 2–36.
Ullman, M. (1969) Dreaming as metaphor in motion. *Archives of General Psychiatry*, 21:696–703.
Ullman, M. (1973) Societal factors in dreaming. *Contemporary Psychoanalysis*, 9:282–292.
Ullman, M. (1996) *Appreciating Dreams: A Group Approach*. Thousand Oaks, CA: Sage.
Vallar, G., Sterzi, R., Bottini, G., Cappa, S. & Rusconi, M. (1990) Temporary remission of left hemianesthesia after vestibular stimulation: A sensory neglect phenomenon. *Cortex*, 26:123–131.
Van de Castle, R. (1994) *Our Dreaming Mind*. New York: Ballantine.
Vaschide, N. (1911) *Le Sommeil et les Rêves*. Paris: Flammarion.
Velikovsky, I. (1934) Can a newly-acquired language become the speech of the unconscious? *Psychoanalytic Review*, 21:329–335.
Vendler, Z. (1977). Wordless thoughts. In: *Language and Thought: Anthropological*

Issues, ed. W. McCormack & S. Wurm. The Hague: Mouton Publishers, pp. 29–44.
Vogel, G. (1978) An alternative view of the neurobiology of dreaming. *American Journal of Psychiatry*, 135:1531–1535.
Volta, O. (1989) *Satie Seen Through His Letters*. London: Marion Boyars.
Vygotsky, L. (1934) *Thought and Language*, trans. A. Kozulin. Cambridge, MA: MIT Press, 1986.
Wagner, C. (1978) *Cosima Wagner's Diaries, 1869–1877, Vol. 1*, ed. M. Gregor-Dellin & D. Mack (trans. G. Skelton). New York: Harcourt Brace Jovanovich.
Waldhorn, H. F., reporter (1967) *Indications for Psychoanalysis: The Place of the Dream in Clinical Psychoanalysis. Monogr. II* of the Kris Study Group of the New York Psychoanalytic Institute, ed. E. Joseph. New York: International Universities Press.
Watson, R. (1994) The clinical use of the analyst's dreams of the patient. *Contemporary Psychoanalysis*, 30:510–521.
Weiskrantz, L. (1986) *Blindsight*. Oxford: Clarendon Press.
Weiskrantz, L. (1997) *Consciousness Lost and Found*. New York: Oxford University Press.
Wells, G., Malpass, R., Lindsay, R., Fisher, R., Turtle, J. & Fulero, S. (2000) From the lab to the police station: A successful application of eyewitness research. *American Psychologist*, 55:581–598.
Whitman, R., Kramer, M. & Baldridge, B. (1969) Dreams about the patient: An approach to countertransference. *Journal of the American Psychoanalytic Association*, 17:702–727.
Whorf, B. (1956) *Language, Thought, & Reality: Selected Writings of Benjamin Lee Whorf*, ed. J. Carroll. Cambridge, MA: MIT Press.
Williams, M. (1987) Reconstruction of an early seduction and its after-effects. *Journal of the American Psychoanalytic Association*, 35:145–163.
Williams, P. (1999) Internet discussion review of "Dreams that turn over a page." *International Journal of Psychoanalysis*, 80:845–856.
Winnicott, D. W. (1988) Chaos. In: *Human Nature*, ed. C. Bollas, M. Davis & R. Shepard. New York: Schocken Books, pp. 135–138.
Winson, J. (1985) *Brain and Psyche*. New York: Vintage.
Winson, J. (1990) The meaning of dreams. *Scientific American*, November, pp. 42–48.
Wolf Man (1957) Letters pertaining to Freud's history of an infantile neurosis. *Psychoanalytic Quarterly*, 26:449–460.
Wolstein, B. (1967) *Theory of Psychoanalytic Therapy*. New York: Grune & Stratton.
Wolstein, B. (1976) A presupposition of how I work. *Contemporary Psychoanalysis*, 12:186–202.
Wotiz, J. & Rudofsky, S. (1984) Kekulé's dreams: Fact or fiction? *Chemistry in Britain*, 20:720–723.

Yamamoto, J., Okonogi, K., Iwasaki, T. & Yoshimura, S. (1969) Mourning in Japan. *American Journal of Psychiatry*, 125:1661.
Young, A., Reid, I., Wright, S. & Hellawell, D. (1993) Face-processing impairments and the Capgras delusion. *British Journal of Psychiatry*, 162:695–698.
Zeki, S. (1990) A century of central achromatopsia. *Brain*, 113:1721–1777.
Zeki, S. (1993) *A Vision of the Brain*. Oxford: Blackwell.
Zimmerman, W. (1967) Psychological and physiological differences between "light" and "deep" sleepers. Unpublished doctoral dissertation, University of Chicago.
Zimmerman, W. (1970) Sleep mentation and auditory awakening thresholds. *Psychophysiology*, 6:540–549.

INDEX